Personal BEST

THE FOREMOST PHILOSOPHER OF FITNESS SHARES TECHNIQUES AND TACTICS FOR SUCCESS AND SELF-LIBERATION

GEORGE SHEEHAN, M.D.

MEDICAL EDITOR, <u>RUNNER'S WORLD</u> MAGAZINE
AUTHOR, <u>RUNNING AND BEING</u>

Rodale Press, Emmaus, Pennsylvania

Printed in the United States of America on acid-free paper ∞

Cover and book design by Acey Lee
Cover illustration by Michele Byrne

If you have any questions or comments concerning this book, please write:

Rodale Press
Book Reader Service
33 East Minor Street
Emmaus, PA 18098

Library of Congress Cataloging-in-Publication Data

Sheehan, George.
    Personal best : the foremost philosopher of fitness shares techniques
and tactics for success and self-liberation / George Sheehan.
        p.   cm.
    ISBN 06-7857-858-7   hardcover
    ISBN 0-87857-995-8   paperback
    1. Physical fitness—Philosophy.   I. Title.
GV481.S474   1989
613.7'1—dc20   89-35357
                                                                       CIP

Distributed in the book trade by St. Martin's Press

    6 8 10 9 7 5   hardcover
2 4 6 8 10 9 7 5 3 1   paperback

To Mary Jane and our sons and daughters, who waited with patience and love while I sought the light—and finally found my way home.

CONTENTS

PREFACE

PREFACE

"Why did you start running?" reporters ask again and again.

I never find an answer that satisfies either the reporters or myself. It's difficult to reconstruct my situation more than 20 years ago, almost impossible to know for certain what was going on in my body and mind—and more particularly my soul.

It's difficult also to reconstruct my environment, the predicament I was in. Forty-five is a decisive age, an age for change. But when asked for particulars, the people who go through those changes aren't sure what the spur was.

A study on alcoholism by Harvard psychiatrist George E. Vaillant brings this question into sharper focus. Alcoholics, Dr. Vaillant found, have a marked tendency to become ex-alcoholics. Many more of them are able to return to abstention or social drinking than was previously thought.

When asked why they quit drinking, though, they had difficulty pinpointing the causes. They gave general answers to this specific question. They recognized that they were no longer in charge.

I started running for much the same reason.

Recovery from alcohol begins when drinkers realize they are no longer consciously in charge, that they have become passengers on a ship whose destination is beyond their ken. This is the required revelation, the necessary self-knowledge.

I can say in retrospect that my running was a response to the same sort of self-discovery, that there was a deeper reason for turning to running than I had always supposed.

It was not merely a substitute for tennis and squash. It was not simply a way to join my children in their high school sport. It was not a method of reliving my college triumphs, such as they were. I ran to regain control of my life.

In a sense, I was like a closet drinker. My deterioration was masked by the assumption of those about me that functioning *adequately* means you are normal. But one can function adequately while using only about 10 percent of one's potential. And I was locked into a routine that utilized only a small percentage of my capabilities, imprisoned in a physical and professional and social existence that no longer allowed me to express my real personality.

I ran to find myself.

Once I returned to running, why did I continue? People don't ask me that. They should, since it is an even more important question.

Dr. Vaillant asked that of his alcoholics. Once they decided to change their lives, to take charge, to assume control, what sustained them in this choice? What forces helped them make the decision stick?

Dr. Vaillant reduced these factors to four: (1) Behavior modification, usually with supervision of some sort; (2) substitute dependencies, such as candy, Valium, or cigarettes; (3) increased religious involvement, which provides a stable source of increased hope and self-esteem; and (4) new relationships.

The last element, Dr. Vaillant noted, is crucial. The new life needs new people. New relationships, he says, are uncontaminated by the old injuries, resentment, and guilt alcoholics inflict on those who care for them.

It is quite evident that running provides all four of these factors. The running body modifies its own behavior. Running then becomes a substitute dependency, an addiction that has positive rather than negative effects. It becomes a religious experience that gives renewed hope and self-esteem. And it bestows on each runner a new circle of similarly minded, nonjudgmental friends.

This leads to my response to the next most frequently asked question: "When do you plan to stop running?"

Never, of course.

CHAPTER

1

LESSONS IN EXCELLENCE

The philosophy of running is the philosophy of holism . . . to function as you are supposed to function, to achieve your personal best.

TO BECOME AN ATHLETE

I had arrived at the running camp late in the morning. The campus of this exclusive New England prep school was deserted. Somewhere inside the beautiful Georgian buildings were 300 people devoting a week to learning more about their sport. Almost 200, I later learned, were of high school age.

I went into the lounge to get a can of soda. When I came out, the runners had broken for lunch. Three of the high school boys were standing by my car, peering in at a trophy I had won the previous day. They were staring at my prize with wide-eyed concentrated interest. The trophy, I realized, was the reason they were there.

The philosophy of running camps is based on that reasoning. The goal is performance. The emphasis is on getting the most out of your ability. This entire week would be devoted to improving time and place in competition. The curriculum was designed to bring a runner to the starting line in winning form.

This is a natural atmosphere to both coach and athlete. Coaches train runners to excel, and runners want tangible evidence of that excellence—improvement on the stopwatch, for one, but finally, the trophy.

So, this rapt inspection of the trophy in the back of the Honda was to be expected. It was the prize so greatly desired, the reward for this week of effort and for the months ahead of putting this instruction into action. Seeing the trophy, the runners could imagine it already theirs. They could savor the moment when they would eventually become winners.

My lecture was late in the afternoon. Three hundred sat there, filled with the pleasant tiredness that comes from prolonged use of your body. They had done interval miles in the morning, and a long run in the woods after lunch had put everyone in a relaxed, happy mood. It was a day of instruction and practice that would help me tell them the real reason for attending camp.

I began by telling the audience of the three young runners and my trophy. That trophy, I told them, was of little consequence. A race is won and forgotten. The trophy is received and rusts on a shelf. There is nothing briefer than the laurel. "So soon they forget," you will say. But so soon *you* will forget as well. The memorable thing is not to excel against others but to excel against yourself.

One woman Olympian who took a gold in the sprints said her joy lasted for only a few minutes. Chris Evert told a reporter that less than two hours after winning at Wimbledon, she was alone in her hotel room feeling depressed.

The real contest is within. The real trophy is the self. This camp is here, I said, to help you win the big race and receive the best of all prizes—becoming a person you can be proud of.

We were there to become athletes. The word comes from a Greek word meaning struggle and prize. The struggle is for the prize which is ourself. That is the prize we all seek. That is the trophy beyond any trophy: our total self—body, mind, and spirit. Running would become the means to that end. It would become an end, as well. But not in a way these youths suspected. In time, we would have the joy of becoming the running. We would find in running those peak experiences, the alterations of consciousness that contemplatives write about, and that more fortunate common folk know firsthand.

The philosophy of running is the philosophy of holism. The running camp is a place where we develop our whole personality, where we strive for the excellence the Greeks called *arete* (pronounced ar-ay-tay) — to function as you are supposed to function, to achieve your personal best. Not to be the best in the camp or on your team, but the best *you*.

The body is the starting point. We see the body as the Greeks saw it, clean and wholesome, good and beautiful, twin sister to the soul. In turning to our bodies, we turn to our minds and souls, to the whole that is ourself. We are here, I told them, to become good wholes. To do that, we must become good choosers. To make the choices that lead to more and more wholeness, more and more self-realization.

This does not make interval miles unimportant. It makes them more important. If we are to excel, we must be competitive. Competition, by definition, is the road to excellence. Our coaches will teach us how to become the best runners possible. They will give us the bodies we were meant to have. Doing these interval miles with others also allows us to share a common purpose with people we would otherwise consider opponents. We come to realize that each us is striving for his or her own personal best, and that that best is entirely separate from anyone else's personal best.

The long runs in the afternoon add contemplation and conversation. This was running in its purest form — we were out there learning about our mental and social capabilities. It gives us new opportunities to develop and perfect our personalities. This day was putting my (and their) purpose in focus.

I am trying, I told them, to be the best possible George Sheehan. Win or lose, that is the only trophy I want or hope for. Running in many ways has helped me in striving for this goal. It has even prepared me for the fact that the thrill of victory is the briefest of human experiences.

The best I can wish you, I said, is that you win your first trophy soon . . . and then get on to the real reason for attending this camp. To begin the lifelong task of becoming an athlete, and achieving *arete*.

LIFE: A WINNING GAME

The normal life is one of continual expansion. We are forever occupied with expressing or discharging what is latent in us. We are maximizers, always trying to make whatever is potential in our personality a living reality. If there is one word for human nature, it is *more*.

This growth does not occur in a haphazard way. We proceed through stages, probably best described by psychologist Erik Erikson.

Each stage is an achievement that requires a special gift. There is a basic virtue needed, an ego quality to be acquired. Experience tells us that reaching each plateau is not easy. Nor, having achieved victory can we assume it permanent. Each day is a reenactment of this lifelong struggle. Each day requires the virtues and values of our entire life.

This growth is not automatic. We cannot assume that at some particular age, each of us will reach a particular stage. Some arrive early, some arrive late. Some miss a stage completely, and eventually must return at a later date. It is as if life is a game board. Each of us must reach each goal to win the game. Fortunately, life is a positive sum game—losing is not *required* by the rules. It is possible for everyone to be a winner—not easy, of course, but possible.

Erikson described this game. George E. Vaillant, in his *Adaptation to Life*, has analyzed what it takes to be a winner. Basic is the successful completion of each task. Equally basic is the continuing presence of the virtues and values gained in each stage. The dominant values needed in infancy are still necessary in old age.

We begin as infants needing hope and trust. Present then and present in all stages are the opposite values: The infant is faced with mistrust. The good beginning in life is one filled with trust—the feeling that life is good and true and beautiful—and living can be filled with joy.

This is the spirit of play, which must be incorporated and continually renewed while we progress through each of the following stages. Hope and trust and play will always be essential.

But they are no less essential, of course, than the gifts and virtues and values of the next stage, or indeed any of the others. Next, as we enter adolescence, we need self-control and willpower, initiative and purpose. Now we must master more difficult developments in ourselves and our relationships with others. The child must have trust. The evolving adolescent must have faith. The mature adult must care. All three major stages in life require hope and fidelity and care.

"We should not be surprised (although we were at the time)," wrote Erikson, "at the similarity between these three and the traditional credal values of faith, hope, and charity."

Indeed, we should not be surprised that Erikson's outline of the life cycle mirrors others that have been presented to us for centuries and contains the consensus experience of the evolution of the human spirit.

In a real sense, it is not necessary to know the history of the psychiatry behind Erikson's concept since the important points are universal. Nineteenth century German philosopher Arthur Schopenhauer made this point in writing on philosophy: "The true philosophy of history lies in perceiving that, in all the endless and motley complexity of events, it is only the self-same unchangeable being which is before us."

Human nature has not changed. We have common feelings and needs. With thought and a little guidance to elevate our consciousness, we can make use of our immediate experience. In fact, we must make use of our immediate experience. Only then will we learn, only then will we change our behavior.

There is, indeed, nothing new under the sun. Life is a permanent boot camp. We must always be in training—and training not only our bodies but our minds and spirits as well. Erikson's game plan is as good as any. What it takes to win are the virtues and values that have come down to us over the centuries. They are embodied in the athlete, the artist, the hero, the saint, the sage—which is a simple description of the evolution of the common man.

Life is not a skill sport. It does not require hand-eye coordination. It is not determined by our intelligence quotient, not dependent on a beatific vision. It is a game anyone can play and play well.

The requirements are those bedrock qualities we all possess. Their development demands no more than our time and effort. Our particular and peculiar genius will manifest itself if we devote ourselves to that project.

The diligent use of our allotted life span is the secret of the successful life. "There is only one road to greatness," said Sydney Smith. "Hard labor." But the right labor done in the right way. Effort is the measure of a man. But it is effort concentrated on the creation and development of the ideal self. Our energies must be directed toward the shaping and making of the total personality. We must unflaggingly pursue personal excellence—*arete*—the goal of the Greeks.

Basic to *arete* is harmony. We are body, mind, and spirit. We cannot stress one function of the self to the detriment of the others. When that happens we become unbalanced. Our lives become dis-rhythmic. The self suffers.

We must, therefore, be impartial with our daily expenditures in time and effort. We should allot the necessary hours and energy to each area of being. There are laws that govern the body and the mind and the spirit. There is a science of this life that will give us predictable results. Exercises to get the most out of the human machine and the body/mind complex that expresses the soul.

We know how to get the most out of our bodies. The rules for physical performance are well-established. They have changed little over the centuries. Consult any text on exercise physiology and you find the do's and don'ts of fitness.

For models, we can look to the athletes. They are humanity at its physical best. Theirs is an experiment in human cultivation, the Olympics, a giant human husbandry fair. Every four years, nations from all over the globe bring their best and say, "Here is what we can become."

The road to that greatness is indeed hard labor. Those of us who would be athletes know that. I do everything an Olympian does. I experience the same fatigue and pain. I, too, have days when I wonder if it is worth it. I remember the joys of indolence. I want to go back in the stands and watch.

As luck would have it, or the Creator intended, the sportive use of the body brings its own joys. My body has found in running all it needs to know, or do. I am not upset that it has no other skills. My life needs nothing more.

2

THE GAME THAT IS LIFE

Life is a positive sum game. . . . Everyone from the gold medalist to the last finisher can rejoice in a personal victory.

PERSONAL HEROICS

George Sheehan, one critic wryly said, is a legend in his own mind. Of course I am. And you should be, too. Each one of us must be a hero. We are here to lead a heroic life. When we cease to lead such lives we no longer truly exist.

It's not easy.

Susan Cheever wrote of her father John's endless battle to escape the constant pressure to achieve, "to leave behind the torpid stability of the suburbs and the responsibilities of a house and family and most of all to escape the pressure to continually surpass himself as a writer."

Each of us knows those urges. We look to a future where we are free to do as we please with whom we please. We look to the time when work and effort, duty and obligation will cease. To a day when we can take our ease and enjoy the fruits of our labors, no longer in contention with the most difficult of rivals—our youthful selves.

We should know better. The battle is never over, the war is never won. Today's bare landscape is always and ever the arena where we contend with ourselves: We say our prayers and go to combat.

No one else may be aware of this struggle, but it does not matter. The hero needs no recognition: The deed is done, the audience of one is satisfied. A poet, serene in his own pursuit of the heroic, wrote, "Commemorate me with no hero-courageous tomb." The heroic act, the courageous act, is its own reward.

The potential for heroism of the common man is firmly planted in our tradition. It was a basic tenet of the transcendentalist philosophers and the Emersonians who followed. There is a story that nineteenth century feminist and Emersonian philosopher Margaret Fuller once read a passage describing Correggio, the Italian known for breaking tradition by painting ordinary people, as "one of those superior beings of whom there are so few." Fuller, in response, wrote on the margin, "And yet *all* might be such."

A young artist who read these lines said, "These words struck out a new strength in me. They revived resolutions, long fallen away, and made me set my face like flint."

That stony strength is there in all of us. That flinty determination is part of our higher nature. And we only need read nineteenth century American philosopher William James to have these qualities renewed for us. "Mankind's common instinct for reality," he wrote, "has always held the world to be essentially *a theater for heroism.*"

That quality — life as heroism's arena — is the reason, wrote Pulitzer-prizewinning sociologist *(Denial of Death)* Ernest Becker, that we still thrill to Emerson and Nietzsche. "We like to be reminded that our central calling, our main task on this planet, is the heroic." The universal human problem, said Becker, is the fear of death, and only through a superlative cosmic heroism can we overcome it. "What one is doing to earn his feeling of heroism is the main self-analytic problem in life."

"It begins to look as though modern man cannot find his heroism in everyday life anymore," wrote Becker. Do not for a minute believe it: Heroism is ever available, and in fact it is through ordinary experiences that the ordinary man can become extraordinary. Heroism, Danish philosopher Kierkegaard said, means being great in what every human can be great in — simply doing the best we can.

So life does resolve into finding the way we can best be heroes — to finding our personal arenas, what it is we do best. Cheever had found that and wanted to put it aside. We are likely to do the same, but we should *not* deny our true talents, our authentic vocations. We all must be heroes, but in our own ways.

My legend will not be your legend. Neither one will be John Cheever's. We are about the business of making a unique self, and a heroic one. How we can best do that is next on the agenda.

WAR SPORTS: PEACEFUL COMBAT

The common man reaches excellence by making demands on himself. Nobility, wrote Spanish philosopher José Ortega y Gasset, is synonymous with a life of efforts, ever set on excelling oneself, in passing beyond what one is to what one sets up as a duty and obligation. Cease in that effort and so will the laughter and tears, the happiness and the joy.

The demand for excellence sport imposes on us may account for its popularity. Save for war, there is no better theater for heroism. Nicholas Fox, an Australian journalist, made this point well.

"Some of the most pure moments in memory," wrote Fox, "moments when men stood ennobled beyond possibility, when all that is grand and magnificent in them is distilled and proffered to those who will accept it, have occurred in sports."

In sport, the heroic is commonplace. It is common not only to do one's best, but to risk failure in the attempt to go beyond it.

"It is a rare thing," Fox wrote, "in our everyday lives to see a man commit himself, expose his frailties, prostrate himself in despairing endeavor. Yet in sport it is seen constantly."

And that commitment, that exposure, is required of everyone in sport, not merely the champions. I spoke once at a postmarathon banquet in Boston. Joan Benoit was the guest of honor, and the videotape of her victory in the Olympic marathon was shown. This, said the master of ceremonies, was one of the great moments in sport. When I rose, I said that *everyone* in the room who on this day had finished the Boston Marathon had their own great moment in sport — each of us on this one day had achieved greatness.

Happiness is always connected with action. Sport is pure effort for the pure enjoyment of it. We use ourselves to the utmost, calling on, as philosopher George Santayana said, "all the primitive virtues and fundamental gifts of man."

The union of body and mind in action reaches its height in sports, where there is no legalistic quibbling, no sophisticated debates. The reason, in Jean-Paul Sartre's view: "Only in games is man free, because only in games does he understand what is going on."

When Heisman trophy winner Dick Kazmaier was asked what he

had learned from playing football, he said, "I learned all the lessons you don't learn from a textbook. I learned about dealing with people, with adversity, and a competitive climate."

Was it football or Princeton that shaped Kazmaier? His words leave little doubt: "Football is a wonderful training ground to learn how to respond to discipline, to pressure, to maintain a balanced approach while you're trying to compete."

Sport involves us more than any other interests except sex and religion. "The very names of a cricket bat and ball make English fingers tingle," wrote English essayist William Hazlitt. He told us of the great Long Robinson who had a screw fastened to his hand to hold the bat after two of the fingers of his right hand had been struck off by the violence of the ball.

"I have myself," wrote Hazlitt, "whiled away whole mornings in seeing him strike the ball to the farthest extremity of the smooth and level sunburnt ground, and with long awkward strides count the notches that made victory sure."

Boxing does not appeal to me. I find it too brutal. I believe in its long-term bad consequences. But I find accounts of the bare-knuckle days exciting, and no lover of any sport could ask for a better book than A. J. Liebling's *The Sweet Science.*

Hazlitt, a thorough-going enthusiast of most sports, had a wonderful account of the fight between Bill Neate and the Gas-Man. He found their recuperation in the half-minute allowed between rounds almost incredible. "To see two men smashed to the ground, smeared in gore, stunned, senseless, the breath knocked out of their bodies and then before you recover from the shock to see them rise up with new strength and courage, stand ready to inflict or receive mortal offense. This is the most astonishing thing of all: this is the high and heroic state of man."

Hazlitt defended this admittedly brutal spectacle against those who despise it. "Do something to show as much pluck, or as much self possession as this, before you assume a superiority which you have never given a single proof of by any one action in the whole course of your lives." Hazlitt himself found sport his own spur to action. "I crawl around the fives-court (handball court) like a cripple until I get a racket in my hand, and then I start up as if I was possessed by the devil: I now have a motive for action."

Sport is a motive for action. Few other things that are not sinful or ruinous deliver us from inertia. Nothing else this side of war and adventure and the religious life will help us evolve into the selves we wish to be. If this world is a vale for soul-making, sport is one of the better ways to engage in the enterprise.

Fives was Hazlitt's way. "It is the finest exercise for the body and the greatest relaxation of the mind. He who takes to playing fives is twice young. He feels neither the past nor the future. Debts, taxes, nothing can touch him further. He has no other wish, no other thought, from the moment the game begins but that of striking the ball, of placing it, of making it."

Everyone who has found their sport knows that feeling. We can take as our own the motto placed over the door of the fives court: "Who enters here forgets himself, his country, and his friends." We become heroes in the making.

THE PURSUIT OF EXCELLENCE

What bothers people about runners is our almost arrogant acceptance that through and in running we are fulfilling our destiny. We runners tend to regard ourselves as born-again heroes and saints. If runners possess anything to a greater degree than endurance, it is self-esteem.

This is a great possession. Self-esteem is the subject of a recent book by the Reverend Robert Schuller, who commissioned the Gallup Poll to study its prevalence and effects on the American public. The survey showed that people with strong self-esteem (Schuller defined it as "the human hunger for the divine dignity that God intended for us") were healthier, happier, and more productive then their neighbors without it.

Self-esteem is present when there is little discrepancy between a person's ideal and actual self. It follows from the progressive development of the self into the heroic self it was meant to be.

I have been asked how the puny distance runner could possess such self-esteem. The fact is that running is an ideal way to develop the self. The runner can say, "I now am the body I was meant to be—trained, capable, and able to respond to any demands made upon me."

And that's not all. Achieving the capable body leads to the same search for the capable mind. The obsession—some see it that way—with training the body leads to an obsession with training the mind as well. And in such an enterprise, talent and wealth, beauty and station, learning and lineage count for little. We already possess all we need: It is *effort* that brings us to greatness and the fusion of what we are with what we can be.

I am guided in this by Ruskin's Law. Writing of the qualities that distinguished great artists from their less gifted brethren, John

Ruskin, Victorian writer and critic, cited sensibility and imagination and, finally, industry. This last, he said, was of great importance.

"When I hear of a young man spoken of as giving promise of high genius, the first question I ask about him is always 'Does he work?' "

That is our measure. Our sensibility and imagination have limitations, but our industry—the work we put into achieving our goals—need not. It is sufficient to pursue excellence, to be dedicated to something, to give ourselves to some project, wholeheartedly.

In this pursuit of excellence we runners do something that upsets some observers: We reset goals. Runners are never satisfied; we are always in process. For me, that is a test for normalcy. The normal person is *constantly* striving for some ideal self.

Is there anyone out there who isn't concerned about self-worth? About an uncertain identity and low self-esteem? Is there anyone not on a constant search for autonomy, mastery and control? The runner is no different from others in these needs. The question then becomes how to satisfy those needs—and is running the way to do it? Or is it really a negative addiction that costs more than the benefits it confers?

Some health-care specialists think so. The dogma goes something like this: Running is acceptable when done for health or to relieve anxiety. It is not acceptable when it is accompanied—as it is in many runners—by the intensity and exclusiveness usually reserved for religious fanatacism. At that point, appropriate preventive and therapeutic measures should be instituted. Runners must be saved from the maladaptive behavior that has taken over their lives.

I don't dispute the description of the typical runner as a person *intensely* committed to his sport. But I also accept the findings of researchers at California State University at Fullerton. Runners, they found, were "more reserved, more intelligent, more dominant, more aggressive, more socially reticent, a bit more suspicious, more shrewd, more self-sufficient, and more unconventional than nonrunners."

It is not the details of our behavior that are in question, it is the judgment made from them. What some see as a problem I see as the solution. For me, running has narrowed the distance between what I am and what I can be, between the actual self and the ideal, between aspiration and reality.

THE GAME OF LIFE

Although there are bad times when it takes a philosopher to explain why, life is a positive sum game. Everyone is a winner. And, therefore, all our other games by which we learn how to play the life game are positive games as well. Everyone from the gold medalist to the last finisher can rejoice in a personal victory.

I have written to that theme for years, but it wasn't until recently that it became something I had experienced myself. Over the years, I have always been near the top in my age group. I have rarely come home without a medal or a trophy. And more often than not, I would finish ahead of two-thirds of the runners in a race.

Doing well has always been important to me. But life has taught me a new lesson about what "doing well" really means—and winning has little to do with it: *Trying* is everything. One week, I severely strained a calf muscle in a 5-miler with two enormous hills. One week later, my cancer struck. One day I was fine, the next I was in agony with pain.

A month later, I'd planned to run in the Sandy Hook triathlon: a half-mile swim, 12 miles on the bike, and ending with a 10-kilometer run. The twin disasters, leg and cancer, now made it out of the question—at least that's what *I* thought. Two of my friends thought different. They cornered me and told me to enter.

"You have no excuses," said one of them. "You swim and cycle— then skip the run." I didn't want any part of it. Then he said, "George, you've always excelled. You've forgotten that the important thing is to *compete.*"

So I competed. And it was worse than anything I had imagined. The swim was an absolute horror. The pack of almost 300 set off for a buoy about 200 yards out. Unfortunately, there was a strong tide going south that made reaching the buoy extremely difficult for the weaker swimmers. After a while I realized that I was in a group of about a dozen who were swimming in place—we were making no headway. The others had rounded the buoy and were heading south at a good pace for the final buoy and the return to shore.

Finally, a lifeguard on a surfboard told us to forget about the first buoy and head for the second. I kept getting farther and farther behind. When I headed for shore I was the last swimmer in the race. One lifeguard on a surfboard shepherded me to shore. "Do you need any help?" she kept asking me every few minutes.

As I emerged from the water and trotted to the transition area, I decided that enough was enough, I was going no further. But when I got to my bike, another friend, a former wrestling coach, came over with water and encouragement. He had no reason to think I was going to quit. So—I didn't. I got on my bike and set out on the two 6-mile laps. In short order, I was lapped by people who were 6 miles ahead of me. They kept zooming by like swallows, while up ahead I could see a few stragglers like myself pumping away and *still* losing ground.

In time, the ordeal began to wind down. A mile out, I passed the winner as he was ending his 10-kilometer run. Up ahead at the finish line, the crowd awaited this young hero—and as I came through, having completed only two-thirds of the race, they gave me a great cheer. They did not know I was going into the transition area and not coming out. Even madmen have moments of sanity. I had done what my friends had asked. Now I could wait for them to finish.

But the cheering did it. I was ashamed to stop. I got off the bike and ordered my body to start running. After a while it didn't hurt anymore. I even caught a few people ahead of me. And two hours and 22 minutes after I had entered the water, I finished.

My two friends were at the finish. There were hugs all around. One said I was a winner. The other said I was a giant. I would not have exchanged that moment for all the trophies I have at home.

As I stood there watching the last of the winners cross the line, I thought to myself, I've finally learned how to play this game. With a little help, of course, from my friends.

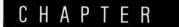

3

THE MANY LEVELS OF MOTIVATION

N*o motivation can live where faith and courage are absent.*

BE A GOOD ANIMAL

When the nineteenth century English philosopher Herbert Spencer spoke on physical sin, he was referring to offenses against the body. In his treatise on education, Spencer stressed the necessity for physical training and the development of the body. "If you wish to be a success in this life," he writes, "you must first be a good animal."

Implied in this statement are deep moral and ethical reasons for being a good animal. Success in Spencer's eyes, which is to say the point of view of a philosopher, was no less than the fulfillment of our natures — becoming what we are meant to be. Unless we become good animals, we will fail and that failure will affect our entire personalities.

The present rush to fitness is a response to this consciousness of physical sin. The morality that impels people to take care of their bodies proceeds through the same stages that mark our usual moral thinking: from fear to selfish interest and ending with an abstract principle—fitness is good because it's the right thing to do. Analysis of the reasons people have for exercising will show the usual progression of why people repent and turn their backs on evil and error, whatever its source.

It begins, as does most morality, in fear. We are bombarded daily with statistics of the mortal effects of our profligate lifestyles. We are constantly warned of the dangers of smoking and drinking and over-eating. Our sedentary lives are not merely sins against the Holy Ghost, it will lower our life span as well. If we become sick or die before our time, it is on our own heads.

Obeying the rules at this level is a childlike morality. It is a version of the old motivation, "If you don't do it, I'll kick your butt." It is little more than forced labor. Exercise is done against one's wishes and maintained only because the alternative is worse.

Morality, a notch above this, occurs when the exercise produces rewards. Exercise helps us lose weight and gain energy. It dispels fatigue and improves appearance. We begin to take pride in our bodies, the way they look and move. We are becoming good physical animals —and enjoying it.

This purely selfish stage leads to one derived from higher impulses. Hans Selye called this the level of selfish altruism. In order to play our parts in society and contribute to the common good, we accept the obligation to be fit. We want to do well for others as well as ourselves. We acknowledge the responsibility to be part of the team effort.

The good animal becomes the good social animal. We succeed by contributing to the success of the common effort. At this stage of morality, we accept law and order. We follow the rules because that is the way the world works.

The third and highest degree of moral impulse comes from the belief that it is the true and good and beautiful thing to do. We are now in pursuit of our best and deepest selves. We are beyond the structures of tradition, the rules of science, the regulations of society, the duties toward our fellowman.

We are now impelled by a new consideration. Our human machines, the interactions of body and mind that manifest our souls, must be brought to their earthly best. The good physical, social animals also become good in the philosophical sense—we become the external manifestations of our inner persons. These animals are now no less than *our selves*, finally and ultimately revealed. When we put on the new body, we put on the new men.

And the good animal finally finds its true habitat.

THE BODY IN MOTION

A body at rest stays at rest. No one knows this Newtonian principle better than fitness specialists. The immobile remain immobile. The sedentary continue to be sedentary. Education fails. Arguments go unheeded. Persuasion does not persuade. Is there any method by which we can induce friends and family to start on a fitness program?

Surveys have shown the various reasons people give for remaining inactive. One of the most thorough surveys was published by Fitness Canada. The predominant reason given by Canadians who were polled was not enough time. Over 40 percent cited the time factor as the key reason they do not exercise.

The excuse of not enough time is true for all of us. None of us have enough time to do everything we want to do. We must make a choice. Establish priorities. Decide which of these presumably good things are better. If our bodies had ombudsmen, they could demand equal time. If we think it through, we would concede it. There is also a bonus when we exercise. Fitness may take time, but it makes time as well.

Nevertheless, the complaint is true. We cannot tack an exercise period onto our usual day. If we are putting something into our life, we must take something out. If we get up early to jog, we will have to retire that much sooner at night. In order to lift weights at lunch hour, we must give up lunch. A late afternoon or early evening session of exercise must replace whatever we did at that time.

Following close on the heels of too little time was the lack of convenient, well-equipped, and inexpensive facilities in which to exercise. Better facilities would encourage Canadians to become more active. At least 20 percent of them feel that way. The rural vote was even higher—an even 30 percent.

That depends, of course, on the activity. Except during severe weather conditions, runners need no athletic facility. I once made that point during a speech at a YMCA fund-raising dinner. "I will probably never set foot in the new Y after it's built," I told the audience, watching the chairman of the committee turn pale. "But," I continued, "there are great numbers of people who will find the Y absolutely essential to their fitness programs."

Fitness should be play. And for many, play needs a playground. Play needs courts and pools, activity rooms and weight areas. Play needs space and equipment and variety. Play should be convenient and inexpensive, suitable to differing physiques and different temperaments. The key to starting a fitness program is to find your play. And the key to a successful fitness program is to find a place and people to play with.

Nevertheless, motivated people find ways to exercise regardless of the proximity, equipment, or cost of facilities.

I know of one corporation in Tennessee that has a successful fitness program without an instructor or fitness facility. Almost half of the employees participate, many with their spouses, and the attrition rate is less than 10 percent. Why is this company so successful? It screens its employees to detect potential medical problems and, at the same time, sets their baseline level of fitness. This is usually motivating information. Next, and possibly most important, they earn cash for their efforts—different amounts for different exercises. Apparently, when you are paid to exercise, you *find* a place to do it.

The next most prevalent reason given for not exercising was the lack of people with whom to play. Almost equally important, and undoubtedly part of this, was the failure of friends or family members to be interested. Gregarious people want company. Shy people need support. And there are those whose main reward from fitness activity is social. Other aspects can be important, but it is the conversation, camaraderie, and human contact that lures us into doing something we would otherwise not do.

The shy and possibly inept exercisers will venture into these athletic areas only when encouraged and accompanied by family or friends. They have usually avoided sports and physical activity in the past. So this is an entirely new world to them, which they perceive to be filled with possibilities for embarrassment and failure.

Both reasons suggest that example is a great force. Where few people exercise, even fewer people are likely to take it up. Where few people demonstrate the values and virtues of fitness, there will be only a limited few who follow their example.

People are herd animals. If we see others doing something (like getting fit) and apparently enjoying it, it boosts our own desire to follow suit. If this is so, our missionary efforts should never cease. But proselytizing can turn a person off perhaps even more easily than turning that same person on. *Example* is still the most effective way to make a lasting convert.

A major factor is ignorance. Ignorance of what constitutes exercise. Ignorance of how much is required. Ignorance of the global effect of exercise on the personality. And ignorance of the specific values that are the motivational force behind the successful exerciser.

More leisure time, better facilities, the interest of others are indeed facilitators. But the reason for getting fit is the realization that life is motion—and a body in motion stays in motion.

FITNESS FACTS

Action is always impelled by some good we want to attain. The question is the choice of which good. Shall we move toward the immediate good at hand, or are we able to see a higher good in the future? Reason, it seems, is almost always in favor of gratification denied. The good we will possess later is better than the one we can have right now.

Fitness programs follow that reasoning. The benefits come from denying our pressing desire to enjoy ourselves this minute. The appetites we have are good, but there are also higher appetites and higher goals. Nevertheless, fitness programs—especially our own—have hard going. We tend to backslide, return to the physical habits that marked our previous lives. And in so doing, settle for less than our bests—and diminish our lives and our possibilities.

Part of this pattern comes from ignorance. There is a saying that no one will do something just because it's good for them. Whatever the action, it will have to appeal to some other motive. I'm beginning to doubt that. It is evident that millions of people are now in fitness programs simply because it is good for them. They have stopped smoking (a tremendously enjoyable practice) for no other reason than that it is good to do so.

What is needed for such action is knowledge. To make a change in one's lifestyle for the better, one needs instruction in three areas. What is the wrong thing to do? Why is it wrong? And what can be done about it? Or, to put it positively: What are the goals in our lifestyles? Why do we need to achieve them? And how can we bring them about?

An analysis of your present situations could include many elements of our daily lives, including such items as whether we wear seat belts and how much sleep we can get. We should see immediately that the first necessity is the consciousness of the basic elements of health.

Let me suggest some indicators of a healthy state: a normal blood pressure; body fat less than 18 percent in a man, 25 percent in a woman; cholesterol no more than 160; freedom from drug abuse, including nicotine and alcohol; sufficient sleep; adequate adaptation to stress; a normal work capacity; freedom from guilt and anxiety; normal memory and problem-solving skills; having a goal above and beyond oneself—something that transcends our routine concerns.

Deviation from any of these attributes will penalize us in some way. So, knowing the rules, we must also know the penalties that occur if these good things are not attained. Although the consequences in some instances may be immediate, most are down the line—out of sight of our immediate experience and therefore not considered.

Many of the good consequences of a healthy lifestyle are immediately evident. Exercise gives us more energy. It increases our productivity within weeks. Progressive weight loss is another quickly noticed benefit, and the improvement in our performance is readily apparent.

Some aren't, however—lower cholesterol and blood pressure. To convince people who don't believe in benefits they can't see, physicians should use the "worst outcome" scenario. It is going to happen to *you*, not your neighbor down the street. Your high cholesterol is eventually going to do *you* in. And the effects of that elevation are already being felt in your arteries. Contrast that with the present cavalier attitude that says the risks are small and only truly high levels are important: Any number of people enjoy rich food, have high cholesterol, and die in car accidents at 90.

That may well be so. But we follow that advice at our peril. Hardening of our arteries is most often the way we become disabled or die. It can be forestalled by simple changes in our lifestyles. We will not only increase our absolute life expectancies, we will increase our *active* life expectancies, as well.

Learn the facts and act on them. It is not a question of being an optimist or a pessimist—the object is to become a realist. There is a way to get the most years and mileage out of the human machine. Leaving it to chance raises the likelihood that you will be shortchanged.

DESIRE: THE IMPORTANCE OF WILL

Motivation is the need, drive, or desire to act in a certain way to achieve a certain end. Basic needs are strong motivators. When I am hungry or thirsty or cold, or when I am in obvious danger, I am impelled to do something about it. I am willing to attack the problem head-on: I do what must be done.

Whereas drives push, desires pull. I have desires for many things. I want self-esteem. I would like to be a hero. I wish to have peak experiences. I pray for that perfect communion with another person. And as I sit here at the typewriter I am trying to write a perfect essay.

Making allowances for differences in vocation and avocation, I presume you would say much the same. Our needs, drives, and desires —the stuff of our lives—do not vary to any great degree. Yet our motivation does. I see about me people who, in philosopher William James's expression, lead lives inferior to themselves. And I suspect that I do the same. We could all be artists and athletes and heroes. We could all care for orphans and widows and visit the sick. We could all be catchers in the rye, each in his or her own unique and particular way announcing the Creator's intentions at our births. We could be our best. But we are not.

Our only excuse is ignorance. We are unaware of our capabilities. We do not realize that each one of us is the marvel of the universe. We should read the geniuses of our past. Heed Emerson: "I preach the infinitude of the common man." We sell ourselves short, and our lives as well. When our horizons narrow, our goals do also. We settle for a comfortable passing grade. We groove through life, effortlessly passing our days. But the intensity of our art—our life—and therefore our joy, passes as well. But that is part of the bargain.

I know of one crew coach who retired because he had a different breed of rowers. "They are no longer," he said, "looking at the hills." When people look at the highest goal, the intensity of motivation increases in two ways. First, in the strength of the desire to achieve. Whatever is necessary will now be done. One look at the grandeur of the Matterhorn gives the true mountaineer all the inspiration he needs! The year's preparation that precedes his climb is now automatic. The climb becomes the reason for existence.

I am reminded at the start of each new year of the reasons why I should try to do better than I think possible. New Year's Day, however, is but one of 365 mornings each year that can afford me a new start toward glory. Life, to this runner, is an uphill race that becomes progressively more difficult. There is no time for dallying. Each day requires its own spur.

I recall toiling up a mountain in a 10-mile race in Durango and having the runner beside me say, "It's so beautiful here." I took a brief look at the peaks around us and the river in the canyon a thousand feet below, said "Yes," and got back to work.

My end is not simple happiness. My need, drive, and desire is to achieve my full and complete self. If I do what I have come to do, if I create the life I was made for, then happiness will follow. The problem in motivation is not the dedication and effort and sacrifice needed to get what we want, it is knowing what it is we could and must want to begin with.

The Declaration of Independence states unequivocally that all men are created equal. Yet every day I find reason to believe this to be untrue. I run in a race and half the field beats me. I attend a seminar and can't follow the reasoning of the speaker. I read a book and I am unable to understand what is evident to others. Daily I am instructed in my deficiencies. I do something, physical or mental, and realize how far I fall short of what other people accomplish.

Despite the Declaration, we are apparently not born equal. I cannot aspire to win the Boston Marathon. I most certainly will not receive the Nobel Prize for literature. I am surrounded by people who know more, do more, and make more than I do. But, like many others, I identify myself with my performance. I become my marathon time. I become my latest book. I become the last lecture I gave.

I am all those things, of course. They are part of the self. They are the various ways I have of expressing who I am and what I believe. These are the operations that reveal the body-mind machine that I am.

But I am more than a body-mind complex. I am a soul as well. I share with everyone on this planet one power infinitely more important than talent: willpower. In this power of the soul, all of us are created equal. Each one of us is capable of the ideal or moral action, which William James defined in this way: "It is the action in the line of the greatest resistance."

Anyone so inclined can decide on ideal action. The will considers the question, Will you or won't you have it so? And in that decision you can be the equal of anyone else. "Effort is the measure of a man," wrote James.

How well we know that. I am never content with contentment. I am uneasy when things go easy. "Don't take things easy," said a great physician, "take things hard." Doing one's absolute best becomes the criterion.

"I am writing the best I can," said the author of some bestselling popular novels. "If I could write any better I would. This is the peak of my powers." It matters little that she cannot write any better. It matters, more than life, that she is doing it with all her might.

Running in races has made this whole subject plain to me. I am thinking now of Palmetto Road, the long steep hill at the 5-mile mark of the Bermuda 10-kilometer run. For most of the race, I am running in the lee of a gentleman my age wearing plaid shorts. Just before the hill I pass him and go into second place in my age group.

It is a short-lived moment of triumph. The hill suddenly puts urgent demands on my body. I forget the imperative of beating anyone in my age group and especially one in plaid shorts. It becomes the hill and me. My legs are heavy and filled with pain. My breath comes in short gasps. I am bent over almost double. The battle shifts. It becomes me against me. My will in a duel with my mind and my body. A contest with that part of myself who wants to stop.

All around me, runners are engaged in the same struggle. Pushing themselves as if their lives depended on reaching the top of this hill. The leaders have already finished, and the race, you might say, is over. But not for us. A spectator who could see this race for what it truly is, would see not bodies but wills straining to reach the crest. Here indeed is "action in the line of the greatest resistance."

A jockey, speaking of a champion horse, said, "He makes the effort and makes it more often." The uncrowned champions at the back of the pack do the same. Unconcerned with what others are doing, driven by the need to do our best, we make the effort and we make it more often. And for those few moments, we become the equal of anyone on this earth.

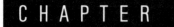

CHAPTER

4

FITNESS FOR LIVING: BEATING THE ODDS

H*ealth makes for the happy pursuit of happiness, and it gives us a longer time to do it.*

VOTING FOR HEALTH

There were five million more Americans counted in the 1980 census than projections from the previous census had predicted. My guess is that this five million are alive today because they're fit. But what triggered this mass movement toward fitness? Only one thing's certain: It came from the people. Fitness is an instance of participatory democracy, with each individual casting a vote for health.

I suspect there have been as many reasons for this change in lifestyle as there are lifestyles.

But beneath all of them, there's a major philosophical change: We've gone, in two decades, from self-gratification to self-*improvement.*

During the 1960s, sexuality, drugs, and pleasure-seeking ruled the roost. The basic ploy was to drop out. There was nothing worth doing well—not government, not God, not even greed. Technology was the enemy, so we retreated back to the cave, in part because we felt the civilization we had inherited was not worth maintaining.

That has all changed. When people become interested in a better way to live, it means they consider life worth living. And when life's worth living, there is only one thing more important than doing something well—doing it *better*.

Since 1968, more and more Americans have put the desire for health at the top of their priority list. We began then to have a sense of duty and even sacrifice. The self-gratification of the Me Decade went down for the count under a new quest—our pursuit of well-being and physical health.

And this shift is still going on. A demographics expert reported that 43 percent of Americans still organize their lives around material well-being. Another 38 percent focus on security as their prime purpose. However, a full 17 percent have become trailblazers: They look to competence and challenge as the requisites for the good life. "We are witnessing," he stated, "an outburst of sheer vitality and ingenuity and ability to cope." It is a global change that is occurring—vitality of the body, ingenuity of the mind, and the ability of the soul to cope.

The spur to this change in our lives has not been longevity, but rather our perceived need to develop bodies and minds to the utmost. Health, we can also see, is not a product of this pursuit, it is a process—an ongoing state of *being* maintained by discipline and commitment. Health makes for the happy pursuit of happiness, and it gives us a longer time to do it.

Whether we're healthy or not is largely our decision: We need no new drug or surgery or expert or medical discovery to do it.

LIVING FOR LIFE

Lifestyle has been described as "the set of habitual behaviors adopted by personal choice." Physicians since the time of Hippocrates have appreciated the importance of these behaviors in the prevention of disease. They have, however, been pessimistic about changing them. The only effective preventive medicine to date has been social medicine —major advances achieved through public health measures such as treatment of water supplies and vaccination of huge numbers of people.

But we have come to an era where aberrant lifestyle—the bad habits we make part of our lives—can no longer be ignored. It has been estimated that in time more than half of all annual deaths in the United States will be the result of our living habits, and for this we have only ourselves to blame. A healthy lifestyle is within reach of practically everyone, regardless of economic circumstances. In fact, it would cost *less* than the way we live now.

How prevalent are high-risk habits? A Massachusetts survey of four of them is revealing. This study concentrated on four basic life-style variables: exercise, smoking, weight, and alcohol use. The people who were questioned had mean educations of 11.9 years, and mean reported household incomes of $17,662. The 1,000 who participated were a cross-section of the state in terms of age, sex, and marital status.

The results? The number overweight was 43 percent; the number smoking, 33 percent; the number getting no exercise, 28.3 percent; and the number guilty of robust alcohol use—more than two drinks daily—was 11.7 percent. Not so good. And women reported more high-risk behaviors than men in virtually all areas except alcohol. Older persons reported less smoking and alcohol use than their younger counterparts, but they had a marked prevalence of overweight and generally exercised less.

Education, not surprisingly, proved to be a significant indicator of healthy lifestyle. Those with higher educations reported less heavy drinking, less overweight, and less smoking. It appears that people in the upper class take physical health more seriously than their blue-collar brethren—a finding borne out by other studies. This difference has been apparent since early in the running boom. When *Runner's World* magazine was getting started, only *one* subscriber had a union card: Middle-class intellectuals dominated the ranks of runners throughout the sport's phenomenal rise in popularity.

And age perhaps *does* bring wisdom: 36 percent of the exercisers in the Massachusetts study preferred walking or jogging, but most were over 65—elderly exercisers who chose walking as their daily constitutional.

The findings of this study are in line with my own experience. When I was in active practice a decade ago, I, too, found admonitions to stop smoking and lose weight to be fruitless most often. And the medical community was partly to blame. Most physicians then had a lifestyle they would deplore in patients. Doctors, as everyone knew, smoked, were generally overweight, and played golf once a week. And only a little further back, in the 1950s, a cigarette company advertised its brand as the winner in a poll of 110,000 physicians.

Now all that is changed. Only 22 percent of physicians smoke, much less than the national average of 33 percent. Practicing physicians are becoming practicing athletes, with the thin, *exercising* physician the new image projected by the medical profession. In my first

Boston Marathon in 1964, I was 1 of only 3 physicians. In 1987, there were over 600.

But the doctors are only mirroring the people. This nation has made a 180-degree turn in its attitude toward health practices. The populace has become sensitive to the importance of lifestyle, and has begun to adopt a healthy one. What should be noted, however, is that the same group that constitutes the majority of the new converts to running—those with more education and more money—is still leading the way.

But neither high income nor a college degree is necessary. The rules of health require less money when you abide by them than when you break them. And you don't need college physiology to understand them. The rules of fitness are known by every schoolchild, or at least should be.

The bottom line: A healthy lifestyle doesn't cost a penny. All you have to do is *choose* it.

EVERYTHING NEW IS OLD

Over the centuries, the rules for health have been constant. Only the reasons for observing them have changed. And, while there have been major advances in public health, few have occurred in personal health. When we read of the latest ways to take care of our bodies, we can be sure that people long ago were given the same advice.

What does change is motivation. Mass movements are set in motion by particular interests at a particular time. People are inspired by the ruling ideas in their culture, and different generations generate different provocations to action.

These two aspects of health, its unchanging principles and its ever-changing incentives, were easily seen in a New York museum exhibit devoted to fitness in the United States in the last century. "Fit for American Health: Fitness, Sport, and American Society (1840-1930)" demonstrated the constancy of methods and materials used to attain health. Then, as now, various forms of exercise were emphasized. People were encouraged to walk, play golf, use rowing machines, train with Indian clubs, move to music. The only thing missing that we do today? Jogging.

Diet was central then, too. Low-fat and vegetarian diets headed up the recommendations. High-fiber food was widely advertised, and bottled water was an even bigger seller than it is now. And Americans were amply instructed in the dangers of alcohol, coffee, and tobacco.

Stress management wasn't ignored, either. The breakdown from stress was called "nervous exhaustion," and the sages of the time considered it an especially American disease: "Americanitis," they called it. An early neurologist said that it resulted from "over brain-work in business, literary, or professional pursuits." To combat this decline in vigor, *active* steps were proposed: Fitness of the body achieved through exercise restored its vital force.

This exhibit displayed real counterparts of the equipment and programs we use today. The astonishing thing? Nothing seems dated or ancient. Our methods of attaining health and fitness are simply new versions of what have always been fundamental ways of achieving maximum body function.

But the reasons for this interest in excellence of the body have changed from era to era. "The exhibit," the *New York Times* stated, "reveals that America's current preoccupation with health, fitness, and dietary improvement *pales* in comparison with the intensity of the nineteenth century."

Where did that passionate intensity come from? Today's health and fitness leaders would like to know, because motivation in the past could be the key to motivation in the present. And it is motivation that is the principal stumbling block to successful fitness programs—the dropout problem is enormous. People can be threatened, coaxed, and enticed into *starting* fitness activities, but all too often, starting has nothing to do with *staying*.

The curator of the fitness exhibit had made an intensive study of the philosophies that powered the early forces of fitness. He divided more than a century of attention to lifestyle into several epochs. In each, people accepted fitness as necessary to life, but for very different reasons.

Spirituality. In the 1830s, fitness was considered part of one's Christianity—preparation of the body for the second coming of Christ. People were enjoined to attain combined physical and spiritual perfection, with health not merely a physical quest but also a spiritual one.

Health and stress management. As time passed and Americans moved into cities, they became anxious about the effects of urban life on their health. The philosophy of health changed to an emphasis on the environment and its dangers, and the problems of stress, as well. Fitness programs thus became a defense against the stresses and strains of this new life.

Strength of character. With the country's growing economic success came the belief that Americans were getting *soft*. The result: a new emphasis on "roughing it." People were encouraged to get outdoors and go back to nature. Hiking and climbing, hunting and boating became fashionable. Even houses and furniture were representative of this urge to return to some vestiges of the pioneer life: Log cabins and rough-hewn tables were all the rage.

Immortality. Finally, as work became the religion of America, there came a belief in fitness as a means of personal salvation. "By the end of the Depression," said the curator, "you see a real, almost desperate fear of dying. I don't think our present concerns are that different."

This exhibit was therefore a recapitulation of our deeper motives for fitness—those that go beyond cholesterol levels and percent of body fat: spirituality, health, strength of character, and immortality.

The study of motivation goes back to the Greeks. Their sports were essential to their education. They saw in sports the integration of body, mind, and soul, the creation of beauty, the mastering of athletics, and the challenge of competition. A French sociologist pointed this out. "Sports," he wrote, "was part of the *education* of the citizen. He was expected to engage in exercise for a whole series of reasons that had to do with the shaping of a citizen; the relation between moral good and physical good; and the growth of a person."

The point: We don't need new ways to become fit and healthy. What is necessary is already known. What we must pursue are the deeper reasons for seeking fitness. Fortunately, these inner urges are the inherited wisdom of the race. Know thyself, and you will know them.

EFFORT IS EXCELLENCE

Folklorist Garrison Keillor's description of Lake Wobegon invariably got a laugh. "It's a place," he said, "where all the women are strong, all the men are good-looking, and all the children are above average."

The last statement is the key to the laughter. The audience knew then that Lake Wobegon did not exist, because our common sense tells us there is no place on earth where *all* the children are above average.

Humor, however, always has two faces. It tells us truth that is not logical, truth that comes from deeper sources than the evidence of our five senses. Life is not a matter of statistics: Our final report card will not give our class ranking. The fact of the matter, the hidden truth, is that everyone can be above average.

Becoming above average is not all that difficult. To put it bluntly, the average person has *settled* for less, has *accepted* mediocrity—and has the status to prove it.

The real goal in life? To be above average—to be *normal,* which really means being the best you can be. Being average is living in the past; being normal is striving in the present.

Normalcy has little to do with being witty and wealthy and good-looking. Those are qualities dictated by chance and circumstance. Being normal is chiefly a matter of making the most out of what you were born with, and it follows from acknowledging an *obligation* to pursue excellence. But it's important to note that the pursuit alone counts just as much as the achievement—and possibly more.

Consider: There was a time when I was special. Back in the 1930s, not many people went to college. Few went on to medical school. A college graduate had status, but a physician stood even higher on the scale. In everything from income to vocabulary, I was above average.

No more: College graduates abound, physicians are in oversupply, and my vocabulary can't get me through a crossword puzzle. I am now officially average. But that doesn't make me truly average, and whether I am or not has to be *my* call, not yours. What really counts is how hard I try—and here, the struggle is all.

We lead lives inferior to ourselves, said philosopher William James —lives that don't reflect our real ability. One reason we do: It's more *comfortable* not to try hard. But life is, or should be, a struggle: Comfort should make us uncomfortable; contentment should make us discontented.

Runners embrace that philosophy. In common with most practicing athletes, we are responding to a basic trait in nature—to be number one. And in this regard also, the struggle is all. I am not deterred in my *pursuit* of excellence by the fact that hundreds of other runners beat me. It's the race that challenges me, not the finish line.

I am not yet "normal," but I'm trying—and that's what makes the difference.

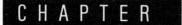

CHAPTER

5

EXERCISE EXPERTISE: MAKING IT WORK

*W*hat *it pleases you to do as an exerciser will be the lifestyle you should have adopted in the first place.*

DETECTING A DEFICIENCY

Are you feeling run-down, sluggish, low in energy? Is simply getting to school or work becoming too much for you? Are you exhausted by three o'clock in the afternoon? Do you feel depressed? Have you lost your initiative?

If you answer yes, you may be suffering from a lifestyle disease that, surveys tell us, affects about one-half of all Americans. It is called exercise deficiency, it is undoubtedly a leading cause of ill health, and no household is exempt.

Exercise deficiency—the sweat deficit—is a self-inflicted disease. It is an old and familiar story: Our greatest tendency is to cheat on ourselves. We think we can enjoy the fullness of life without paying for it. But that is not the way the world works—or the human machine, either: *Nothing* is free.

31

Full-blown exercise deficiency states are evident to the most inexperienced observer—sufferers are manifestly out of shape. These extreme cases usually fatigue easily and early and spend most of the day in physical and mental torpor. They are much too tired when they get home at night to even consider taking any physical exercise. For them, repose is the natural state, and any activity is an effort.

Many people with exercise deficiency are unaware that they have it. They expect no more from their bodies than they are getting. They believe their lack of energy and enthusiasm goes with age. They think they are normal. The reality: They are *average*, because it's average to slow down, average to become less productive, average to have less energy—and since that's exactly what happens to most of us, we confuse the two. But average is *not* normal. Normal is the *best* you can be.

The notion that loss of physical vigor is inevitable usually comes in the mid-thirties. At the FBI Academy, where recruits are placed in a fitness program to get them back in condition, one aspirant complained to the director, "I'm 35. I'm too old for this stuff."

But we are never too old to be fit, and never too young to start preserving fitness. We *need* to be physically fit whether we are 20 or 35 or even 70. Being unfit at any age is settling for less than your best and is a classic example of the sort of thinking that is behind the widespread incidence of exercise deficiency.

Fortunately, the movement toward fitness is equally widespread. Half the people in this country now realize the need for physical exercise. They know there is no need to lose the gleam in their eye, the bloom in their cheek, the lift in their walk, and the life in their day.

And all it takes is sweat.

ENJOYING THE EFFORT

English clergyman and writer Sydney Smith, a man of original insights about the conduct of life, once wrote that he had nothing new to say about the care of the body. No one has, since health has no history. It always was, is, and will be. While the world has changed in remarkable ways, the repertoire of health has remained the same over the centuries: Whenever humans turn to health and fitness, they repeat regimens that date back to ancient Greece.

Ronald Reagan's fitness program is a case in point. In an interview, the former President stated the eternal truths of exercise. "I have found," he said, "that one key to exercise is to find something you enjoy." That has *always* been the first principle in fitness: What you do must be enjoyable, or you will not persist in it.

"The other key," said Reagan, "is to keep the exercise varied." Routine leads to boredom. Monotony makes for loss of interest. The process itself must be stimulating. Even dedicated runners, who find running a self-renewing compulsion, vary their training routes and take runs that differ in distance and intensity. The same thing—yesterday, today, and tomorrow—will defeat even the most enthusiastic exerciser.

It was Reagan's view also that every exercise program should have an outdoor element. This is fundamental: Indoor exercise is always a substitute, something to be done in inclement weather or to save time. But the great outdoors is infinitely preferable. There, we have the earth and sky, the wind and the rain, to awaken our animal instincts.

When one has to be indoors, the exercise prescriptions should be varied and brief. Reagan followed this rule. In his little gym in the White House he had a treadmill, an exercise bike, a machine with weights and pulleys to work on arms, legs, shoulders, and stomach, and something he called "a leg-lift contraption."

His program consisted of 10 minutes of calisthenics followed by 15 minutes on one of the machines. During that time he watched the evening news on TV. Each day he did something different, alternating exercises and machines. And each day he got out of there in a half hour.

These are the hallmarks of the successful fitness program. Another must is making it an integral part of the day. Necessity often dictates when a person can exercise, but it appears that it is best done between noon and 6:00 P.M. This is the high point in the daily trajectory of our body's natural rhythms.

I like to do my running in the early afternoon. Reagan looked forward to working out before dinner. His strenuous exercise dissipated the frustrations and aggravations, the tensions and anxieties, that developed during the presidential day—or, indeed, every person's day. It has been no different since Greeks in the fifth century B.C. spent an hour every day working out in the gymnasium, or *palaestra*. The message for modern man: Go with what works for you—*but make it fun.*

THE EXERCISE EQUATION: PART ONE

The simplest way to preserve health is to exercise. It is the only lifestyle change that does not raise additional questions: Exercise equals health, period.

In contrast, the arguments about what we should eat are endless.

The last word on food is the *first* word of yet another debate. What is dogma to some is heresy to others. There is no truth, no certainty, while nutrition books proliferate—and with them, our doubts about what's real and what's not.

The same might be said for alcohol. After two centuries of civilized life, we still can't make up our minds about whether or not we should drink. If we do drink, what should it be? If beer, what kind of beer? If wine, what sort of wine?

If we decide to limit ourselves to water, can we even be sure of that? Should it be hard or soft? Should it be bottled? And if so, should it contain, as the French say, *gas?*

Other lifestyle changes also share these varieties of opinion about what should be done. But they all have a common thread: Whatever the health professionals suggest requires willpower of the highest order.

Exercise does away with all the uncertainties. It answers all the questions. It replaces all the other lifestyle changes. Whatever you do wrong, knowingly or unknowingly, will be corrected by exercise. Eventually—and even without the use of willpower—all the prescribed alterations in daily living take place. In other words, you naturally start doing what's good for you, whether it's eating breakfast or going to bed early. It just *happens.*

When you exercise, your body determines your diet. You eat when you are hungry, you drink when you are dry. If you try to indulge yourself, the body will not permit it. For myself, I eat what I like, and the exercise takes care of it. I maintain my weight, have a normal blood lipid (fat) profile and a low percent of body fat. If I want to splurge on food and eat something rich, I go out and run 10 miles, and *then* I eat it. And even drink is no longer a problem: Two beers will give me that good feeling it took a six-pack to get in the old days.

Exercise now regulates my life. I travel unscathed through this babble of conflicting opinions by simply letting my body make these decisions for me. I recommend it to you: If you *can't* stop being a lush or a glutton or a two-pack-a-day smoker, exercise is your dish. Why? The exercising body does not *like* to smoke. It is moderate in its drinking and has definite ideas on diet. With exercise, you put on the new man. Exercise, and then you can do as you please.

The reason is simple: What it *pleases* you to do as an exerciser will be the lifestyle you *should* have adopted in the first place.

THE EXERCISE EQUATION: PART TWO

If you decide to change your life and go for health and fitness, what is the most important thing to do? Suppose you were given the following list and asked which of these measures you should do first, what choice would you make? (1) Stop smoking; (2) reduce alcohol intake; (3) diet; (4) get enough sleep; (5) learn relaxation techniques; (6) manage stress; (7) exercise; (8) all of the above.

The answer is exercise.

"The easiest way to preserve health and with greater profit than all other measures put together is to exercise well." So wrote Cristobal Mendez in his *Exercise Book,* published in 1553. Nothing has changed in the interim. Exercise is and always will be the single best thing to do about your health. Like charity, exercise covers a multitude of sins.

The most striking feature about it is its *immediate* benefit. I met a colleague who had been using the stairs in the hospital instead of the elevator. In two weeks, he had already noted an increase in energy and a reduction of fatigue. His evening hours no longer exhausted him.

In contrast, programs carefully designed to improve health frequently *cause* other problems. Consider smoking. All too often in practice, I see the usual aftermath of a successful attempt to stop smoking: The exsmoker gains weight, loses emotional equilibrium, is easily angered or depressed, and in general becomes hell to live with.

Dieting may not cause such catastrophic side effects, but it can destroy the enjoyment of life. It is never far from consciousness, and the thought of food occupies the mind most of the day. This rising-to-retiring battle diverts much energy that might be better spent on other productive efforts, and it has a negative effect on the true development of the self.

And so it goes. Anything we take out of our lives was there for a reason; we remove it at our peril. Exercise, on the other hand, is something we add to our lives — something that should have been there in the first place. The result — unlike the result of dieting or giving up cigarettes — is equally simple. We are more than we were, not less. And we are naturally better — better in fitness, better in health.

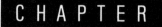
6

SCIENCE OF THE SOUND MIND

I*n running, motion becomes a mantra for this altered state of consciousness.*

THE BRAIN GAIN

Physicians who've concentrated on making life last longer through exercise tend to ignore the very important contribution physical activity makes to the mind.

Dr. Roy Shephard, a Canadian physiologist, cites an 18-month conditioning program at the National Aeronautics and Space Administration that makes the fact clear: Participants in the program all showed *major* gains in self-image. And it didn't stop there. With self-esteem came an increase in stamina, feelings of positive health, and a greater ability to cope with stress. Not bad for a little sweat.

The positive effect of exercise on anxiety and depression has also been reported in frequent studies. Joggers have been shown to have low scores in body manifestations of anxiety such as elevated heart rate and muscle tension. Running has been actually used as therapy in depression, with surprising results. It *surpassed* the results received from *drug* treatment.

Given those kinds of gains, it's obvious that exercise is a potent and powerful tool in stress management. My own experience in medical practice backs that up. Time and time again, when I felt like punching the next patient in the nose, an hour's run would purge me. I would return to work full of sweetness and light, almost *incapable* of anger or irritation.

Another generally unrecognized consequence of exercise is an increase in the ability to learn. There is an immediate and long-range improvement in the capacity for concentration. One study was done in a Canadian school where a physical education program (which reduced classroom time by 12 percent) was given to some students, while other students used as controls were not given the additional five hours of physical activity a week. Those in the physical education program scored consistently higher classroom marks than those who were not.

Studies are, of course, only studies. You and I are each an experiment of one, and we must find what works for us. Will exercise do for you what Dr. Shephard claims? Will it give you a sound mind in a sound body? Will it give you the human machine you need to make your life a work of art?

You'll never know until you try.

MIND GYMS

"A sound mind in a sound body," said seventeenth century English philosopher John Locke, "is a short but complete description of a happy life."

Neither is given to us; both must be acquired through effort. We know the rules for a sound body well. There are exercise protocols for speed, strength, and stamina, as well as programs for flexibility and coordination. We have learned the nutrition that makes our body work best, and we are aware of its requirements for sleep and relaxation.

The sound body is the athletic body. And, therefore, the training for the sound body is athletic training. It doesn't matter how old you are—training *works*. Read what the Roman philosopher Cicero had to say about old age and you will see that he expected the aging body to do great deeds. Our current interest in age-group competitive sports has confirmed his opinion.

But what of the sound mind? Are the rules for the mind as

straightforward as those for the body? Are there clear-cut principles on the care and feeding of the brain?

Of course. The first rule for the brain, as it is for the body, is to remain active. We are all aware that people who stay active, mentally and physically, appear much younger than their contemporaries who do not.

While on a ski trip, a friend of mine had breakfast with an elderly man who had performed extremely well on the slopes the day before. His mind, my friend discovered, was as quick and agile as his body. When he was complimented on this, he said, "When I was in my early sixties, my doctor told me that my daily exercise had kept my body functioning well, and I should give my mind some daily exercise as well. 'Do a crossword puzzle every day,' he told me. That has become my custom since."

There is no question that the brain requires exercise. Not necessarily a crossword puzzle every day, but some sort of regular training program to keep it functioning well—a gymnasium for the mind. The growth and development of the brain can go on well into old age. As long ago as the sixth century B.C.—the time of Pythagoras—thinkers have held that the brain is helped by exercise. Age can be held at bay and even conquered by remaining active. And as with the body, what is required is *maintenance:* the daily renewal of our powers, the regular use of our mental faculties.

The brain needs to be active if it is to function well. The brain stores information and retrieves it. It solves problems and creates solutions. It reasons, imagines, learns, and remembers. But there is a science to all this, there are ways to help the intellect perform best. And the first rule is "Use it or lose it." Use memory. Use reasoning. Use logic. *Use* the mind's many capabilities.

In exercising our body, we maintain the range of motion over our joints and muscles. Unless we stretch to our utmost, we gradually become more and more restricted in motion. Such rigidity is the primary evidence of unimpeded aging. Active dancers, on the other hand, retain their youth into their eighties because their flexibility is unchanged from their prime.

So it is with the mind. We should stretch it to the limits daily. There are various ways to do this. The crossword puzzle is one. But we must, as with the body, be preserving other functions as well. To be mental athletes, we must be prepared to observe, judge, and act, to obtain information, process it through our reason and memory of the past, and come to some logical judgment. Then we must develop some unique response to the present situation.

Fortunately for me, my profession requires continual study. The library at my hospital is constantly being replenished with dozens of weekly and monthly medical journals. The *Index Medicus* contains citations from hundreds more. I renew the information bank in my mind on a regular basis; visits to these stacks are part of my routine.

The hospital library has a role in my mental fitness program. So does my writing and reading. But the mental athlete must also be an artist—and the art can be anything you *love* to do. You need to love it because loving it is the only thing that ensures you'll do your best—and doing your best is the main concern. Love it, and you will learn the necessities for inspiration. Love it, and you will discover the environment and attitudes and practices that help your brain to function well.

The fitness formula for the body is quite simple. Pick your activity, then do 30 minutes at a comfortable pace, four times a week. Follow a similar program for the mind. Pick your activity and then do it for 45 minutes, four times a week.

The one, of course, complements the other. Things usually go better for my mind if I exercise. A run provides the best conditions for thinking. And arranging for an hour of solitude a day, whether exercising or not, is essential, as is finding the time of day that best corresponds to the rhythms of my mind. In this, as with physical exercise, what I choose to do must be play—something I enjoy doing for myself, something I would do even if it had nothing to do with the soundness of my mind.

INTELLECT BY SWEAT

"If you run more than 15 miles per week," said Ken Cooper, M.D., of the Cooper Institute for Aerobic Research in Texas, "you run for something other than aerobic fitness." That statement, and Cooper's implication that many runners are obsessive about mileage, are both true. Aerobic fitness is the ability to do work, and if all you want or require from exercise is the ability to do work, Dr. Cooper is right: 15 miles is enough.

But how far do we have to run for all the other things running brings—sanity and self-worth, for example? That's not so easy to say. Self-mastery and self-esteem cannot be calculated by a treadmill, nor can the value of a spiritual insight be determined by a blood test. But all three are common consequences of exercise. We must *not* ignore the psychological, creative, and spiritual dividends people gain from exercise.

Some runners, for instance, require 5 to 10 miles a day to maintain their sanity, serenity, and good humor. A woman friend, who walks an hour a day getting to and from work, told me she still likes to run 5 miles when she gets home. "I need it for head time," she said.

The reasons for running and other forms of exercise go far beyond fitness. Some people run for philosophical reasons, not finish lines. Running is an entry to another world, a pathway to experiences that cannot always be articulated. Whether you call them peak experiences or mystical events, runners continue to seek them.

"There are other and greater realities," said philospher William James. And it's true: There is more to life than what our senses tell us, and people have sought in many ways to find out precisely what. James, for example, experimented with nitrous oxide. Running is a significantly safer way to pursue the same thing—new understanding.

James also spent considerable amounts of his time investigating psychic phenomena. And it is important to note that the fitness movement has taken place at a time of resurgence in interest in psychics. We now have around us what is called the New Age movement—people focusing on aspects of the self that are beyond scientific proof. They are going into the right brain, into nonlogical areas of the mind to explore the possibilities.

Even television is showing the effects. Advertisers are asking us to "be all you can be," "master the possibilities," and "perfect the experience." These are slogans that James would have loved. One of his greatest works is *The Varieties of Religious Experience.* This book, composed of the Gifford Lectures he gave in Edinburgh, is no less than a continuous account of human beings going beyond the ordinary human experience—a New Age bible of sorts written in the last century.

Fitness can be an attempt to go beyond the ordinary human experience. It begins with exploring the limits of the body, and it then explores the limits of the mind. Ultimately, it explores the limits of the whole person. One discovers from hand-to-hand combat with the self—or through a transport to indescribable areas of the soul—that there are indeed other and greater realities.

And, frankly, I'm not at all sure you can find this other life on Dr. Ken Cooper's 15 miles a week.

MENTAL MUSCLE—THE RUNNING WAY

So where do you find the life of the mind? Within yourself, the self that is nurtured and freed by running. When you come down to it, what running does is give you the basic skills to live well. Each one of us is obliged to live his or her own life, without precedent or design. We arise each day to act out our own dramas, write our own individual novels.

We must prepare for this daily act of creation in much the same way an athlete trains for an event. The basic skills are all-important. Coaches are forever stressing the fundamentals. Football players must learn to block and tackle. Baseball players practice to improve running, throwing, and hitting. Tennis players develop serve, volley, and ground strokes.

These primary abilities usually carry the day. True, the athlete enters the event with a game plan. But more often than not, that evaporates. Factors beyond our control enter in. It's at that point— when things go awry—that the ability to do the basics—*not* the tricks —then determines the outcome.

To play the life game well, there are some essentials: Energy is one. Physical energy is necessary for whatever we do daily. Without it, whatever we do will be done badly or not at all. The 24 hours we're given each day shrink to a good deal less when we lack the endurance and stamina to actually use them. Running develops that energy. It can make the end of your work the beginning of your day.

Why, then, should we settle for the fatigue and lassitude that so often sets in late in the day or early in the evening? There is a cure: It's called motion, motion of almost any sort, provided it is vigorous and persistent. Walking, cycling, swimming, rope skipping—and, of course, running—all fit the bill.

Running produces fitness of muscle but it also produces another fitness, a fitness beyond that. It allows for meditation, the *sine qua non* of creativity and contemplation, which provides a sense of where we fit in the scheme of things.

The life game requires physical energy, but it requires other energies as well, such as creative energy. This means learning how to work with the stream of consciousness. The ability to free-associate is vital to pursuing the self. Human potential movements *all* stress this need to free oneself from consequences and enter the world of mind play. In running, motion becomes the mantra for this altered state of consciousness.

The life game does not operate solely through reason, but reason and logic are necessary. We cannot go through life as pure animals; physical energy is not enough, nor is creative energy sufficient of itself.

There is a place for discipline and self-control, for gratification denied—the orderly actualization of the unruly, playful thoughts that come on the run. All human potential movements should also instill the need for reason and order. The athlete, said Plato, grows unbalanced in the absence of education.

Running gives one the self-control, the discipline needed to profit from the lessons it offers. It prepares for hardship; it teaches about pain and guilt. But it also demands logic and teaches the runner how results are obtained—through work, over time.

In facing life, no one knows exactly what is going to happen, what is going to be needed, where the search for the grail will lead. The best we can do is be prepared. Running makes us athletes in all areas of life, trained in the basics of living and ready, therefore, for whatever comes—able to live each day, fill each hour, and grapple with the critical moment.

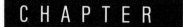
7

RUNNING: ROAD THOUGHTS

There it is — my why of running, my reason for exercise — no less than the creation of the human being I become. I am my word made flesh.

THE RUNNER'S RATIONALE

When I lecture, I often begin with a short film on running. The opening scene is the start of the Boston Marathon. Thousands of runners stream toward the camera. Meanwhile, the narrator remarks that these marathoners are the visible elite of millions of runners now lining the roads and filling the parks. "The nonrunner watches," he says, "and wonders — *why?*"

The audience almost always laughs at that question. To one group, running is normal; to the other, running — especially marathon running — is a mystery. When the film ends and the lights go on, I ascend the stage and address the question: Why do people run? And why do additional millions pursue other forms of exercise?

My answer is direct: Their lives depend upon it. People begin running for any number of motives, but we stick to it for one basic reason—to find out who we really are. Running or some other form of exercise is essential in the drive to become and perpetuate the ultimate self, because finding out who we are means finding out what our limits are—and we have to *test* ourselves to do that.

I run because my life in all its aspects depends upon it. The length of my life, certainly; the hours in my day, just as surely. The person I am, my productivity, my creativity, my pursuit of happiness—all are conditioned and determined by my hours on the road. There is not one aspect even of the very moment that I stand up in front of that audience that does not relate to my running experience.

Most non-exercisers are unaware of this global, whole-life effect of athletic training. Fitness experts carve out particular territories in which they operate. Each is an advocate of a relatively narrow view of this enormous subject. Physicians, physiologists, psychologists, sociologists, teachers, even philosophers, understandably concentrate on effects with which they feel competent. They focus on special parts of our lives, but not life in its totality—not life with a capital L. Their little *whys* end where the really big one begins.

The physician tells me that my life span is related to my lifestyle. When I began running, my "coronary risk factors"—smoking, excess drinking, extra weight—all disappeared. I stopped the rare cigarette, my weight returned to what it had been in college, and my blood pressure didn't rise as expected as I got older.

Running added hours to my day—my physical work capacity is four to five times higher than it was when I was 38 years old and (presumably) at my prime. Whatever I ask of my body—within reason—it is capable of doing. Clearly, my body benefits from fitness.

But my mind does, too. The psychologist tells me that. The negative feelings—anxiety and depression, anger and hostility—are all reduced by training. My emotional stability is due in great part to the running I do. Concurrent with the lowering of these destructive feelings are gains in the constructive ones. There are also other effects frequently mentioned in psychological studies: An increase in self-esteem, improvements in self-image, the development of self-confidence.

And the public me benefits also: The sociologist argues that my professional success is linked to the fitness I earn from running. It is no longer simply survival of the fittest, it is also success to the fittest. Fit people occupy the upper echelon in education, position, and salary. They are the leaders in the information society, the people in author John Naisbitt's *Megatrends* future. My running, the sociologist says, enables me to compete in a highly competitive society.

So it goes: Each specialist sees the place of exercise through the prism of that particular specialty. The educator is aware that, through my running and racing, I experience firsthand the values and virtues that form the evolving self: My sport is a laboratory where I learn about such things as sacrifice and solitude, courage and cooperation, victory and defeat.

The intellectual then reminds me that creative thinking requires the inner and outer solitude that running confers. Running provides all the elements necessary for contemplation, and through this process I arrive at the life I will lead when I am home and showered and ready for society.

I explain and illustrate this fragmentation to the audience. And then I tell my listeners that no one of them is enough. Each of these experts see only a bit of me. But I am not a cholesterol level, I am not a lipid profile. I am not an ergometer test, nor am I a Rorschach or an IQ. I am a physician, a student, a problem solver, a philosopher. I am also a parent, a sibling, a lover, a friend. But none of these names entirely defines me. "I absolutely deny," wrote English author D. H. Lawrence, "that I am a soul, or a body or an intelligence, or a nervous system or bunch of glands, or any of the rest of the bits of me. The whole is greater than the sum of my parts. Therefore, I, who am a man alive, am greater than my soul or spirit, . . . or anything else that is merely a part of me. I am a total living human being."

I look out over the audience and ask them, "Are you content with this total living person you are now?" American social philosopher Lewis Mumford once remarked that today might be a fair sample of eternity. If so, this would be the eternal you, the final product of your years on earth. If this were your last day would you be satisfied?

There it is—my *why* of running, my reason for exercise—no less than the creation of the human being I become. I am my word made flesh.

THE MYSTERY OF THE MARATHON

The athletic experience can be divided into three parts. One is the preparation, the training of the body. Two is the event, the challenging of the self. And three is the aftermath. And for the runner, the ultimate athletic experience is the marathon. It takes training and challenging and creating to the absolute limits.

Running has been described as a thinking person's sport. The reference is to the predominance of middle-class, highly educated people who have taken up this activity. But it is also true that it is a sport that requires extensive study of the workings of the body. Runners in training acquire extensive knowledge of how the body operates best. In coming to one's peak, a good working knowledge of exercise physiology and nutrition is necessary.

But the application of that science is both intellectual and intuitive. Runners have an expression: "Listen to your body." Basically, it means that your body can tell you things all the sophisticated hardware in the world never will. Runners understand that biofeedback machines only amplify messages that should be heard without them. They develop *biological wisdom:* Experts in their own bodies, they become good animals.

This listening and learning is often done by playing with the edge of self-inflicted pain. Doing hills and speed work, for example, means repeatedly pushing to the limits of tolerance of oxygen debt. This is painful. There are times, however, when even training like this can be a pleasure—days when I get tremendous enjoyment out of the effort and the sweat and competence I feel. Like Thoreau, I occupy my body with delight.

In training for the marathon, I grow in physical wisdom. I learn how my body works best. I read the texts, of course, but then I take these bookish theories out on the road and test them. I filter them through my exercising body and come up with my own truth. I prepare myself for an exploration to my outer limits—the marathon itself.

The marathon is the focal point of all that goes before and all that comes afterward. The long-distance race is a struggle that results in self-discovery. It is an adventure into the limits of the self, representing for runners what has been called the moral equivalent of war—a theater for heroism, where the runner can do deeds of daring and greatness.

Life is made in doing and suffering and creating. All of that is there in the marathon—the doing in training, the suffering in the race, and finally, the creating that comes in the tranquility that follows.

This stage on which we can be bigger than life is a place where we can exhibit all that is good in us. Courage and determination, discipline and willpower, the purging of all negative impulses—we see that we are indeed whole and holy. We have been told time and again we were born to success, but a truly run marathon *convinces* us of that truth.

The marathon fills our subconscious with this gospel. Taking a well-trained body through a grueling 26.2-mile race does immeasurably more for the self-concept and self-esteem than years with the best psychiatrist.

Robert Frost once said that to write a poem you have to have an experience. To do any creative act, you must have an experience. Any race is such an experience, but the marathon is that experience raised to the nth degree. It fills the conscious and unconscious with sights and sounds, feelings and emotions, trials and accomplishments. And in the end, we know creation.

THE RUNNER'S HIGH: A ROAD TO REVELATION

"There is no such thing as a runner's high," wrote runner and radiologist David Levin in the *Journal of the American Medical Association.* "Anyone expecting a high or mystical experience during a run is headed for disappointment. I don't attain them, nor do the marathoners with whom I am acquainted."

Levin is pro-running. He averages 60 miles a week and has run seven marathons, including a 2:38 performance in the 1981 Boston Marathon. He is no stranger to the running experience. The reasons he runs are many and varied. They do not include the runner's high.

He sees this state as a figment of someone's imagination, a myth perpetuated largely by those who stand to gain financially from it. This euphoria—if it occurs at all, he says—comes when the run is over and you know you don't have to face it again. Running for Levin is tough, tedious, tiring, and often painful. The payoff comes from being a runner, not from running itself.

I believe all the particulars in Levin's article. I know he is speaking his truth. But he has made the dangerous leap from his personal experience and the experiences of his friends to that of all runners. He has concluded that if his group does not get a runner's high, no one else does.

I suspect that dogged, determined, 60-miles-a-week marathoners are actually the *last* ones to ask about mystical experiences. For them, running is indeed tough, tedious, tiring, and often painful. But for those of us who do half that mileage, who train at two minutes over our race pace, who run to think, and reserve pain for the race—for us, the runner's high is an integral and essential part of our lives. It draws us again and again to escape our humdrum, ordinary, and commonplace real lives. And in its absolute form, it is undoubtedly what sociologist Abraham Maslow described as "peak performance."

In his later years, Maslow qualified his definition of this phenomenon. He originally thought it occurred to few people and then under very special circumstances. He discovered that this was not so: Any *number* of activities could result in this feeling. There were, in fact, multiple methods of achieving a sense of timelessness, of oneness with the universe.

He also recognized that there were lesser versions of this variety of *satori*—"plateau" experiences, where the emotional response was calmer, the experience more a feeling of peace of being in control.

"They seek retreats for themselves," wrote stoic Marcus Aurelius Antoninus, "a house in the country, seashore, and the mountains. But this is altogether the mark of the common man, for it is in thy power whenever you shall choose to retire within thyself." My day's run becomes that retreat. There I discover the truth of the meditation of the great Stoic Epictetus: "Nowhere, either with more quiet or freedom from trouble, does a man retire than into his own soul."

My body permits this to happen. At two minutes over my race pace, my body is virtuoso. It requires no guidance, no commands, no spur. It is on automatic pilot. My mind is free to dissociate, to wander on its own. On some days, this brings on another type of high—a creative one. My mind becomes a cascade of thoughts. The sights and sounds, the touches and tastes, the pains and pleasures of my entire life become available to me. I am able to read a journal I never knew I'd kept.

At times, these thoughts center around a common theme, the one I am then in the process of writing. Other times, there is a kaleidoscope of new and exciting arrangements of past experiences. I sometimes return from the run with an entire column that arose *de novo* after I reached my second wind.

Then there are the days—or perhaps the day—when I have that elusive runner's high. By strict definition, mystical experiences are rare. The French philosopher and scientist Blaise Pascal admitted to one. St. John of the Cross was said to have had only three. But by Maslow's standards, mystical experiences can be quite frequent. Children probably have them daily, since childhood is a state of enlightenment much like that sought by the Zen masters: "There are no categories, no words, no time."

Athletes, whatever their level of performance, are also a favored group. "There is no word in English for that feeling," said pitcher Mark Fydrich, describing his emotions in his comeback attempt in a minor league game in Pawtucket, Rhode Island. He was talking about how he felt when the crowd spurred him on in the last few innings.

Words fail when we are attempting to describe what is, by definition, mystical—beyond words. The runner's high is such a state. But if there is one word that approximates it, it is ecstasy—ecstasy in the original Greek sense of "standing outside." Running takes me out of the world and my role in it. For a brief hour, it gives me the freedom to do everything or nothing, to become or just to be, and all without censure or praise. I am, for those 60 minutes, a new Adam, number one in my own universe. And I taste the immortality I thirst for every minute of my waking day.

THE RUNNER'S HIGH: FURTHER REVELATIONS

The person that I am is a body and a mind expressing a spirit. When I run, my entire personality participates to a greater or lesser degree. My highs, therefore, vary from a purely physical reaction to the deepest spiritual experiences. My feelings span the spectrum from simple sensual pleasure to joy, from contentment to a peace beyond understanding.

The simplest way to describe these varying phenomena is to say they are peak experiences. Each is a state of being lost in the present, of becoming timeless, selfless, outside of space, history, and anxiety. Maslow said this state was a diluted, more secular, and more frequent version of the mystical experience.

When one enters this state there is a loss of the self, a fusion with the reality observed. "A oneness," said Maslow, "where there was a twoness." This leads to further interior revelations. People report seeing formerly hidden truth. Almost always, the whole experience is expressed as bliss, ecstasy, exultation.

There are many ways besides running to trigger such events. "The list becomes so long," wrote Maslow, "that it becomes necessary to make generalizations. It looks as if any experience of real excellence, or real perfection, of any moving toward perfect values, tends to produce a peak experience." Maslow mentioned childbirth, music, art, dancing. "A love for the body, awareness of the body, reverence for the body are good paths to peak experiences."

I begin in the body. But the highs that follow range from animal to angelic, from pure body to pure spirit. It is possible in the span of an hour to be a mindless body or a bodiless mind: to be constantly monitoring my senses, or to be deep in the recesses of my subconscious. An afternoon's run can take me from the ground below my feet to the heaven above my head.

On most runs, there is a progression. I go from being totally the observer to becoming completely inside what I am thinking about. As with sleep, such a falling away from the outside world takes some time. First I become comfortable. The warm sweat comes, the muscles require less and less effort. The running is now automatic. I enter the world of my thoughts.

Another word to describe this experience is centering. This has been defined by psychiatrist Stephen Kurtz as "the process by which we move from the agitated periphery of our lives to a silent interior space that, however empty it may appear, will reveal itself as indescribably full." The agitated periphery, that hurried, harassed life, is where I live. It is the painful and anxious and frustrating interaction between me and myself, me and my environment, and the most difficult part of that environment, me and other people.

Running has already helped me center that life. It is, to be sure, a centering of another sort. When I run, I am able to distinguish the important from the unimportant, what must be done from what can be put aside. I return from the roads with a revised game plan, once more on compass toward my own goals. My hour alone reminds me of what is essential for the good life; I have learned what to do at the agitated periphery.

But Kurtz saw centering operating at a much higher level. It is not merely a method of arriving at a game plan for successful living. This center is a *place,* and a return to this place is essential for the self. We must, he said, go back into this silent interior space and find God. Only then, reborn and renewed, powerful and lovable, no longer alone and lonely, can we deal with the agitated periphery. The good self begins in this meeting with God.

Just more words from a psychiatrist? Perhaps. But running—which has, in fact, centered *my* life—does in the very act bring me to this quiet cove Kurtz described. My running takes me away from that disturbed circumference and into silence, the center of my being. God is there—he whose center is everywhere and whose circumference is nowhere.

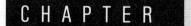

8

DANGER SIGNALS: RUNNING WITH HEART DISEASE

Sudden cardiac death from running is a major concern only to a very select group of runners.

SUDDEN DEATH ALARMS RUNNERS

The death of Jim Fixx while running on a Vermont road has raised questions about the safety and efficacy of jogging. Evidently, heart disease can develop despite an intensive running program. At autopsy, Fixx had severe coronary disease and evidence of an earlier nonfatal heart attack. Here is an instance of a dedicated high mileage runner who collapsed and died, ignorant of the fact that he had serious heart disease.

Runners and nonrunners wonder, Why run if it isn't going to stop me from having heart disease? Why run if I am in danger of dropping dead on the road? This leads to one further question, Can I be sure it is safe for me to run?

Let me begin by looking at the circumstances surrounding the death of Jim Fixx. He had an extremely bad family history. His father had his first heart attack at 35, then a fatal one at the age of 43. This is a highly significant risk factor. A study in Utah using the Mormon genealogy tables showed that 50 percent of heart attacks occurred in 5 percent of the families.

Like other runners who died while running, Fixx was a prime candidate for heart disease. Indeed, many of the casualties already had documented coronary obstruction or insufficiency. In a survey of nine jogging deaths in Auckland, five of the victims already knew they had heart disease and the other four had major risk factors such as smoking.

Secondly, Fixx, as most others, had warning. He told his fiancée that for several weeks he had been experiencing a tightness in his chest while running. It was troublesome enough for him to vacation in Vermont, to see if the air in Vermont would relieve it. "If I get to Vermont and I'm still having it," he said, "I'll go see someone." The first day there, he died.

My experience is that most people who suffer a heart attack or collapse suddenly have these prodromal symptoms. We are animals and nature gives us warnings. Unfortunately, many people ignore them, or, perhaps better said, deny them. I have had patients who were awakened from sleep with chest pain night after night, never told a soul, and then had the heart attack. They lived to tell me, but had they died immediately, no one would have known of the warnings they received.

I receive phone calls from runners who tell me of experiencing chest pain three to ten minutes into a run, then slowing down, or even—it seems incredible—running right through it. The pain then subsides, and they finish the run. Invariably this has been going on for a while, and they have not yet told anyone else, much less a doctor.

In studying the cases of two South African ultra-marathoners who died of heart attacks, Timothy Noakes, M.D., came upon this same phenomenon. Their training journals revealed that they had been having typical angina pectoris while running. Other than making an entry in their logs, they had not spoken to anyone about it.

The final characteristic of people who die suddenly while running is the presence of serious heart disease. Almost all autopsies show marked narrowing of the coronary artery, often with evidence of prior heart attack. Runners with healthy hearts can be assured they are impervious to such episodes. For them, running is a safe and sane way to preserve health.

We should know that sudden death is limited to individuals with the following characteristics:

1. They have serious heart disease, in many instances already documented.

2. They have significant risk factors for heart disease, such as smoking or high blood pressure.
3. They receive warnings that their coronary circulation is about to fail.

Given all these factors we can see that sudden cardiac death from running is a major concern only to a very select group of runners. Further, it is a catastrophe that can be avoided. When the entire circumstances of such an event are analyzed, it is easy to see it was not an act of God. There were already reasons to be on one's guard, evidence of peril ahead. These people apparently ignore the body when it sounds the alarm. As is often the case, they let the mind overrule the messages they receive from the body.

The presence of serious heart disease does not preclude running if it is done according to the dictates of the body: jogging within the perimeter defined by pain; jogging in the comfort zone; jogging at a conversational pace. When running is done in this sensible, civilized, humane way, there is no danger. A doctor in Toronto has thousands of heart patients running. A number of them with two- and three-vessel coronary artery disease actually run marathons. But they are trained to let their bodies, not their minds, dictate their programs.

So runners should be reassured. It is extremely unlikely that you have serious heart disease without being already aware of it. Further, it becomes a hazard only when you get the warning symptoms, and you certainly shall, that you are pushing yourself too much for the current status of your cardiovascular system. Then you are in jeopardy and must make the necessary adjustments.

A case can be made that running caused Jim Fixx to live longer than he would have without it. He outlived his father by ten years. I suspect it would have been even longer if he had listened to the danger signals he was receiving out on the road.

A LIFE SENTENCE

In my medical infancy, I viewed a heart attack as a death sentence. The victim, as I saw it, was like a mortally wounded animal awaiting the inevitable fatal ending. This would come soon and, in any case, certainly within five years.

Decades of practice have changed my mind. Coronary heart disease is not the killer I thought it was. People who die of heart disease do so because they have not learned how to live. They die, as nineteenth century French poet Charles Pegúy once said, of their entire life. A person with extensive disease may live for decades, while another with much less arterial obstruction will be snuffed out.

To live a long life, said Supreme Court Justice Oliver Wendell Holmes, get a chronic disease and take care of it. Living with coronary disease means becoming an athlete. Regular exercise, a low-fat diet, and sufficient rest are essential ingredients to that training. Stopping smoking is a must.

The heart patient must follow the lifestyle that ensures peak performance. And then must listen to the body so as not to go past that peak into the valley of death that can follow.

It is close to astonishing to observe what a consistent program of comfortable aerobic exercise can do. It is also reassuring to see the effect of a low-fat diet on high-risk cholesterol levels. What is happening, of course, is the patient is becoming an athlete.

For most heart patients, their athletic event is getting through the day. They are looking to fill their waking hours with happy, healthy, productive activity. This is clearly an attainable goal.

A heart attack need not be a death sentence. It can be the beginning of a long and productive life.

INTERNAL INTERACTIONS

Few patients require less medication and more advice than those with coronary disease. Despite the almost incredible gains in pharmacy and surgery, the fate of most coronary patients is in their own hands. Their life span depends on their lifestyle. The judicious use of the new drugs and bypass surgery undoubtedly adds to such gains. All, however, is for naught, if patients persistently misbehave.

Attention to smoking, diet, exercise, and weight control are imperative. Management of stress is no longer optional. Mental and spiritual health become essential. Some cardiologists see certain areas of lifestyle as primary, but most agree that it is a return to an ideal lifestyle that remains the primary force in the prevention and treatment of coronary disease.

Three of the more prominent proponents of this point of view are doctors William Dock, Meyer Friedman, and Peter Nixon. Dr. Dock, a trained pathologist, directed his major concern to abnormal blood lipid patterns. Although drugs hold some promise, the only long-term effective way to do this is through diet (essentially low-fat, low-calorie) and steady, quiet exercise. Dr. Dock stressed that the chief factors that tend to increase the deposit of these blood fats in the blood vessels are smoking, hypertension, obesity, and food allergy. He is a pragmatic scientist and deals in specifics. His is a no-nonsense, unyielding position on hard facts that can be easily charted.

Meyer Friedman thought the Dock approach was hacking at the branches. The root of coronary artery disease, according to Dr. Friedman, is a personality disorder. These victims have a Type-A personality. They are suffering from the "hurry sickness," and have a demonstrable free-floating hostility and a disordered time sense.

Dr. Friedman's goal in therapy is to modify or change this behavior. This means more than a change in lifestyle—it means a change in life goals. These people, said Dr. Friedman, must be shown the error of their ways. They are the perfect but sad example of psychoanalyst Erich Fromm's modern man, who has everything but is nothing.

Since this is then a spiritual problem, only a conversion will lead to salvation. William James had similar ideas about the same problem. In his speech, "The Gospel of Relaxation," given in 1898, his description is almost word-for-word Dr. Friedman's hurry sickness.

In this talk, James advocated physical training and exercise to provide a background of sanity and serenity and good humor. There was, he said, a peace and confidence that rose from every muscle of a well-trained body. This represented an element of spiritual hygiene of inestimable value.

Friedman urged his patients to reconstruct a new mode of living in which friendship, affection, and joy will serve as a new focus for many of their activities. In most instances, time urgency and hostility, the two basic characteristics of the Type-A personality, disappear.

Dr. Nixon, too, saw diet as secondary. He drew his lesson from the Victorian period, when the treatment of the patient was the recommended way to treat the disease. The patient with coronary disease is overloaded and breaks down. The object then is either to improve capacity or lower the load.

Right living, with cessation of smoking, weight loss, and exercise, improves the capacity of the system. A proper attitude is essential. Confidence is the key. A feeling of control is the result. The patient becomes able to do more and more with less and less effort.

There you have it. The fact is that we are wholes: body, mind, and spirit. We must attend to all aspects of the personality because they interact to produce disease or make it symptomatic. The concept of lifestyle, therefore, includes our physical, mental, and social lifestyle. Some experts concentrate on one area, others on another. Be assured that all are equally important.

9

RACING:
SPECIAL EFFECTS

*The race is pain taken in measured amounts—
pain that reaches my physiological limit. If I
would endure more pain, I could not.*

MEDITATIONS ON RACING

Racing takes running and transforms it from play to sport. A free activity becomes something of consequence. The race is a theater where we willingly suspend our disbelief, and there we act out our *own* drama.

In the race we are all children. Only a child can reach a state of doing with the whole heart, without thinking of anything else, without hesitation or doubt or fear of criticism. The race is such a state. It is pure, perfect, and spontaneous.

At the finish of a race there is a feeling of wholeness, of integrity, of realizing the ideal. The runner experiences in a minor way that wonderful state described by philosopher William James, "A new reach of freedom with the struggle over, the keynote of the universe sounding in our ears, the everlasting possession spread before our eyes."

Racing is the lovemaking of the runner. The runner develops an appetite for running, a hunger for racing. Racing is a passion, a fever that burns in the blood as the weekend draws near. And the race itself is an ecstasy. It is a new relationship with yourself. Truly, the race is no more and no less than falling in love with yourself.

Despite the ecstasy, all races hurt. Each hurts in a different way. I have endured heat in Mobile, battled winds in Bermuda, struggled up hills in Central Park. I hit the wall at 21 miles in Boston. In each instance my body was undergoing a different trial, reacting to a different kind of stress. There was that same global fatigue, but there were also the specific symptoms connected with heat or hills or wind or those last 6 miles.

Pain is the mystery of life. It is the reminder of our finitude, and anticipates our death. We find it hard to understand the nature of pain. We may understand why Adam and Eve had to work, but we do *not* understand why Job had to suffer. Yet we find we must not merely accept pain, we must *seek* it: The race tells us so.

If pain is the mystery of life, the race is the mystery of running. The race is pain in its purest form. It is pain sought and isolated from any countervailing sensations, pain that fills my body and takes possession of it, pain from which only my will is free.

The race is pain taken in measured amounts—pain that reaches my physiological limit. If I would endure more pain, I could not. My body would fail to function. For those rare moments when I push beyond this limit, reaching for the crest of a hill, I look and act like a man *in extremis*. My breathing is that of a dying man, my legs move like someone infirm, my arms are pleading for help.

Our primary instinct, they tell us, is self-preservation. The race tells me otherwise. There is an equal and balancing drive to do something heroic. Effort, said William James, is the measure of a man. I would amend that. The pain sustained in making that effort is how I measure myself. The nearer I can come to the maximum, the more heroic I become.

The race is the tournament. It is the trial. The race for me is what the mountain is to the climber, what white water is to the canoeist. The race, where I can be a hero, is a contest where I give my word of honor to go out and do battle with myself.

I do not question this impulse. I know it is basic and true. It is the attempt to be myself. I take the risk, seek the challenge, invite the pain. Peace lies beyond the finish line, on the peak of the mountain, just past the rocks, and across the turbulent water.

THE RACE: AN ACT OF FAITH

The race, I told the runners sitting at the tables in front of me, is not rational. We were in the University of Wisconsin field house, the night before the Crazy Legs Run. The spaghetti dinner was over, and the runners were waiting for me to tell them why we raced.

I wasn't sure I could. There is hard evidence on the value of *running* in making us sound of mind and sound of body, but racing? There is no proof that a race is necessary, no scientific evidence that racing is good for us.

But I race almost every week and find new and unexpected rewards each time I do. A race is a place for self-discovery—even when that discovery cannot be expressed. And a race is play—play elevated to an intimate encounter with the self, and, as such, occupying unchallenged high ground in our journey through life.

The race is like religion and play. It resembles art and music. It fills an area of life that is of tremendous importance but no practical value. And like those other similar activities, the race is among our most important functions. It helps us discover and form the self, and we find where we are and where we are going. We learn who we are and what we might be.

I think the essential factor is that win or lose, do well or do badly, I feel at home in the race. The race is a place where I renew my faith in myself, and in life itself. The hundreds or thousands around me are, I am certain, having the same experience. French existentialist writer Albert Camus put it this way: We are at home in our games because it is the only place we know just what we are supposed to do.

We have practical reasons for running, but only the most impractical for racing. The race stirs us, moves us, fills us with emotion but we have difficulty telling *why.* Just before dinner, for example, the Wisconsin band had played a number of rousing pieces. Can we explain the effect of that music? We are moved and don't know why. We feel sentiments and cannot establish their cause. We see the world and ourselves a little differently. But this learning experience resists analysis.

We run to perfect the body-mind instrument. But we race to learn our innermost self. In the race we get down to bedrock. We find courage and strength we never knew we possessed. Just as in a revival meeting, where we discover sentiments we did not believe possible, generosity quite beyond our nature, in racing we give witness to a person we have never been before.

A race is like the river Heraclitus spoke of: We are never in the same one, the Greek philosopher said. The river is always different when we cross it and so are we. The race is the same way—it's never the same, and neither is the runner.

The race, I told those who would be at the starting line the next morning, is where we keep the faith—our faith in the child and artist and saint inside each of us.

THE HILL

When I came out of the woods at the halfway mark, I was 100 yards behind the two leaders. One was evidently better than me, the other *surely* so. He had beaten me in a previous 7-mile race by more than two minutes.

This was the National 10,000 Meter Cross Country Championship for 60-and-over, two loops over a demanding 3.1-mile course. It was a true challenge for a championship race. The terrain had a proper mixture of hills and flat areas, asking for strength uphill, stamina on the level going, and speed downhill. The footing was as varied as the terrain—dirt and gravel and grass occurring intermittently. Those in the younger age groups who had been in the earlier race had been asked to compare it to Van Cortlandt Park, the benchmark for championship courses.

"This one is tougher," they reported.

It was. The long initial upgrade was followed by a series of short hills. Then came a long flat area. About midway, we came out on a large meadow about a half-mile in circumference. The route dropped gradually to the midway point and then rose again steeply in a 300-yard-long rise. Following that was a succession of downhills, which eventually took us out of the woods at the end of the course.

I had fallen behind on the upgrade at the start, then recovered some ground on a long downhill, close to midway. I was still 30 yards behind when we reached the long steep hill at the 2-mile mark. When I reached the summit, I was out of contention for first or second place, and beginning to worry about the man behind me. But if I could hold my pace through the long upgrade and manage the monster hill, I would end up with the bronze.

It felt good to be in a race where the competition was so explicit. Every race I run in has age-group divisions. In every other race, I am in a sea of runners, never quite sure of where my 60-year-old competitors are. I never know whether there is someone up front I must catch, or someone close behind trying to run me down. I find out where I placed at the awards ceremony.

Here, I was dealing with certainty. There was nothing but space between me and the two runners I had to catch. Nothing but empty trails between me and the man trying to run me down.

The second loop began as a replica of the first. I lost ground on the upgrade, made up for lost ground and more in a succession of short downhills. And then, in a flat-out sprint through a long descent, I suddenly came within challenging distance of the front runners.

But just ahead lay the monster hill. This was surely my highwater mark, I thought—the best I can do. But then two spectators at the crest of the hill entered the drama. They began shouting at me. "George, work this hill! This is the race right here! Harder! Harder! You can do it! You can do it!"

And I did. I passed one man and came to the summit not more than a yard behind the leader. It took horrendous effort: I put everything I had left into the ascent of that hill. When I got to the top my legs were paralyzed with pain, my head was at my knees, my eyes focused on my shoes coming and going only inches away. I was breathing 60 times a minute and still not getting enough air. Every part of my body was screaming, *No more! No more!*

You must realize how unusual this occurrence was. Hills are my nemesis. When I am beaten, I am beaten on a hill. "I caught you on that last hill," a runner would tell me. If it wasn't the last hill, it was the first or the second or one in between. In my years of running, I rarely recall passing anyone on a hill.

But I had reversed that outcome by listening to those exhortations. I knew the two spectators were correct: You win or lose on a decisive hill. And so it was here. I lost a little ground in the recovery. The man behind me passed me back and joined the front runner some 20 yards ahead. But I had tasted blood and the series of downhills that were left were my specialty.

I swooped down the first and was at their backs. The second one put me in the lead. Then came a third and I was running like a deer, free of pursuit. There was a short, quick uphill where the trail narrowed, which I took in stride. By now I was flying, feeling as I did when I was a teenager outclassing a field in my first race.

Then I burst out of the woods, still accelerating. Up ahead was the chute and the digital clock and the gold medal. Far behind me, now struggling, were the two men who had been in charge of the race up until that decisive hill.

It pays to *listen* once in a while.

A FITTING STAGE FOR HEROISM

When I returned to running some 20 years ago, it had nothing to do with health and fitness. I wanted to relive my competitive years in college. I wanted to feel again that competent, responding body, the excitement of the race, the struggle down the homestretch, neck and neck with an opponent.

I wanted once more to be a hero.

I did not realize then that this drive toward immortality is universal —that I would be followed by millions of other Americans. But I and the other runners who followed me were simply repeating something that has occurred over the ages: Men and women answering the ascetic impulse, the inborn need to do the heroic.

James felt that this drive to asceticism was characteristic of the twice-born—those who saw the evil in the world and knew it could only be dealt with on an individual basis, through meeting pain and guilt and death squarely. Mankind, James said, has taken it as a reality that the world is made to be a theater of heroism.

If so, we are like so many out-of-work actors. There are very few chances, it appears, to find such a part. The call to do a heroic deed occurs rarely, if at all, in day-to-day life. American poet James Dickey once said that you could go through your entire life in these United States without ever finding out whether or not you were a coward.

I now have that chance offered to me every week. The race has become my theater for heroism, and of all the races there is no better proscenium—no better stage—for heroism than a marathon.

Each marathon is a stage on which I must write and act out an epic drama—one that, as American philosopher George Santayana said of the football game, involves all the values and virtues of the race. And while every marathon stirs my soul, and every marathon inspires my best, none stirs the heroic more than the Marine Corps Marathon.

This race begins and ends in Arlington National Cemetery. The start is at the foot of the hill where the Iwo Jima monument stands, the finish of the race is at the monument itself. As we make our final preparations, we can see across the Potomac the various memorials we will pass on the course. Surrounded now by the graves of heroes, we visit tributes to other heroes along the way.

Getting to the starting line in battle trim is itself a heroic enterprise. Marathon training, for someone who works for their daily bread or is raising a family, is little different from going to Marine Corps boot camp.

In one of his earliest works, *Meditations on Don Quixote*, Spanish philosopher José Ortega y Gasset discussed the hero. "The hero," he wrote, "is someone in continual opposition to the status quo. The hero is always becoming himself." As I stood on the line at the Marine Corps Marathon, I was surrounded by such people—no longer satisfied with the status quo, desperately involved in the heroic project of becoming themselves.

I had met many of them the evening before at the clinic I give here every year. Some came up and visited after the program finished. We talked about tomorrow and the three-hour barrier, of what we hoped to do. The year before, a man in his early thirties, with a sturdy build but quite trim, came up to me and said, "Last year I was three-oh-seven." Close, I thought, this year he might enter that charmed circle of marathoners who have broken three hours. What did he expect this year? I asked him. "I'd like to get down to one-sixty-eight." He was talking pounds, not minutes, but it meant the same thing: His preparation had transformed him into the classic athlete, the hero waiting-to-be.

Around me at the starting line, I am sure there were many such stories. Raw recruits, now fashioned into warriors. Ordinary citizens, whose previous lives had held little more than boredom, frustration, anxiety, or depression, now filled with the martial virtues. Common-variety human beings, ready to take on the most grueling challenge devised by man.

And I do not exaggerate. World-class runners approach the marathon with trepidation. Olympians fail to finish. Record holders collapse. This contest has consequences in pain and fatigue and exhaustion unrivaled in sport. And all the more so because this agony is self-inflicted. At any moment the runner can yield to the body's demand for relief. The end of the marathon—and the end of heroism—is always just one step away. You can stop anytime you like.

But on this day, the heroes were out. At the halfway point, I turned to the runner next to me and said, "I have never seen such mass competence in my life." I had reached Washington's Union Station in one hour and 35 minutes. My pace was just as I planned—7:15 a mile. If held to the end, this pace would usually guarantee me a finish in the top third of most marathons and especially this one—a marathon for the ordinary runner.

But this day, it was evident the ordinary runner was no longer ordinary. The runners, almost 12,000 in number, seemed like marines themselves. They'd taken basic training, gone through their own equivalent of boot camp, and had been, in effect, their own drill instuctors. They were combat-ready and showed it.

When the cannon boomed, they'd set out in full cry, streaming past me right from the start. I covered the first mile in under seven minutes, but hundreds upon hundreds had gone flying by in that short stretch.

When I slowed to my planned pace, those numbers *increased*. There were thousands of ordinary distance runners, a people's army, ahead of me at the halfway mark. These were everyday human beings, people you would recognize as neighbors and friends. The Marine Corps Marathon is known for its organization but not for its runners—it's a marathon for first-timers and those in the back of the pack, people who run before work in the morning or after it at night, people who a few years back viewed a walk to the store as an inconvenience.

But now these first-timers and back-of-the-pack runners were easing past me looking like experts—and experts is what they had become. A race-tested veteran of 20 years, I was positioned far in the rear and *still* losing ground. I was having my consciousness elevated with every step. Here were thousands of people running for more than 90 minutes at a speed that in the past would have winded them in a minute. They were going at a rate they had previously reserved for emergencies like crossing a street in traffic, or catching a bus—and even more, planning to maintain it for over *three hours.*

Forget that disaster might lie ahead. Forget that many would eventually slow down. Forget that some might even have to walk. Forget that the last 6 miles would take its usual toll. There at Union Station, all I could see was evidence of heroism and the marvelous endurance of the ordinary human body.

At mile 17, we set out on Hanes Point, and I began to see evidence of the marvelous power of the human will. I had yet to pass a tiring runner. I was, however, now moving with a flow that was slowing just as I was. I had lost the lift in my legs. My stride had shortened. I had become conscious of my calves and thighs, my shoulders and my arms. Soon the consciousness would turn into outright pain.

Runners were now taking longer at the water stations, and were slower to start up again. But start up again they did, and they continued to crank out the miles. Their bodies were faltering, but not their minds.

Mass competence had become mass determination.

An hour or more of this ordeal and mass determination became mass courage. Every runner was having the same experience: The body had forgotten how. The will could not remember why. The heart supplied the strength that kept us going. And the driving force was the heroic passion that we had almost unknowingly brought with us to this struggle. This race had become a commitment beyond pain or exhaustion or indeed any argument the body or mind could bring to bear.

We had begun this race in the burial ground of ordinary men who had become heroes—soldiers who in the end had found in themselves a competence and determination and courage they never knew they possessed. When we returned, so had we.

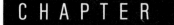

10

THE INNER RUNNER

When we take to the roads, we place ourselves in a setting that fosters our art — which is no less than the self we make and the life we live.

OUR FINEST HOURS

The speaker who preceded me was a world-class runner. His topic: "How to Improve Your 10-Kilometer Time." His formula: hours of interval training, fartleks (sprints), and speed play. His only surcease: an occasional easy run, and now and then a day off. "Arriving at your best 10-kilometer time," he told the audience, "requires continually challenging yourself in practice."

When it came my turn, I took an opposing view. I agreed *in toto* with his training program. What gave me pause was whether it was worth it. "Do we want to give up what we have," I asked, "for a few seconds on the digital clock at the finish of a race?"

What most runners have in their daily run is a very special place for mental and spiritual life. But it comes with *easy* running, at a pace that frees the mind to create and the spirit to soar. The physical challenge a racer inflicts on himself has no place here.

My training run is an exercise for my body. But even more, it is an exercise for the mind, a time of unparalleled mental activity. The river road I run along becomes an unequaled haven for concentration and creativity and problem solving.

I have a friend, a writer like myself, who runs 45 minutes each day. His pace permits him to shut out all but the thoughts that stream through his mind. Then he returns home to his word processor and pours out everything that came into his consciousness during the run.

Such mental activity is the rule rather than the exception for distance runners. My correspondence contains instances of lawyers who wrote briefs, physicians who made diagnoses, even a coach who devised game plans, during their daily miles on the road.

I have heard from artists who developed new and unusual approaches to their work; from researchers who finally caught the drift of the laboratory data they had amassed. And one psychologist wrote me to say he had dictated an entire *book* using a tape recorder while he ran.

A survey confirmed that these extraordinary happenings are, in fact, quite common. They occur with regularity to the majority of runners. It is one of the reasons 56 percent of runners come to see running as an important—and even a very important—part of their lives. It is also unexpected, since this increase in mental activity is never mentioned as one of the reasons they began running.

Although unexpected, 96 percent of the 424 runners interviewed in the survey noted significant mental and emotional benefits from running. The enhancement of mental powers is most marked in the creative process. Runners describe the typical impact as a sudden insight, rather than step-by-step problem resolution, although that also occurs.

We runners, it seems, have stumbled on the secret of many great artists. English poet William Wordsworth, who was a prodigious walker, said that poetry took origin from "emotion recollected in tranquility." The requisite of the creative act then is solitude. We must reach tranquillity by removing ourselves from ordinary cares and actions of the day.

"Art," said Irish poet William Butler Yeats, "is a fountain jetting from the entire hopes, memories, and sensations of the body."

When it comes, it is just so. Wordsworth called it "a spontaneous overflow." It gushes forth.

When I run, I join those geniuses of the past who found their creativity in similar if not identical circumstances. I have discovered that my tranquillity develops about 20 to 30 minutes into the run. It takes that much time to detach myself from a preoccupation with my body and from dwelling on the cares and concerns that filled my mind before I suited up. By then my body is on its own: Competent, relaxed, virtuoso, and I am off into my head.

From then on, I am likely to have sudden and varied insights that illuminate whatever I am thinking about. At no other time does my mind move so swiftly and in such various ways. Like my body it becomes virtuoso: It perceives from all sides, opens doors to rooms locked over the years, brings long-forgotten events to view. And then it takes all this and makes a new vision of me and my world.

I tried to pass the synthesis of all that on to my audience. "Our finest hours," I told the runners in front of me, "are during those easy comfortable miles on the road," When we take to the roads, we place ourselves in a setting that fosters our art—which is no less than the self we make and the life we live. We should not be willing, I told them, to sacrifice all that to a stopwatch.

THE SUN AT NOON

Man's highest activity, said Thomas Aquinas, a thirteenth century Italian philosopher and theologian, is contemplation—and then putting the fruits of that contemplation into action. Runners do just that. They become contemplatives who then make real the vision that comes to them on the road.

Contemplation is a creative act. When I am deep in thought on my run, I have a new awareness of myself and my world. What follows will eventually change my day and even my life. This time in reverie, this dreaming while awake, will be translated into action in my real life.

The seed at the heart of productive contemplation is experience— something deep inside of me, something of import that I've heard, felt, seen, or lived through. Ideally, it is something positive, something that reveals me and my values as if the sun at noon was shining on them. Contemplation is preceded by action, just as it must be followed by action. When I go off in my mind, I must take some material with me. To come back transformed, I must have a transforming event to contemplate.

The source of that event can be anywhere—home, work, or play. I find it most in my races. In a race, all sense impressions are heightened. The race itself assumes an importance beyond any of my pursuits in real life. Every moment in preparation, race, and aftermath is registered. The sights and sounds, the people and the pain, the thoughts and emotions, all make a deep imprint.

The race is not the only place this occurs, just the best. These learning experiences are present, potentially at least, during my entire day. They are being stored in my conscious memory, true, but most particularly in my subconscious memory. "The freedom to create," writes the great naturalist Loren Eiseley, "is somehow linked to a facility of access to those obscure regions below the conscious mind."

There you have it. The relationship between contemplation, creativity, and the subconscious mind. Contemplation is seeing a better, truer, and more beautiful way to manifest my person—the first step toward *becoming* that person.

FINDING THE CENTER

"Our destiny," wrote Thomas Aquinas, "is to run to the edge of the world and beyond, off into the darkness." There are days I do that. I run to the edge of the world and beyond. But not off into the darkness: I run into the light, the light of dawn and dusk—light that at times holds promise, at others, peace. And there I contemplate.

While out on the roads, I am engaged in what Aquinas called man's highest activity—contemplation. Later I put the fruits of that contemplation into action. One need not be a trained philosopher to do this. It is the nature of man to go inside himself and examine himself and the world. And fortunately for me, it is the nature of running to free me to do it.

We have this tendency to sell ourselves short. We do it daily. We do not believe we can become athletes, so we become spectators. We do not believe we can become heroes, so we become followers. We do not believe we can become philosophers, so we never find our truth.

But contemplation is not something reserved for the favored few. True, the specialists in such pursuits have private places where nothing can disturb them. The monks take to their cells; writers also withdraw to secluded spots. Emerson would go periodically to a New York hotel to work on his words, and Thoreau hid away at Walden Pond. But when I run I have found my personal equivalent of Walden Pond: I lose myself in inner space, that microcosm that contains the macrocosm— all of outer space and beyond.

In using my body, I become disembodied. I become pure intellect. My life becomes thought. Motion has made time stand still. I am totally and completely in the present. This is, if I believe Roman philosopher Plotinus (an expert on such matters), a mystical experience. He compares such events to the condition of a person so absorbed in reading that he is unaware he is reading. For the moment, reason, evaluation, judgment are suspended.

Josef Pieper, the German theologian, claimed that man's ultimate happiness consists of contemplation. And this, he said, is not a special happiness reserved for the philosophers: It is available to the whole, earthy, *human* man or woman.

For Pieper, contemplation was a freedom from workaday busyness, an escape from harried rush, from mad pursuit, from unrest, from the necessity of care. The elements of happiness and of contemplation are the same: repose, leisure, peace. "The contemplative person," said Pieper, "needs himself alone."

And when I run, I am Pieper's contemplative. There are no disputes, no arguments. I step out of time into a reposeful *now* My body is off on its own, it needs no direction. My mind enters a new kingdom and I am, for the moment, one with Aquinas, one with Plotinus.

11

AMERICAN DOCTORS: THE NECESSITY FOR A NEW BREED

The medical profession has virtually no under-standing of why people are becoming fit, and so little understanding of how to become fit, that they've been almost useless in telling them how to do it.

IN THE LAND OF THE BLIND

In the early 1970s, the people in these United States began a 180-degree turn in lifestyle. Millions of Americans stopped smoking, went on diets, started exercise programs, and lost weight. Eventually more than half the country became involved in this free-living experiment in health and wellness. Now, almost 20 years later, only one-third of Americans smoke and almost half have a personal fitness program. A fit, trim, and fully functioning body has become part of our culture.

The oddest aspect of this rush to fitness? The failure of physicians to lead it, or even join in. One would think that doctors would be the natural instigators and directors of this movement. Not so: The opposite has been the case. The reason seems to be that the medical profession has virtually no understanding of why people are becoming fit, and so little understanding of how to become fit, that they've been almost useless in telling them how to do it. The result? Ordinary, exercising citizens know more about the psychology and physiology of fitness than their doctors do.

Health is, of course, a large subject. English writer G.K. Chesterton said health was the study of the universe. No one can hope to master its entire scope. Nevertheless, it is obvious that physicians can and should have a working knowledge of exercise physiology—the science of human performance.

The reality is that many don't. If they are to become the leaders of this trend, they must *master* the clinical use of exercise and be conversant with its good and bad effects.

That day is coming, I have no doubt. It has already arrived at the Medical University of South Carolina at Charleston where I serve as an assistant professor. My role is to advise the administration and faculty on a curriculum that will make the study of exercise part of the medical student's program.

As I envision it, the freshman class will be instructed in the fundamentals of exercise physiology—how maximum human function is attained. This is new to medical schools. Students have learned about the normal and the abnormal, yes, but not the supernormal. They have had no courses on the development of maximum steady states, or reaching peaks in physical work capacity and oxygen uptake.

That gap in medical education shows that not one physician in a hundred now practicing understands the myriad of adaptive changes that occur in the body when it trains. It is a rare doctor who is aware of the metabolic rehabilitation that occurs with exercise. Even rarer is the one who realizes that the major changes due to exercise occur not in the heart or lungs, but in the cells of the working muscles.

Continuing the natural sequence would be teaching the pathology of exercise—the damage it can cause—in the second year. Future physicians would learn about the variety of exercise-induced diseases, and the illnesses that can occur in virtually every system of the body with exercise.

Finally, in the third year, when patient care becomes the major interest, the courses will cover the clinical applications of exercise, the actual real-world uses of exercise in the practice of medicine. These budding doctors will come to see how exercise can help each and every patient they treat.

What we really propose to do in South Carolina is to train a new breed of physician, one well-versed in the science of exercise and its application. This new breed will understand its good and bad effects, and be able to offer an exercise program to every person who comes for advice or treatment.

Those of us caught up in the fitness movement have learned one thing: Everyone, regardless of ability or the presence of chronic disease, is capable of improved physical performance. It is time our doctors learned that as well.

PHYSICIAN, TEACH THYSELF

When I was a medical resident at Kings County Hospital, I once had charge of a diabetic ward. I found it almost impossible to get someone to cover if I wanted an evening off. My colleagues who had never dealt with diabetics before were reluctant to do so.

I believe that much the same reluctance exists in the medical community about exercise. Physicians feel inadequate when asked to prescribe it. They are unsure about the basic tenets of fitness, uncertain as to what exactly is happening in the body. And rather than be put in that uncomfortable position, they avoid the problem completely—sorry, I don't do that—or send the patient off to an organized program (a health club, even) for someone else to handle.

But if it's easy for doctors to avoid diabetics—they can just specialize in something else—exercise is something else. Virtually *everyone* who comes into a physician's office could benefit from exercise. In fact, exercise prescriptions should be automatic—given *pro forma* to everyone in for their annual checkups, health maintenance, insurance physicals, or to those just asking doctors questions at cocktail parties.

The best method of incorporating exercise into the doctor/patient relationship is to do some on-the-job training. The physician can become an experiment of one and undertake a fitness program. Charting energy, weight, percent body fat, morning pulse, and some easily done performance tests can be an illuminating experience.

Such an experiment not only brings knowledge, it brings confidence—the confidence a physician needs to make exercise part of his or her practice. Exercise physiology itself *can* be intimidating, but, like most things in life, it can be distilled down to essentials. The fundamentals fit on a single index card.

What makes prescribing exercise difficult is that physicians have not been taught those fundamentals. Physiology, yes, but not *exercise* physiology. The marginally functioning body, but not the exercising body, the fully trained body. The truth is that medical schools don't teach students how to make people fit.

Fortunately, there isn't much to know. But the little there is is very important. Exercise physiology is, for one thing, the study of the functioning muscle. A runner in training—or any other fit person—chiefly improves the efficiency of his working muscles, not his heart and lungs. Other organs enter the fray only secondarily. The heart is a muscle and shares in the effects, but it is not the primary reason for the fitness that follows training.

Consider the Tarahumara Indians of Mexico: These *very* fit runners engage in leisurely, 50-mile-long games of kickball, but have hearts the same size as yours and mine.

Fundamental One is: You don't need to work hard, but you *do* need to work. And Fundamental Two: You don't have to work *hard* to become fit.

We know this from two major advances in exercise physiology that were made in 1968: the muscle biopsy, and the Perceived Exertion Scale—a product of Swedish researchers who proved that our sense of how hard we're working closely matches the scientific definitions of the same thing.

Muscle biopsies showed that fitness—the increase in physical work capacity—occurred at the cellular level. The perceived exertion scale, which gears training rate to the body's perception of *light, comfortable,* and *somewhat hard,* told us that comfortable exercise—just enough to make your breathing speed up—was all it took to make fitness happen.

Armed with this knowledge, the fitness formula has been worked out: thirty minutes of a comfortable muscular activity, four times a week. A person following this regimen for three months will *invariably* become fit. The activity itself can be a personal choice, but the bigger the muscles used, the more fitness that results—and the biggest muscles we have are in our legs. Fundamental Three, then, is: Use your legs, since utilization of large muscle groups is necessary. Walking, jogging, swimming, cycling, aerobic dancing, rope skipping, rebounding, cross-country skiing, racquet sports, karate, golf (without a cart) all qualify.

To summarize, the three fundamentals are all a physician needs to know to effectively prescribe exercise:

1. Work.
2. Work comfortably.
3. Work the legs.

And to really condense it—for the doctor with *no* spare memory space—remember this equation: legs = fitness = *great* legs.

PHYSICIAN, TEACH THYSELF MORE

A physician who knows the three fundamentals can effectively prescribe exercise. But the doctor who knows just a bit more can prescribe exercise with even greater effect.

The key variable in the three fundamentals above is the concept of *comfortable*. Since this is subjective, while time and frequency is objective, it may require other descriptions for the patient. Comfortable is a pace at, or just below, the point at which you start to breathe more quickly. Some suggest it is the point at which you begin to breathe through your mouth.

Taken any of these ways, it is clear it is an almost leisurely pace. It is reminiscent of runner Alfie Shrubb's suggestion that the perfect marathon speed was a pace at which you could fall asleep. Training, the physician should know, is not a case of no pain, no gain.

This comfortable pace maximizes two desired results: (1) the mobilization and burning of fat, and (2) the development of endurance. Both muscular and metabolic rehabilitation is maximal. At higher levels of activity, the body burns more and more carbohydrates. In fact, once in the anaerobic level—working *hard* on the Perceived Exertion Scale—carbohydrate is burned exclusively. But at slower paces, more *fat* is burned—ideal for people interested in fitness and endurance work. Translation: For maximum fat burning, working long and slow is infinitely better than short and hard.

The initial minutes of the training period should be done at an even slower pace. This warm-up is necessary to allow the body to make the necessary changes to exercise efficiently. These changes include:

1. Shunting of blood to the muscles, heart, and skin
2. Reducing intestinal and kidney flow
3. Increasing cardiac output
4. Increasing oxygen utilization by muscles

This adaptation takes from three minutes for world-class athletes to as much as ten or more minutes for ordinary human beings. It's basically the body getting ready for serious work. It's usually accompanied by a rise in temperature. You literally warm up—a light warm sweat, which tells you you're there, and a feeling of competence.

There's a definite need for a warm-up: A warmed-up body is a flexible body, which protects us from injury. But there seems to be *no* need for a "cool-down." Cooling down occurs naturally in any case. The important thing immediately after exercise is position. Standing can result in syncope (fainting), while lying flat increases stress on the heart. *Sitting* is therefore the preferred position.

The time of day is unimportant from a physiological point of view. Morning, afternoon, or evening runs have the same effect. But our circadian rhythms—our internal biological tides—tend to make us more flexible and efficient in the early afternoon, so exercise at that time of day is generally more enjoyable.

Exercise can lower our rate of aging to about 5 percent per decade. If weight is maintained, the decline may be even as low as 2 percent. I am in a study of 60-and-over people that indicates my maximum oxygen capacity has declined only 15 percent since I competed 40 years ago in cross-country.

The bottom line? Exercise does not confer immunity from coronary disease or from serious and even fatal arrhythmias. But neither does the sedentary life. The evidence is that exercise *does* improve the odds *against* these developments. Translation: You're safer if you exercise—period.

A POSTSCRIPT ON PATIENTS

"The next breakthrough in medicine," said American writer John Knowles, "will be the patient taking responsibility."

I like that idea. It means we don't have to wait for some potential Nobel Prize winner working on drugs in a laboratory, or some super surgeon devising a new operation, for the next advance in medical treatment. It can occur tomorrow morning in your kitchen: What you eat, as well as what you do and how you conduct your life, can produce astonishing new levels of health and fitness.

The truth of this is evident to anyone who has tried it. It was also evident to a group of physicians who tried it on patients with chronic lung disease. With virtually no change in medical therapy, researchers at the University of California School of Medicine, Davis, were able to reduce symptoms, shorten hospital stays, and prolong life. The answer: a holistic approach to the patient and the patient's lifestyle—treating the whole *person* instead of the sick *part.*

The difference in outcome is not due to experimental drugs or to new surgical techniques. The improvement has come about because of a return to basics, a concentration on fundamentals: Rely on the patient, not the physician.

The medical therapy used in the research was the same used by almost everyone in the field. The only innovative treatment was the daily use of oxygen for prolonged periods and even continuously. And even this was reserved for those with very low oxygen levels.

The mainstays of this program were holistic measures: smoking cessation followed by weight control, proper nutrition, and adequate fluid intake (eight to ten glasses of fluid per day)—all, of course, essentials in health as well as disease.

Exercise was equally important. "This should be a routine component of any pulmonary rehabilitation program," one researcher said, "so that the patient can achieve a higher level of endurance."

The researchers were not particular about which exercise was used—walking, swimming, bicycling—as long as it was readily accessible and something the patient was willing to do.

I'm not surprised. My own experience with pulmonary patients is that they're woefully out of shape and suffer from poor nutrition and muscle wasting. They're often in such bad shape that exercise at first has to be intermittent, with many rest periods, before the full 30 minutes usually recommended can be attained. Initially, I would have them pedal a bicycle wheel attached to their chair for two or three *minutes*, rest, and then repeat, until they reached up to half an hour.

Nutrition is also a problem. Many don't eat enough protein, potassium, or magnesium, while most eat too much fat and not enough complex carbohydrates. A little guidance in diet can have major results.

Of major interest was the typical patient's failure to show improvement on pulmonary tests. Hospital stays dropped from an average of 16 days to less than 2, but, nevertheless, the forced expiratory volume of the lungs—a standard measure of lung function—continued to decrease at the usual rate. This is important for two reasons. It shows that the program can be successful regardless of changes in pulmonary function. Secondly, the program improves the overall capability of the patient rather than the disease itself.

The message: Physicians who've previously directed all their attention toward tests should realize that the one aspect of disease they need to focus on is lifestyle—the patient, not his pathology.

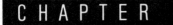

12

CORPORATE CARING: MEDICINE AS INDUSTRY

It has produced physicians who get A's in medical school and flunk in life.

THE DISEASE MACHINE

When King Albert died of typhoid, the English press termed medicine "the withered arm of science." Not so now: Medicine has the biceps of an Olympic weightlifter. Disease after disease has succumbed to the type of research being done at the National Institutes of Health (NIH). Great advances have been made in understanding and treating all sorts of pathological processes. The 13,000 dedicated people at the NIH have continued the never-ending war on disease.

But what bothers me is the absence of a similar emphasis on *health*. Health is not the absence of disease. Indeed, health can exist when disease is present. Health is an active process whereby we attain maximum performance from what is available to us.

Health despite disease is especially evident in handicapped people —the wheelchair athletes, the children in the Special Olympics, the woman with multiple sclerosis who completed the New York Marathon.

76

We recognize that people are not unfit because they are handicapped, they are handicapped because they are unfit.

And that handicap in life extends to millions of Americans. Our emphasis on disease has blinded health-care specialists to this shortfall in medical research and practice. "Let this institute be truly an institute of *health*, not disease," I told an NIH audience once, "and to justify that original name, begin to study health and how to enhance it." Do away certainly with unnecessary morbidity and mortality, as the NIH is doing now, to give us the years we are entitled to. But let us not neglect true health: the filling of those years with happy, productive activity. And that takes fitness.

It cannot be said too often that exercise may not change disease, but it does change patients. It improves performance *regardless* of disease, and that simple fact cannot be stressed too much.

Healthy means whole. It means healed. It means a way of living. Its presence does not depend on the absence of disease. Indeed, the absence of disease does not necessarily mean you are healthy.

Health by definition is *total* physical, mental, and social well-being. That well-being is a state of action, not repose. A day of health is a day of action as a fully functioning human being.

Whatever his or her handicap, any person can attain health. One can bring body, mind, and spirit to a superior level of well-being and performance. Exercise is the key. With exercise, one becomes a good animal. Other necessary qualities follow: endurance, energy, physical work capacity—and the sound mind joins the sound body.

PATIENTS OR PRODUCTS

A few years ago, I was invited to speak to students at a well-known medical school in the Midwest. When I arrived, I was ushered into a small amphitheater. Instead of the student body I expected, I was faced with 15 or 20 people, predominantly faculty members. When I asked my host where my promised audience was, he replied, "Each student has a television set. Anyone interested can dial you in."

As my talk went on, I became increasingly disturbed with this whole procedure. I wanted my listeners in *front* of me. I wanted eye contact and the contact of personalities that goes with it. I wanted the rapport between audience and speaker that stimulates both thought and actions. And I wanted the intimacy that makes for an experience that lives forever in memory.

But what bothered me most was that these future physicians saw no *need* to look at me—to feel my presence and, in a real sense, know me. And not needing to see me in my three (and indeed, many other) dimensions meant that they would have no need to see the living, three-dimensional *patient*, either.

This was scary. I could see the medicine of the future, where there is no necessity to deal with *people*, just disease. The patient need only appear on the screen, followed by his test results. The diagnosis would be made, therapy prescribed, and then — click — the next patient would appear on the set.

Decades ago, Spanish philosopher José Ortega y Gasset had seen this trend in medical education. It was based, he said, on a fallacy. Medical schools were educating doctors to be scientists when in fact they were meant to be *practitioners*. Medicine was a profession, not a science. And doctors, Ortega y Gasset thought, should know general concepts of science, not the details that would make them true experts. Being an expert, he believed, would get in the way of caring for patients.

Ortega y Gasset did not see professionals being educated that way, however. There was probably no medical school the world over, he stated, that was seriously occupied with thinking out what it *really* means to be a good physician.

Now there is. Harvard University's president, Derek Bok, appraised medical education and the way physicians practiced medicine. He concluded that physicians are inadequate, both professionally and personally. The result: An experimental curriculum devised by a faculty-student committee, to teach the attitudes, knowledge, and skills needed in the practice of medicine, is in place at the Harvard Medical School now.

Harvard, where the brightest are taught by the best, was rated the most prestigious medical school in the nation by two surveys of those institutions. Yet Bok had compiled a long list of deficiencies due to what he saw as inadequate professional training. Being number one does not necessarily mean you are doing things right.

Physicians, Bok said, lack in psychosocial skills; have been taught little or no preventive medicine; are generally unaware of financial problems caused by tests, procedures, and patient care; and cannot deal with the torrent of information in the scientific literature.

Ignoring this practical approach to medical practice and placing tremendous emphasis on science instead has taken its toll. It has produced physicians who get A's in medical school and flunk in life. Our current crop of doctors are in real difficulty — difficulty understanding and motivating patients, and difficulty understanding the impact of what they do. They have been unable, for example, to adapt to the concept of cost/benefit monitoring—balancing the cost of a procedure against the good it may do. The staggering cost of medical care has risen year after year, but only a minority of physicians ever ask, "Are the patients getting their money's worth?" The vast number of unnecessary hospitalizations, the needless use of antibiotics, the mindless ordering of unproductive tests—these are all now-familiar abuses. Doctors clearly need training in the most economical way to practice effective medicine.

They also lack training in preventive medicine. Less than 2 percent of the typical medical school curriculum is devoted to this subject, even though it is estimated that 50 percent of illnesses are due to the patients' lifestyles.

And even the material that *is* being taught, Bok said, is being taught wrong. There is evidence that by the time they graduate, second-year students will forget 90 percent of the factual items they have learned. And what about the 10 percent they retain? In this rapidly changing scientific world, is that small percentage of factual items still true?

There is additional concern about the personal qualities of medical school graduates. Bok cited one study showing that almost half of the people who dropped out of the premed studies did so because they were *repelled by the attitudes of their classmates.* Another survey reported that 88 percent of medical students admitted cheating in college. Such conduct, Bok said, has been proven to have further consequences.

In this light, it's not surprising, for example, that an Institute of Medicine report found 64 percent of a large sample of families unhappy with their doctor-patient relationship. An even more damaging fact? One-third to *one-half* of the families surveyed had changed doctors because of dissatisfaction over the physician's *personal* qualities.

The curiculum study team at Harvard put together a program that emphasizes the desired personal qualities. These include compassion, honesty, integrity, dependability, sensibility, and responsibility.

The physician who has these qualities and also knows what makes people tick, who understands the principles of preventive medicine and who makes good calls on cost/benefit ratios—that is the graduate Harvard is looking for—and so are we.

MEDICAL MECHANICS

In medicine, practice does indeed make perfect. Only in practice, in the daily involvement in the lives of their patients, do physicians become the *doctors*—the true teachers—they were meant to be. The science taught in medical school has its place, but scientists treat diseases—*doctors* treat *people.*

When I face a patient across my desk, I should bring much more to that encounter than what I've learned in school or read in the journals. Reason, as philosopher George Santayana pointed out, is much more than logic and intelligence. It is the synthesis of logic and intelligence with emotion and experience. I must see in the patient what 30 years in practice—not 3 years in med school—has taught me to see.

Medical schools pay lip service to this ideal, but *teach* the opposite —they persist in training *scientists.* It makes me doubt that the administrators of medical schools ever even think about what constitutes a good doctor.

Consider: They begin by making superior intelligence a criterion for admission. This is an egregious error. "Intelligence," said Dr. Richard Cabot, one of the great clinicians, "is unnecessary and even dangerous to the physician."

Doctors need not be quick learners but they must become *thorough* ones. More than anything else, they require common sense. They must be able to read people just as well as they read books.

"I use tests," my father once told me, "to keep the family quiet while I'm trying to make the diagnosis." It took me a while to learn that lesson: to spend time on the patient instead of on the laboratory results.

I recall an incident when I was serving a student clerkship in a city hospital. I was making rounds on the patients in my usual way. I would take the chart off the foot of the bed, go through the laboratory results, order some more studies, and then continue to the next bed—never looking at the patient. I was caught in this by a senior attending physician, who gave me a dressing-down that made me feel like a delinquent deckhand facing an admiral at sea.

Still, class after class of medical students go out into internships and practice with the same attitude I had after my graduation—that numbers matter more than the people they're attached to. Science does in fact have some answers, but not nearly enough. Science deals with the known, doctors deal with mystery—and we need solutions, proven or not. We learn things in practice *decades* before the scientists have a clue as to why they work.

It does not surprise me, for example, that despite our skill, the most accurate way to diagnose angina is the patient's history, not his test results. The patient is willing to tell us what is the matter, and the *good* doctor learns how to listen. And in fact, the good doctor who listens learns a lot of things that my surgeon uncle used to say, "are not in the story books."

The practicing doctor learns how to treat the whole patient; comes to understand that there are questions with nonscientific answers; realizes the role of common sense; and begins to trust experience.

A doctor, finally, is so much more than a physician that true doctors should glory in the name.

RETURN OF THE MEDICINE MAN

There is an old adage that scientists tend to become religious as they age, but that poets end up as nonbelievers. The knowers realize there are things that cannot be known, "another and greater reality" as philosopher William James put it, while mystics have their world shrink to a lesser and unfriendly universe.

Perhaps this is nowhere more evident than in medical practice. The longer physicians practice, the less science they use and the more religion. They work less with drugs and more with the emotions. They think more of healing and less of curing. They tend to see a person rather than a disease. They know that there are forces that no drug company or surgical procedure has yet to harness.

One indication of this attitude is an essay by Christopher Magarey, M.D., in the *Medical Journal of Australia*. Dr. Magarey called for healing and meditation in medical practice, citing numerous instances of improvement in disease states brought about by what's known as the art of medicine.

Health, he said, can be equated with openness to life, empathy, and the ability to still the mind—to be calm, to meditate. When such attitudes and practices are used, they are effective not only in bringing about psychological health, but physical health as well.

The doctor, as Dr. Magarey sees it, can actually become a healer—a person whose own meditation and attitude has a profound effect on the patient. And with a bonus to himself.

"Through the daily discipline of meditation, or an equivalent practice, medical practitioners can expect not only to become more effective healers," wrote Dr. Magarey, "but also to find increased health and equanimity and happiness in their own lives."

A great physician once remarked that the longer he was in practice the more he discovered that his patients were much more interested in what had *happened* to him than what he had read. Physicians who do not practice meditation, do not engage in physical activity and play, and do not take a holistic approach to life are *technicians*—mere mechanics who will never truly enter the lives of the people who sit across the desk from them.

13

STRESS
FOR SUCCESS

Coping means to take the initiative, to strike back, to take charge, to dominate.

NO PAIN, NO GAIN

I was at Burlington Northern Railroad's annual meeting to share the morning program with a professor of psychiatry. Our subject was stress—what it was, what caused it, how to manage it. And our job was to tell these corporation executives first how to identify and then how to deal with this most important fact of life.

The psychiatrist spent his 90 minutes on the analysis of the problem—the definition of stress, the varied responses to stress, why some people react one way while others act in another, the factors that increase our vulnerability and those that increase our resistance.

Much of what he said these executives already knew. They were experts at experiencing stress—the same type of individuals, in fact, whose histories were the basis of the psychiatrist's talk. They already knew what caused stress. They knew also that whatever change must come would have to be in *themselves*, not in the corporation.

At the very beginning, the psychiatrist promised to tell his listeners about the resources that could be tapped for this internal transformation. He spoke about *using* stress. He made the crucial point that stress can be good or bad, and that it is up to us to determine its effects. Throughout the body of his presentation, he frequently used the words "control" and "mastery." They were the keys in coping with stress.

In his final minutes, he listed the coping mechanisms: health, exercise, relaxation techniques. He also spoke of some deleterious coping patterns and the various types of substance abuse. But by then his time was up and the executives broke for coffee.

That left the management of stress to me. I had to tell them *how* to achieve the control and mastery that the psychiatrist recommended.

I went right to the attack. You may think coping is a defensive word, I told them, an indication of a willingness to live and let live. It is not. Coping comes from the French word *coup*, a blow. Coping means to take the initiative, to strike back, to take charge, to dominate. When we cope, we are in control—we are masters of the situation.

Coping begins with the care of the human machine, the body-mind complex that expresses the self. The Greeks called that care *Askesis* (athletic training) and believed that we all must become athletes in every sense of the word: physical athletes, mental athletes, spiritual athletes.

Athletes use stress to become *better*—to run faster, throw farther, jump higher. Through gradually increasing their level of stress, they are able to conquer the maximal stress of competition. And through training they learn that *all* things matter, that nothing is neutral—everything in life adds or subtracts stress in our existence.

MIND OVER MUDDLE

Philosopher William James said that the first lecture he had ever heard on psychology was one he had given himself. And, in fact, his book *The Principles of Psychology* still remains an authoritative text with few equals: The science of the mind has made little progress since.

Those who treat the overstressed mind would have us believe otherwise. Psychiatry has any number of competing therapies, each proclaiming itself the way to a healthy, de-stressed personality. But results good and bad occur with equal frequency whatever practice is followed. People cope or don't cope regardless of their psychiatrists' particular schools of technique.

This might lead you to suspect that learning to cope better is simply a matter of time. But time is not a healer, despite rumors to the contrary. "Time is a test of trouble, not a remedy," wrote poet Emily Dickinson. What heals us is really something else.

"Depression and anxiety are not our problem," the famous physician Karl Menninger said at age 94. "They are simply unwanted visitors and eventually depart. Our difficulties stem from our basic human weaknesses—selfishness, cruelty, and hardheartedness."

So it is the self that is at fault: We fail to cope because we fail to grow. We can see this more clearly in psychoanalyst and educator Erik Erikson's eight stages of life. Each stage requires the development of a basic virtue and mental quality. We do not go from infancy to adolescence to adulthood automatically. Key strengths are necessary at each stage, and remain necessary—although perhaps not most important —the rest of our lives.

What Dr. Erikson systematized has been known—and lived— for centuries. Dr. Erikson's journey of growth and coping begins in hope and ends in wisdom. *Completing* the journey—achieving our full potential—requires will and purpose, competence and fidelity, love and care. Those are virtues no end of talking will confer. They must be earned, and to earn them we must go out in the world: We are engaged in a perilous experiment that requires *living*, not conversation.

STRESS: THE VICTORY WITHIN

It's clear from the foregoing that handling stress, in the final analysis, means handling yourself.

The Stoic philosopher Epictetus saw little virtue in getting away from upsetting individuals or circumstances. In his view, it made more sense to cultivate a state of mind that would prevent these bothersome people or events from stirring up our insides.

Avoid, Epictetus stated, only those things within our control. "For if he attempts to avoid anything independent of his will," said Epictetus, "he knows *sometime* he will fall in with something which he wishes to avoid and will be unhappy."

Dealing with stress is learning what is within our power to change and what is not. All we control, essentially, is ourselves—what we decide to *do*. Things not in our power include our bodies, our health, the rest of the world and all the people in it. And since stress is caused by other people, for the most part it can no more be avoided than life itself.

And, frankly, it *shouldn't* be. "Hans Selye is wrong," wrote psychiatrist George E. Vaillant. "It is not stress that kills us. It is the effective *adaptation* to stress that permits us to live." Dr. Vaillant emphasized that adaptating to stress is not mere adjustment or conformity—it requires both grappling with the problem and personal growth.

I think of adaptation as finding our own ways of preserving physical, mental, and spiritual equilibrium. These ways, as Dr. Vaillant pointed out, may be immature for some, neurotic for others, or mature for those like Epictetus who have made the best deal with life. But what works, works.

How, then, can we increase success in managing stress? Epictetus describes the person making progress. "The condition and characterisic of an uninstructed person is this: He never expects from himself profit or harm, but from externals. The signs of one who is making progress are these: He expects all advantage and all harm from himself. He censures no man. He says nothing about himself as if he were somebody or knew something; when he is impeded at all or hindered, he blames himself; if a man praises him he ridicules the praiser to himself; if a man censures him he makes no defence. He removes all desire from himself, and he transfers aversion only to things within our power which are contrary to nature. Whether he is considered foolish or ignorant he cares not; and in a word, he watches himself as if he were an enemy and lying in ambush."

That life may appeal to a Stoic, but quite possibly not to less spartan personalities. How can we then judge our own ability to adapt to stress and be a success in life?

Dr. Vaillant's criteria are the *external* evidences of health. "Health," he stated, "is success in living." So mental, physical, and psychological health are assumed when an individual does well in life.

"Inner happiness, external play, objective vocational success, mature inner defenses, good outward marriage—all correlate highly," he contended. If our lives are going well, chances are our health and ability to handle stress are in good shape, too. The one requires the other.

Dr. Vaillant is only an observer, too. He is able to predict early on those most likely to do well. But just *how* one learns to adapt better to stress is not made evident. One thing is nonetheless certain: Success hinges on a change in you, not your life. "God has fixed this law," wrote Epictetus. "If you would have anything good, receive it from yourself."

14

NOTES ON SMOKING

In *combating any addiction, the primary decision is not one of method, it is one of will— the will and the overwhelming desire to regain control of your life.*

THE GOOD OLD DAYS

I never smoked for four reasons. I smoked a cigar at 13. I became a runner at 17. I never learned to inhale. And I was too cheap.

The cigar was a classic example of aversion therapy. I smoked it at nine o'clock Saturday night and was still sick at nine o'clock mass the next day. My mother told the curious that I had a touch of the sun.

Becoming a runner in high school really put cigarettes out of the picture. Athletes were known to smoke and prominent baseball players were featured in cigarette ads, but it was accepted that runners did not. Cigarettes cut your wind and were to be avoided.

My inability to inhale also kept me from smoking because it made me look *ridiculous.* One or two puffs and I would explode into paroxysms of coughing. What smoking I did do was therefore all a pose. I simply took the smoke in and let it out again, *looking* like a smoker but not actually smoking.

Finally, I was too close with a buck to consider spending it on cigarettes. The idea of buying something and then burning it went against my grain, so I decided early in life that it was absurd to spend my money on cigarettes.

But these were all personal, not medical, reasons. And, consequently, when I became a physician, I never campaigned against cigarettes. Few physicians did. I recall one professor at medical school who gave lectures showing the blackened lungs of smokers. But like most doctors I went with the culture—smoking then was generally accepted so we accepted it, too. In fact, an advertisement for one popular cigarette stated that it was the choice of thousands of physicians. And I recall an American Medical Association meeting in the early 1940s, where a long line of doctors stood in line waiting for a free metal container in which you could carry a pack of cigarettes.

The acceptance of smoking was almost total then. Men, in fact, were *supposed* to smoke. Women, for social reasons, were supposed to abstain. And young boys waited anxiously for the day they would reach smoking age—a true rite of passage.

In those days men who did *not* smoke were unusual—so much so that it was not a question of whether you smoked but *what* you smoked. Anthropologists did studies differentiating the personalities of cigarette smokers from cigar smokers and both of those from pipe smokers. No mention was made of nonsmokers. And in day-to-day activities, surrounded by smokers, nonsmokers felt like teetotalers at a cocktail party.

Real life was the smoking life. When in doubt about what to give a male relative for Christmas, the easy out was a carton of cigarettes. Ashtrays were another popular item, as were lighters and other smoking paraphernalia.

It is difficult in our present climate to imagine this total acceptance of smoking just two generations ago, but the fumes literally permeated society. During World War II, cigarettes were one of the most popular items dispensed to the troops, and the hero in virtually every movie was a smoker. Smoking often seemed an integral part of film making. The lighting of a cigarette and the manner of smoking it were often pivotal moments in pivotal scenes.

Guests on TV talk shows were expected to smoke, too. I recall watching Jean Kerr, the author of *Please Don't Eat the Daisies*, becoming so nervous during a TV interview that she ended up lighting a second cigarette with the first one still unfinished in the ashtray.

Smoking in those days was not only acceptable, it was the in thing to do. Advertisement after advertisement told us that. You established your niche not only by smoking but also by *how* you smoked. Lighting, holding, and actually smoking the cigarette became as important as your clothes and grammar. When everyone smoked, the way you smoked told people who you were.

I came through that period unscathed. I was an outsider, certainly, who missed the pleasures of smoking, but I also missed the consequences. I never had to kick the habit, a prospect that now confronts the millions still smoking in this country—and the additional millions of teenagers who start smoking each year.

But more importantly, I never had to face the health consequences, either—the damaged heart, the blackened lungs, or the cancer that kills so many smokers annually.

I can offer only one comment: There, but for the grace of God, go I. Smoking in my day was considered at most a minor vice, but we know better now. It's a major addiction and its consequences can be mortal.

THE BATTLE

The battle against smoking can be surprisingly easy or incredibly hard. For some smokers, the simple decision to quit is enough. For others, every campaign is a failure. A lifelong smoker is advised by his physician to give up cigarettes and never takes another puff. Another smoker tries every tactic known to man but continues to smoke.

Nicotine is an enormously potent drug—so much so that in some individuals, no threat of future disease is effective. I've seen patients with Buerger's disease, a circulatory problem affecting the extremities, continue to smoke—even though the smoking—which aggravates the disease by constricting already narrowed capillaries—was causing gangrene. A patient would lose toes, then a foot, and then have an above-the-knee amputation—and *continue* smoking. And even when the other leg started to go, he'd keep smoking.

Such is the sway of nicotine over its victims. Still, two million Americans successfully stop smoking every year. Some of these are undoubtedly hard-core smokers who have attended smoking cessation clinics or had individual therapy. But those treatments can account for only a small fraction of the total number. The great majority have been able to stop without help or major commotion.

"Most people stop smoking unspectacularly and alone," wrote a member of the Australian Health and Research Council, in the *Lancet*. He cited a study of British ex-smokers in which a majority remember stopping smoking as not all that difficult. And in fact, 41 percent found it much *easier* than they had expected.

The big question: What makes it easy for one smoker to toss the cigarettes away and never look back? Why does another stay a smoker no matter what method is used to stop? And is there a way to tell these two types of smokers apart?

Answers to these questions rest on the concepts of habituation and addiction. Smoking first becomes a habit. In this phase, smoking becomes part of one's lifestyle. It is incorporated into the rhythm of the day, the various rituals of rising, eating, working, playing.

It's the nicotine that makes this happen. It gives us a lift for chores, but then helps us relax when the day's over. It is an ideal drug for the contrasting cycles of the typical person's day.

At this stage—still only habituation—stopping smoking produces psychological distress. The resultant symptoms have to do with the loss of lift on the one hand, and the loss of relaxation on the other. The real difficulty at this point in staying off cigarettes depends on how important nicotine has become in the smoker's waking hours. Still, a habit can be broken with a great deal more ease than an addiction.

Addiction is a different story. The word comes from the Latin root *addictio*, which means to surrender. When a smoker becomes addicted to nicotine, that person has given in—is no longer in control. At this stage, quitting cigarettes causes psychological *and* physical problems. While the nicotine is being exorcised, the smoker has to endure a gamut of painful and distressing consequences—anxiety, cold sweats, shaking hands among them. And always, the persistent craving for another cigarette. It takes at least a year to be reasonably certain the cure has worked.

The key distinction here is that while bad habits may be difficult to break, beating an addiction means all-out war. With a habit, you're fighting your brain and your nervous system. But with an addiction, you're taking on your body as well. Your entire physiology fights back to *demand* what is now a necessary substance—nicotine.

Just how bad *is* a smoker's addiction? Smoking cessation programs have failure rates that almost exactly match those seen in *heroin* programs. And at the end of a year, only about one-fourth of the patients in medically supervised antismoking programs have achieved abstinence.

The message: If it's only a habit, you can probably quit by yourself. But if you think you're addicted—get help.

THE BODY BEAUTIFUL: EXERCISE AGAINST ADDICTION

In combating any addiction, the primary decision is not one of method, it is one of will—the will and the overwhelming desire to regain control of your life. The first step for recovery is the realization that your self, your personality, is no longer in command of your life. You are no longer one, no longer whole—no longer, in the full sense of the word, *healthy.*

You will not restore that oneness by simply getting rid of the demon, either. Bad as the addiction was, it satisfied a need. Smoking became habitual because it *sustained* you in some way, it somehow enabled you to adapt and cope with the ever-diminishing life you were living.

Now you've got to replace it with something positive, something healthy, and that requires work. It demands adherence to certain principles—and the knowledge that no war is won in a single day.

Too many people who take one cigarette or one drink have the feeling that they might as well have passed for a sheep as a lamb. They proceed then to saturate themselves with nicotine or alcohol. But one cigarette, one drink, does not mean you've lost the war.

Beating addiction depends on your basic strategy, not on a few minor skirmishes. Exercise is an *excellent* basic strategy. Building the good body gives you the essential of any good fighter—morale. And if you are changing your life, in a battle that calls for every weapon at your command, morale is the sine qua non.

Morale, as Webster describes it, is beautiful: an attitude that is resolute, confident, giving, self-sacrificing, and courageous. There is a buoyant sense of well-being based on physical and mental health, a confidence in the future, and a sense of purpose.

And that is, in large part, the reason exercise works: *It makes you feel better.*

An alcoholic on Antabuse quickly learns that any alcohol intake causes violent nausea and vomiting. The same phenomenon can occur when a person becomes an athlete, training the body for performance. The negative addictions have negative results: They interfere with your physical performance. So the runner stops smoking because his chest hurts and he can't breathe.

This is only the start, but it is the only start. Thoreau put it bluntly. "The first and strongest rule," he said, "is to make yourself a perfect body." When you are in control, you hear and see and smell, you touch and feel and taste. You are back in the now, the present you have avoided for so long. You are living at the top of your physical powers —and it's *there* that you will defeat addiction.

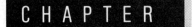

15

ALCOHOL: QUESTIONS AND ANSWERS

What can we do to harvest alcohol's benefits without reaping its negatives at the same time?

EVERYTHING IN MODERATION

In my medical infancy, I learned that there was a relationship between alcohol intake and the state of a person's blood vessels. I was a medical resident on the wards of Kings County Hospital in Brooklyn when a wise old clinician told me, "Alcoholics have the arteries of a baby."

In those days doctors lived by their wits, not tests and technology. They took careful histories and made notes on everything else about the patients while they were talking to them. These physicians were descendants of Sherlock Holmes (Arthur Conan Doyle was a physician himself): *Nothing* escaped their notice.

After he told me that, I began looking more closely at my alcoholic patients. They had other similarities to childhood. They had no hair on their chests and little, if any, under their arms. While their livers and brains were being destroyed, their skin was getting soft and silky—tangible evidence of the youthful arteries below the surface.

There were some who said that alcoholics died too young to develop coronary heart disease. A dedicated drinker usually succumbs in his forties, the toll on his internal organs leading to an early demise. But in my experience, the question was moot—an alcoholic's arteries were *always* younger than the chronological age of these victims of drinking.

Alcohol's apparent beneficial effects seemed of little importance to me then. It might well preserve a person's arteries, but to what avail if it killed him in the process? The life span of the alcoholic—the eventual sum of these positive and negative effects—is all too short. Very few heavy drinkers cash in on the longevity granted them at birth.

Moderate alcohol drinking, however, had long been associated with a happy, healthy, productive life. Studies in 1972 on a large cohort of active, long-lived people found that one important rule of health was to drink moderately.

It appeared, therefore, that alcohol in moderate doses might help in assuring our longevity. We've been offered hard evidence that a limited amount of drinking can also reduce the incidence of heart disease. A study done on 100,000 men at the Kaiser Permanente reported significantly less hospitalization for heart disease in drinkers than nondrinkers. Furthermore, the investigation showed that this protection was just as great in those who had only two drinks a day as in those who had many more.

The mechanism by which alcohol influences the course of heart disease is pure guesswork. Alcohol has multiple effects, including its psychological benefits, which may contribute significantly to the protection that occurs.

"Presumably the sedative effect of a cocktail or highball at the end of a day's work, a glass of wine with dinner, or a glass of beer before bed," said cardiologist Dr. William Dock, "offset to some extent the environmental stress that hastens coronary fatality."

I believe this to be true. I find a couple of beers a good way to end my day. When I have wrapped up everything to do with my vocation and avocation, those two beers calm the internal storms. They restore my inner climate to normal.

But the major effect of alcohol is probably biochemical. It pushes high density lipoprotein (HDL) levels—the amount of *good* cholesterol in my body—up. And experts now generally believe that HDL has a protective action against low density lipoprotein (LDL) cholesterol—the bad cholesterol.

Whatever the reason, alcohol can help prevent or at least retard heart disease. What we are learning now is that this effect can be achieved by moderate drinking—it is not necessary to become an alcoholic to get additional insurance against a heart attack.

SAFELY SMASHED

If two drinks a day is safe drinking—what it takes to protect your heart—what's *sensible* drinking? How far beyond that can we go and still be safe? Is sensible drinking even *possible?* In an address to the Institute of Psychiatry in London, Professor E. F. Kendall of the University of Edinburgh took on this very difficult and important topic.

When the layman asks, "How much can I drink without damaging my health?" Professor Kendall admitted it is impossible to give a simple and scientifically defensible answer. But he did make suggestions, drawing on the opinion of a special committee of the Royal College of Psychiatrists, London Health Council recommendations, and the Royal College of Physicians' own guidelines.

The consensus view in England? Twenty-one drinks a week for a man or 14 for a woman is safe, but anything past 50 for a man or 35 for a woman is definitely harmful. No level of drinking, however, is wholly free of risk.

But it is remarkable how much health-care people working in the field of alcoholism vary in their estimates of what is dangerous. There are readily measurable indicators of bad effects—cirrhosis, for example, and hospitalizations for alcoholism, which seem to follow per capita consumption. But individual effects vary. I have seen heavy drinkers with intact livers but greatly enlarged hearts, and others quite normal in every other way who had no memory for their present lives: One woman, long divorced from her husband, kept insisting she had to get home to make his supper.

It was once thought that if you ate well, you could avoid most of these complications. It was only when you drank your lunch and supper that nemesis awaited you down the road. But the *Bierherzen* (beer hearts) of Austria's heavy beer drinkers—enlarged hearts linked to beer consumption—proved this to be false: Austrians are famous for eating as much as they drink.

But the statistics are not all bad. There are numbers that suggest good things about alcohol. The happy, healthy, productive, long-lived people studied by sociologists in a famous Alameda County, California, project turned out to be moderate drinkers. They averaged a drink or two a day. And subsequent studies have confirmed the protection alcohol gives against coronary disease. A landmark study at the Kaiser Permanente in Los Angeles found a *50 percent decrease* in coronary disease admissions for those who took two drinks a day. Researchers have gone so far as to suggest alcohol *deficiency* is a risk factor.

The drinker's problem, then, is to arrive at this happy medium. Actually *stopping* alcohol is heavy work, and only worthwhile if there is evidence that one is losing control of one's life or health. And from a public health standpoint, as Professor Kendall points out, "There is *no* scope for the zero option with respect to man's favorite intoxicant." Translation: People *will* drink.

Most of us also don't believe we are drinking more than is good for us. And we are abetted in this by the confusion of the experts: Pick almost any number and you can find someone to say it's safe.

Nevertheless, Professor Kendall took the position that most drinkers would do better to drink less. He was inclined, however, to go past the general advice of "Drink less," and offered something a good deal more practical: "Reduce your weekly intake by a third."

He wasn't talking to safety drinkers, though—if you are already taking your two drinks a day and feeling righteous about it, keep going. You are not the target of the Health Council, or the Royal College, or even Alcoholics Anonymous. But if you are drinking a six-pack of beer a night and something extra on weekends—listen to Professor Kendall, because the odds are you're bound for trouble.

Which brings us back to the main question: What can we do to harvest alcohol's benefits without reaping its negatives at the same time?

It is a matter of what the Greeks called moderation, which means much more than our modern concept of moderation. To the Greeks, moderation meant a lifestyle—a system of exercise, diet, and activities that led to *consistent* peak performance. Moderation was the good life in which we did not abolish our desires but used them to arrive at the perfectly balanced individual.

What I am suggesting is that alcohol also has a place in that system—there are uses for alcohol, and if one is already a drinker, that attention to these uses will bring health and longevity.

ALCOHOL AND ATHLETICS: PLEASURE OR PERIL

In the days when running pants came to the midthigh, distance runners would occasionally fortify themselves with a brandy for a race on a cold winter's day. When I came to running, the use of alcohol was still mainly medicinal. When I took a chill after a New York Marathon in the early 1970s, a veteran opened up his equipment bag and offered me a shot of Irish whiskey as first aid.

Otherwise, though, alcohol was absent from our races—before, during, and after. The average runner back then was lean and slight, a mousy loner not given to social pursuits. It was the beefy athletes in the hitting games who made alcohol part of their sports. English poet A. E. Housman wrote it well: "Ale, man, ale's the stuff for fellows who it hurts to think."

For the thinking, solitary runner it is essential that alcohol not interfere with performance. Or if it does, that the costs be minor when compared to its social and psychological benefits. A half-second increase in my 10-kilometer time, for instance, might be acceptable in return for a good time at the party the night before the race.

It's my impression that alcohol in moderation for the athlete was never questioned until the turn of the century. At that time, there was a quantum leap in running performance, and professional runners began to appear. Running for some became the way they made their living. In that light, every part of the runner's lifestyle, including drinking, took on new importance. The great English sprinter, J. W. Morton, wrote in 1906, "The use of intoxicants and tobacco for a fully developed and mature athlete is a point which is causing a *quantity* of discussion."

Morton left no question about his views. "Personally, taken in strictest moderation it may not do a man much harm; nevertheless, a man avoiding these luxuries is capable of better performances." Morton agreed that giving up everything like drinking would take away the pleasure of athletics, but remarked that "a championship is worth practicing a little self-denial."

Alfie Shrubb, a contemporary of Morton's and a professional who was considered the best distance runner in the world, disagreed. Shrubb was accustomed to having an ale for lunch and defended his practice ferociously.

"In the face of teetotalers, I have recommended a glass of ale," he wrote, "and I am firmly under the impression that indulging in an occasional glass will derive greater benefits thereby than a man who observes and adheres to a total and rigid teetotalism."

Shrubb, however, would have nothing to do with hard liquor. "Never touch spirits of any kind," he warned. "That is the worst thing an athlete can do. They are of no earthly use and can only work serious harm."

In the past few years the question of alcohol use by athletes, and particularly runners, has again assumed importance. One reason is simply its increasing presence: Many races are now sponsored by beer companies. Postrace ceremonies consequently include alcoholic beverages. When runners celebrate now, they celebrate like everyone else —and their postrace parties tend to last even longer than the races, quite a feat if the race happens to be a marathon.

I doubt that any of these celebrants view alcohol as helpful in training. The beer and the people, the laughter and the good feeling, are the real *rewards*. If they're not productive of better running, they are nonetheless part of the pleasure of running. So it comes down again to the big question: Does alcohol impair our best efforts?

Here, as in most of life, there are only two cases for action—dogma and personal experience. Either we have faith in the dogma of the scientist, or we draw, through experience, our own conclusions. Believing in science has proven to be a bum show, little better than accepting other people's prejudices (Morton's or Shrubb's, for instance). My message to you: Live your own life, run your own race, and discover for yourself whether alcohol is burden or boon.

THE BIG PICTURE: ALCOHOL IN LIFE

Alcohol is a large subject. It permeates our whole culture. The American College of Sports Medicine did well to limit its position paper to the effects of acute alcohol ingestion on human performance. The college otherwise would have had to enter into a discussion that has been going on since the dawn of civilization: the role of alcohol in life.

The main reason we use alcohol is to alter our consciousness. That alteration may be extremely minor—simply making us perceive this party we are attending as interesting and entertaining—or it may be major, as in having one of sociologist Abraham Maslow's peak experiences.

Ogden Nash's immortal lines illustrate one minor use of alcohol: to break the ice. "Candy is dandy," he wrote, "but liquor is quicker." Of course, the worse the party the more alcohol is consumed.

Painter and author Barnaby Conrad wrote of one incident at a deadly serious tea party after a lecture to a Midwest women's club. He had helped himself several times to the sherry when his hostess remarked, "You know that drinking does not make you more attractive." Conrad drew himself up and replied, "Madame, I do not drink to make myself more attractive; I drink to make *you* more attractive."

Alcohol in some form has always been part of celebration, festivals, and carnivals—at events that are larger than life. "The sway of alcohol over mankind," wrote scientist William James, "is unquestionably due to its power to stimulate the mystical faculties of human nature." In our cups, we perceive a different reality. It makes us, said philospher William James, one with truth. "Drunkenness expands, unites and says yes. It is, in fact, the great exciter of the Yes function in man."

If only we could hew to the line and stop when we have achieved sociability and insight and a new feeling about life. That is, of course, the difficulty: Such states convince the person of this other consciousness, but even though we open a door and go in, we come out knowing no more than when we entered.

My own association with alcohol has taken several twists and turns during my life. I rarely touched it while I was running in college. I preferred a nightly half-pint of vanilla ice cream to my fellow students' couple or three beers. Then came private practice with those rare days off, and with them, some fancy drinking bouts. When I began running at 45, my alcohol intake went down to almost zero: I had no need for a relaxant or a confidence booster or something to produce an altered state of consciousness. Running did all that.

Now, with my practice past, and the running a part of a bigger pattern of writing and lecturing and traveling, I find those two beers at night something I look forward to. They are a fine way to end the day. They do, in any case, *end* the day. I can do nothing creative after two beers.

So when I finally sit down and open a beer, it is the signal that my day is over. I am ready to put this present 24 hours into the history books, and get ready for the new tomorrow. That beer is the seal—and believe this: It beats the heck out of candy.

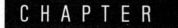
DISCUSSIONS ON DIET

A *person with 10 percent body fat, for example, may burn 500 more calories a day than a person with 30 percent body fat, even though both have the identical work output.*

FIT PEOPLE BURN MORE FAT

On any given day in the United States, half the adult population is on a diet. Almost all these dieters will lose weight. And almost all will gain it right back again.

Why some people stay overweight despite a determined effort not to, and others can eat like a horse and remain thin, remains a scientific mystery. Theoretically, we all follow the laws of thermodynamics: Energy in minus energy out equals energy stored. But the body modifies that equation in unfathomable ways. All calories of energy going into the body, it turns out, are not alike. They are not absorbed or stored or utilized in similar fashion. A calorie of carbohydrate has very different consequences than a calorie of fat or a calorie of protein.

Energy from food is burned in four different ways:

1. The resting metabolic rate (RMR). This is the energy cost of being quietly at rest during the day.

2. The energy required by muscular work.

3. Food-induced thermogenesis (heat production). Just eating accelerates your metabolism, thus burning up calories without any real work output. Carbohydrates and proteins do this far better than fat.

4. Adaptive thermogenesis. This represents energy expended, which yields heat but no work. Your temperature is up. You're burning more calories, but you're not doing anything. This phenomenon is apparently increased by physical training and a diet high in carbohydrates.

Moreover, we know that *what* we eat is as important as how much we eat. It takes only 3 calories to store 100 calories of fat, for example. But eat the same amount in carbohydrates and your body will burn *23* calories storing it—a notable difference. Fat, in other words, is much more fattening than carbohydrate. Combining that with the fact that carbohydrates also make your body burn more calories generally, some investigators have suggested that less than *1 percent* of the carbohydrate in a mixed meal makes it into fat. Protein is the best of all: It makes virtually no contribution to our fat stores, and almost 50 percent of protein calories are burned up by its conversion and utilization in the body.

The obvious conclusions: One, fat stored in the body comes mainly from fat: Eat fat, get fat. And two, the body can deal with protein and carbohydrate, but it can't deal with fat. Therefore, conclusion three: What we eat is more important than how *much* we eat. Moreover, the metabolic consequences of dietary intake are determined primarily by carbohydrate and protein. In other words, the heat-generating effect of food and the adaptive thermogenesis are controlled in the most part by our carbohydrate and protein intake. The body can deal with excess carbohydrate and protein. It has no mechanism, however, to dispose of excess fat in our diet.

We can now understand why exercise is extremely important. Obviously, it increases energy output through muscular energy. It also can increase the resting metabolic rate by increasing the lean muscle mass/fat ratio in the body. Translation: The more muscle you have, the more energy you burn at *all* times. As your percent of body fat goes down—and the amount of you that's muscle goes up—an increase in adaptive thermogenesis occurs—a fit person gets "hotter" quicker and stays hot longer. A person with 10 percent body fat, for example, may burn 500 more calories a day than a person with 30 percent body fat, even though both have the *identical* work output.

It is time we made the diet/exercise connection. That is the solution to losing weight effectively—and the solution to the even greater problem of not gaining it back.

If you are one of the 50 percent of Americans looking for a magic diet, here it is: It's the low fat, moderate protein, high carbohydrate, and high exercise weight reduction diet.

THE CASE OF THE DIETING DIETITIAN

Consider the case of the dietitian who could not lose weight. She was not a dumb dietitian. She had graduated *cum laude* in nutrition from the state univeristy, then went on to a nationally known hospital where she had a meteoric rise in the dietary department.

But despite this demonstrated mastery, her own weight was still a problem. She went from diet to diet. Her weight rose and fell like the tides. No matter how she reduced her calories, she hit an unyielding wall of flesh—the body would give a little and then refuse to budge.

Here was a specialist failing in an enterprise that should have been, if you'll pardon the expression, a piece of cake. Diet was her dish, food was her game, but she could not come up with a winning game plan.

She had it all, too—access to the medical literature on reducing diet, and data on what these diets should contain. And the most authoritative research in the field came across her desk. But even with all this information, she could not lose weight and keep it lost.

"Zounds!" one is inclined to exclaim. "Doesn't anyone here know how to play this game?"

Apparently not. In a conference on human obesity held in New York City, the scientists admitted they were in disarray. The feeling of the group was expressed by a doctor from Paris. "The treatment of obesity," he said, "remains a puzzling challenge." Most of those attending agreed. But physicians *must* expect failure if they treat obesity without understanding the physiology and biochemistry of energy regulation.

Diet is not the answer. Losing weight is a complex process, and diet is certainly part of it. But it is only one-half of the dollar bill. You will need the other half if you are going to buy into a successful program.

So—what's the other half? Let's start the answer by taking a close look at excess weight. It is not bone and muscle and transient water retention. What we have in excess is fat. We are not overweight, we are over*fat*. Here, the real story emerges: why diet doesn't work but exercise—the other half of the dollar bill—does.

Like the dietitian, overfat people who go on diets can win a few battles but they eventually lose the war. Diet alone cannot control the fat content of the body—*because it sows the seeds of its own defeat.*

A person on a diet will lose weight—but *most of that weight will be water and muscle.* Muscle is the most energy-hungry tissue in the body. It becomes obvious then why diets don't work: It's like trying to warm your house by turning the heat *down.*

What happened to the unlucky dietitian? She got lucky. She became friends with a runner and became a runner herself. Then the pounds came off and stayed off. Through serendipity, not science, she finally made the diet-exercise connection.

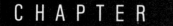
AN EXPERT OPINION ON EXPERT ADVICE

U*nder precisely controlled conditions, we will, individually, do as we damn please. And that, fortunately, is precisely what we should do.*

A WORD FROM THE WISE

The good advice business has never been better. *Counselors* of all sorts are multiplying like rabbits. Whatever the problem, of the body or mind or spirit, they are ready to give us the answer.

It used to be that we were exposed to such well-intentioned admonitions only on Sunday in church or in a weekly advice to the lovelorn column. But not anymore: Now we can't escape it. Advice pours out of the radio, it fills the newspapers, lines the shelves of every bookstore.

And to what avail? How much of this good advice is good for an individual? And if good, how much is followed? And if followed, how much does it change a person's life? The answer to all three questions: very little. Virtue cannot be taught, experience must be experienced, and some things we just have to learn the hard way—on our own.

This, of course, does not stop the preachers from preaching. The sowers of the word are always with us. And there are always listeners, too. P. T. Barnum said a new one was born every minute—people who seek help for choices they must make themselves, people who even *pay* for the help that is offered.

Theodore Roszak, a perceptive social commentator, especially during the 1960s, commented on this phenomenon. "We go to doctors and physiologists to learn what's going on in *our* organism," he said, "and that cuts us off from any direct experience that *we* can have, with a sense of certainty that we know what's going on and that *we* are indeed the best authorities over our inner life and our bodies."

Let that sink in: *We are the best authorities.* That does not mean we do not need information. Even the Pope has his *periti,* his experts, to give him information, to educate him on those things that can be found in the books.

Frankly, we *need* adequate information to live in this world. But information will never replace experience and the wisdom that follows from it.

"The vice of living in a highly artificial social order," said Roszak, "is that you experience through the media, through literature, through books, rather than in a raw and direct way."

There comes a time when you must become your *own* teacher, your *own* coach, your *own* clergyman.

We do share a host of attributes with others: drives and desires, instincts and longings. Under precisely controlled conditions, our overall responses to certain stimuli can be statistically predicted. But we are not statistics. Under precisely controlled conditions, we will, individually, do as we damn please. And that, fortunately, is precisely what we should do.

We need not ask another person, "Who am I?" If we do, we will never engage in the adventure of self-discovery. We will live another and false life. Do not mistake yourself for anyone else—the average American man, the ordinary inhabitant of this globe, the common-variety human being. They exist only on charts.

We must as a result have a healthy distrust and a healthy cynicism for the experts and for authority in general. Each of us is an experiment of one, each an expert in the self and a witness to a personal truth. My advice to the advisors would be, "Do not tell me what to do, tell me what you do. Do not tell me what is good for me, tell me what is good for you. If, at the same time, you reveal the you in me, if you become a mirror to my inner self, then you have made a reader and a friend."

GOD IS WATCHING

It was a sultry summer's day. Hot, humid, and not even a hint of a wind. As I ran past the marina, I saw the flag hanging straight down, draped against the pole.

No one was stirring. The early afternoon heat had sent people indoors. I ran the deserted back streets of this little harbor town alone with my thoughts.

I was sweating profusely. I enjoy that. A running friend once told me, "I sweat to think." Sweating, or what brings me to sweating, does help me think. It also makes me feel good about myself. That day, I was a king running through my kingdom.

Then up ahead, I saw another human being. He was up on a scaffold shingling a house. When I came close, I could see he was wearing only jeans and had a muscular and tanned upper body. I judged him to be in his early forties.

I am fundamentally a loner. But as I have grown older, I have taken to nodding to people as I run by. At times, I even say something like, "Beautiful day." But my inclination is still as in earlier days—to pass right by.

This time I didn't. Perhaps because he and I appeared to be the only living people on the streets that day, I felt the urge to speak to him. As I neared the house, he was shaping the shingle to fit in under the eaves, and I called up, "Do good."

He turned toward me and appeared to measure me and what I was doing. Then he said, "Intend to."

Ordinarily that exchange would be a long conversation to me. I have flown to the Coast and exchanged even fewer words to strangers on either side. Something, however, impelled me to say more.

"God is watching," I called up to him. I had been brought up with the certain knowledge that God had his eye on me, recording misdeed after misdeed. If the just man fails seven times a day, I was assuredly in the area of seven times seven. In my younger days in a Jesuit high school, I had decided my only chance was that keeping track of the millions of sins committed by millions was too big a task even for the Almighty. My transgressions might go unnoticed.

He looked at me then and said, "Hope so."

In one short response he had turned the world around. He had made himself the equal of anyone on this earth and made what he was doing of equal importance to any other human activity. He did that for me, too. We were both doing what we did well and doing it the best we could. His shingling was work. But it was also what my running was to me—*play.* He had reached the level Robert Frost had defined, "when work is play for mortal stakes."

He had gone beyond that even and made it an art. He was defining himself by what he was doing. And I suddenly realized I was doing the same.

"The artist is not a special kind of man," wrote English sculptor Eric Gill, "but every man is a special kind of artist." Our art is living. What we call the arts are secondary. We live our lives in a special way and find in that our own meaning.

I finished my run still thinking of that encounter. Two ordinary people, doing in his instance something mundane and in mine something of no practical value, discovering that art—and meaning, and a glimpse of heaven—can occur to anyone, anywhere, anytime.

"Whether by the ministry of angels or saints, or by the ministry of common workmen," Gill wrote, "we are all led heavenward."

Let's all live as if God were watching.

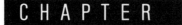

18

SPORT:
THE CRUCIBLE

There is no better arena for evaluating your value system, no better laboratory for investigating motivation—and no better proving ground for demonstrating one's defects. Sport exposes. Sport teaches. Sport develops. Sport becomes my art, my language, my way of being in this world.

THE LION'S DEN: A PHILOSOPHY OF SPORT

I had entered the lion's den—a convention of philosophers. I have been called a philosopher, but I am not. I have had no training in philosophy. I began reading philosophers when I was 45, and then only their diaries and lighter works. A philosopher in full cry after truth is beyond my simple powers. Reading William James when he is seriously pursuing his profession is like racing with an Olympian. In seconds I have lost contact.

Yet I was there to discuss "The Philosophy of Sport." Presumably being called a philosopher of sport meant I was one. The real philosophers sat there prepared to listen to and evaluate my philosophical statements.

At such times, when everyone is an expert in a subject in which I am an ignoramus, I find it best to go to the subject in which I am the reigning expert—myself. There are two ways of knowing: one through thought and study, the philosopher's path. The other—my path— through living. The general knows the theories of war, but the front-line soldier knows it firsthand. Walking point on patrol can teach things people will never learn in war college. So, too, I knew things through myself that were known to no other.

It is also well to remember that philosophy is, at bottom, a justification of your way of life, your view of the universe. In that enterprise, one person's truth is as good as another's. Philosophers, it is true, dig deeper, use language we don't understand, and build systems that climb to the sky. But no other philosophy of sport would be more valid than mine. A philosophy of sport must be lived, not learned. Everyone in that hall—no matter what universals they pronounced, no matter where they saw the place of sport in life—would be revealing their true philosophy, their ideas of the meaning of life. I found it good to remember Emerson's statement, "Philosophers spend their lives trying to put into words what the common man experiences."

The discussion that day touched on numerous aspects of sport— competition, the emphasis on winning, the place of sports in education. One coach asked how he could reconcile apparently opposing forces in sport—individual perfection and team play, for example?

One guest speaker was a professional hockey player. He spoke of the violence in his game and saw it as a natural outlet. It was, if held within reason, a relatively harmless way to release anger and frustration. Most of his listeners disagreed. They found such spectacles distasteful and subhuman, and were unable to fit such displays into their philosophy of sport.

But, frankly, they don't have to. My philosophy of sport is as individualistic as the way I pursue it. And it continues to change and adapt, to grow and mature, just as I change and adapt, grow and mature. The hockey player's more violent perspective is just as valid as mine. And the two views *don't* have to agree.

A philosophy of sport is almost if not quite identical to a philosophy of life. If anything, a person's approach to sport expresses the philosophy of life much more vividly and dramatically then any other aspect of his or her life. It is truly the union of theory and practice that should characterize all our actions but does not.

Sport expresses my philosophy. It also amends and expands it. It mirrors the stages of my life. It also slows and speeds my development. The philosophy of sport is not a subject I have studied, it is a subject I have lived.

It could be argued that sport does not cause personal development, it simply reflects it. That the progressive changes in personality and character it produces are really due to aging, not playing.

I believe otherwise. For me, sport has been the single most important influence in my life. Becoming an athlete has made me become what otherwise I might not have been.

Occasionally an audience asks me what I consider the greatest achievement in my life. I usually reply that it's me. Another question asked frequently is what I would change if I had my life to live over. The answer: nothing. I am here today because of the influence of everything that happened in my past. I am the product of those vectors and forces acting on the raw material that was—and still is—*me*.

Sport has been one instrument in my achievements, part of the various vectors and forces that contribute to the person writing this essay.

There is no better arena for evaluating your value system, no better laboratory for investigating motivation—and no better proving ground for demonstrating one's defects. Sport exposes. Sport teaches. Sport develops. Sport becomes my art, my language, my way of being in this world.

My philosophy of sport? I live it every day.

19

THE GOODNESS
OF GAMES

*The playful child living in a playful world is a
true aristocrat, using school and leisure to
perfect himself and make of his life a work of art.*

TEACHING TEACHERS: THE WISDOM OF PLAY

My audience was made up of physical education teachers, health
professionals interested in fitness. After-dinner speeches rarely disturb
the torpor induced by good food and a few drinks. Nevertheless, I was
there to tell them how important their jobs were, how essential to the
good life. And that today we were lucky to be in a period where the
body was being given its proper respect. That was the good news. The
bad news: They were not making the most of the opportunity.

The reason? They had failed to understand their role. They had
become scientists instead of practitioners—and the difference is a real
one. Scientists focus on the mechanism of fitness, with endless reports
and statistics regarding the physiology of fitness, the inner workings of
muscle. *Practitioners* concentrate on something entirely different—the
why of fitness, the inner workings of *mind*.

I'd read reports on optimum body construction for different athletic events, but few on why someone would want to enter such events; studies on the optimum forearm length to throw a javelin, but little on why people want to throw it; and erudite analyses of rebounding ability in basketball but nothing on *why* people forsake every other activity to play with a large round ball.

Fitness experts have come to know a great deal about the physical state of fitness. But they have left virtually untouched the psychological and philosophical impact of fitness on our lives.

Physical educators see their goal as *fitness* itself, and the process then becomes the body activities necessary to achieve it. We should realize that is *not* the way the human animal operates. Children who love to play physically nonetheless *hate* physical education: We will not do anything for any length of time if it bores us.

After we leave school, the doctors take over. Now, the motivation is fear—fear of silent killers like cholesterol, fear of shortened lives. But the doctors don't know the human animal either. We will not do anything for any length of time simply because it is good for us.

But people will do anything for any length of time if it is *play*. They will accept pain, tolerate exhaustion, be heedless of time. In fact, the only thing they will question is interruption. I recall a race in Midland, Michigan, when we were stopped at a railroad crossing until a freight train passed. This respite from effort was uniformly viewed as an *indignity* that marred the event.

The subject of physical education is play. The process of physical education is learning to play *better*, just as the subject of medicine is health, and the process is learning how to live better. Life—the ultimate game—and man—the ultimate athlete—are the concerns of both disciplines.

The best physicians are practitioners, not scientists. They use faith and logic and experience to guide their patients, not numbers and charts and calculated probabilities. So it should be with physical educators. Science is a small part of what they do, yet they tend to make that science paramount.

The reason, it seems to me, is that physical educators have an inferiority complex. The educational establishment does not recognize that physical education is as important as any other subject on the curriculum. Consequently, physical educators are not considered equals by their peers. The result? They imitate the other disciplines, adopting an overly scientific attitude toward a subject that is as much art as science.

And what they teach *is* important: There are few things in this life more valuable than learning how to play well. We are first and always *homo ludens* — man the player. The person who helps us accomplish that must stand tall — and resist the impulse to imitate others.

ADOLESCENCE:
NATURAL NOBLEMEN AND THE BIRTH OF BOREDOM

A Canadian physiologist investigated teenage fitness several years ago and found something interesting: Fitness seems to *stop* at adolescence. Kids who were in good shape as preteens suddenly *decline* in fitness, by all the normally accepted measures. The obvious question: Why?

The answer, it seems to me, is that primary fact of a teenager's life — high school. They enter high school and they enter a new life and new way to live it.

The change in lifestyle is most obvious in its physical expression. The 14-year-old is a good animal. He is accustomed to hours of movement and play between school-out and supper. The games he plays then are intense, absorbing, transporting experiences. He derives energy from them that makes him capable of what appears to be perpetual motion.

The 14-year-old is enjoying a last year of freedom — the last year of being a child. He has aspects of his life that will never come again: his gang, play, his dreams — heroes and a chance to be one. The 14-year-old plots his own course, his day his own with a minimum of rules: Show up for meals, do your homework, take care of a few chores.

It is in this physical world that the child becomes whole. And this wholeness extends to his entire life. He becomes a seamless union of body, mind, and spirit. He tastes excellence and sees it all around him. This playful child living in a playful world is a true aristocrat, using school and leisure to perfect himself and make of his life a work of art. Living is a game, and perfection the result.

And then suddenly, both the game and the perfection are lost.

This aristocrat, this animal-artist-hero-saint enters high school and meets middle-class minds and middle-class values. The changes then are global: Education ceases to be learning and becomes teaching. Facts become more important than real knowing — comprehension replaced by the need to learn vast compendiums of trivia. The drawing out of what is already within stops. Information is stuffed in instead. Goals and grades become paramount — from now on, the important things are IQ exams, PSAT scores, college entrance requirements. The child who was a seamless whole is fragmented.

To a 14-year-old aristocrat, what counted most was his play. But now he doesn't belong to that neighborhood bunch that played until darkness intervened. Now he has *supervised athletic activity*—play replaced by calisthenics, joy by drudgery, and happiness by boredom.

The good animal begins to die.

Do I overstate the case? Probably so. Perhaps it's true that we should accept this decline in physical activity and say: "It has to be. There are more important things to be done. It is time to put away the things of the child."

But for my part I say we can *never* put away the things of the child. The role of education is to make an adult of a person *without* removing the child. Without play—without that child still alive in all of us—we will always be incomplete. And not only physically, but creatively, intellectually, and spiritually as well.

"Man made the school," said English social scientist Walter Bagehot. "God made the schoolyard." We must not forget it. Play is an expression of the true self—the person the Creator had in mind the day we were born.

THE SERIOUS BUSINESS OF PLAY

Play is nonrational. Like humor and religion, it often doesn't make sense. But we are, as American philosopher William James said, "incurably religious." And also incurably playful. We are endowed with a sense of humor so strong that it can manifest itself even on the way to the gallows.

When we enter the world of play, we are escaping and finding diversion. We are taking a time-out and getting, in effect, a pass releasing us from our regular duties—or the gallows.

But play is, like it or not, serious business. If it never gets beyond this initial freedom it will fail. Play is not necessarily the absence of stress. It is an immersion into activities that may stress us to the very limits.

Play is not retiring from the daily battle. Play is even more demanding than real life. It asks unremittingly for our very best. And as with health, our very best means our physical and mental best.

But if it's difficult, it's also rewarding. Make *anything* play and you'll succeed at it. Consider fitness programs. What distinguishes those who stay from those who drop out? Basically, it is just that they have dicovered *play.* Fitness has become *fun.* They have found something they would do even if it didn't help them lose weight and give them energy. These benefits become important simply because they mean we can play better.

Experts can help people find their play, but it is still an individual decision. There are kinds of play that reward physical skill, other types of play that require neither agility nor coordination. But, in play, "to each his own" is particularly true. The important thing is to keep looking. I know people who tried one activity after another with no success, then finally became lifelong enthusiasts in forms of play that had never occurred to them. Hiking, karate, cross-country skiing, even rowing—all gain adherents who never look back. These people found play—and wonder how they ever lived without it.

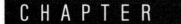

20

THE SAVVY STRIDER

The best exercise is walking. There is considerable evidence to support that statement.

THOUGHT WALKS

Advocates of walking and running have never been reluctant to exaggerate. "If you could run and run and run and never get tired," asks someone in English author C. S. Lewis's *The Last Battle*, "why would you want to do anything else?"

Thoreau took the same approach to walking. "I walk half the daylight," he stated, "but when I tell people, I don't think they believe me."

Statements about walking and hiking always seem to be in superlatives. If the sedentary life is, as Emerson wrote, "A sin against the Holy Ghost," those who are active must somehow possess all the gifts the Holy Spirit will bestow.

For some, running has brought about rebirth. "I find running to be excellent therapy," wrote a recovered alcoholic. "It has brought me a whole new area for my physical health and conditioning." A strong recommendation, but modest compared to what follows.

"I have a personal frontier," he continued, "a place to focus my energies, something that can turn every morning into an adventure. When I finish my little 5-mile run through the park, I can truly say to myself for once in my life, 'Yes, I can,' and that in itself is worth living for."

Others give more scientific reasons for running. "When I was a student," wrote a retired general practitioner in the *British Medical Journal*, "the idealism of youth led me to believe there must be an ideal form of exercise. I do not claim to have found that ideal form of exercise. I am not even sure it exists. I am sure, however, from the point of view of promoting health, though there may be exercises as good, there is no exercise *better* than running."

Runners find this to be a self-evident truth. The ideal exercise exists and they are doing it. Running is second to none for promoting health. It is also second to none in providing pleasure and enjoyment. The inexpressibly good feelings in the body are matched by those engendered in the mind and spirit, as well.

But walkers *refuse* to take second place, although their reasons for walking are very different from those of runners.

"The influences that make one walk more than the other are more ethereal than terrestrial," wrote Thoreau. "It is the quality of the air more than the quality of the ground that concerns the walker."

And, "I have never jogged or run," wrote my old professor of medicine, Dr. William Dock, "because I can't see the flowers, shrubs, and trees." In another letter he explained, "My own form of madness is for strolling and preferably up hills with views and flora. My joy since childhood has been climbing on slopes with trees and shrubs and flowers."

Such walks resemble those the Swedish naturalist Linnaeus called herbalizations. He would take his students on trips that lasted from seven in the morning until nightfall. The time was spent searching out and identifying plants and insects, birds and eggs.

Thoreau, it would seem, enjoyed the best of both worlds. He was a naturalist who filled his journals with his day's catch. But he was also a thinker who pursued an idea down into the labyrinth of his mind and, in the process, lost consciousness of the outside world. I find his notes on nature as dull as his walker's thoughts are exciting.

The common denominator here is *motion*. Life is movement. What that movement will be depends on one's entire personality. In 1555, the early Spanish physician Cristobal Mendez chose walking because he could read, observe, converse, and meditate.

Walking and running justify the solitary state. The geniuses who walked were selfish people: Thoreau, Emerson, Nietzsche, Rousseau, even William James. Rousseau's early concern was for the common good. Then, at age 66, he wrote *The Reveries of a Solitary Walker* and took it all back. He argued for the joys and rewards of isolation, and, like the others, it became clear that he spoke for Man and avoided men.

Creation is a solitary act. Science is *we*, but art is *I*. It is easy to see that walking—where we're often alone with ourselves—can become the place where we become artists. In isolation, we create.

GAIN WITHOUT PAIN

The best exercise is walking.

There is considerable evidence to support that statement, although some would dispute it. Walking, for starters, requires no instruction or at the most, very little. Only if one moves on to competitive race walking is coaching of *any* sort necessary. Walking is also virtually injury-free, unlike many other kinds of aerobic exercise.

And walking is generally preferred by the body. When I awaken in the morning my body rebels against the idea of running, yet it will readily accept a walk of the same duration. The great Alfie Shrubb, the leading runner of his time, began his day with a walk. He also recommended an occasional long walk during the day in place of running.

Walking is a gentle but effective way to become fit. Even for the competitive runner, walking can provide additional training with no threat of injury. Though seldom employed, there is good physiological evidence for its use. Alternate walking/jogging is the preferred program for some morning runners and has been incorporated into the protocol for depressed patients at the University of Wisconsin.

Walking is a very natural activity, too. We do it every day without thinking about it. It's so natural that children begin within the first year and become adept in no time. Walkers have none of the fears and worries that beset the neophyte runner.

But is walking strenuous enough to be good for our health? This is simply a matter of choosing the right pace. It should be stated that all movement is good movement, but there is a minimum pace that will give us the desired benefits: fast enough to make us breathe harder, but not so fast that we can't talk. For most of us, this is about 50 to 60 percent of our age-adjusted maximum—a brisk pace.

Walking, as we know, can be done in a variety of forms and a number of speeds. American playwright Thornton Wilder once listed 200 different ways of saying a person was drunk. Any writer of similar gifts might be able to come up with nearly that number describing ways to walk: saunter, stroll, amble, plod, stride, step, pace, strut, stalk, prance, putter, tread, bounce, march, shuffle, mince.

It is probable that all of these types of perambulation, if done long enough and frequently enough, will lead to fitness.

THE BOREDOM OF BACKPACKING

I took up hiking to humor a friend. She was a member of the Adirondacks Mountain Club and taught me all I needed to know. She knew the best places to hike, and the best times to do it. We covered some of the most beautiful trails in the Hudson Valley area. I wore the right shoes, the correct clothing, and I was tutored in when to eat, what to eat, and what should be in my backpack. A novice, I received instruction from a master. And presented with hiking at its best, I found it a bore.

The whole business surprised me. I had thought I would like hiking. I enjoyed walking, and hiking seemed to be little more than a different way of walking. My mentors, Emerson and Thoreau, appeared to be hikers as well as walkers. Why, then, was I out of my element hiking?

The reasons go deep. The main reason, however, is that I am not a hiker: I'm a runner. To me the landscape is a matter of indifference. To the hiker, it is all. The hiker is completely occupied with the environment, whereas I am completely occupied with my thoughts.

This preoccupation with everything about you is an absolute necessity when hiking. Every step must be made with care. The footing can never be taken for granted. The ground below your feet is constantly changing. There are rocks and even boulders, fallen tree trunks and overhanging branches. A retreat into your mind is as dangerous as dozing at the wheel of a car.

You must also stay on the trail. You must be ever on the alert for the markings on the trees. Miss one and you are lost. Half the time I spent hiking was in retracing my steps to find a turn in the trail.

Hiking at that level is an animal existence. It demands the undivided attention the animal gives to everything around it. The briefest lapse can bring on disaster. You have to keep your head up and your eyes moving. There is no time for reverie, no time to retire into one's mind and think.

There is more to hiking, of course, than survival. Emerson suggested there were two companions one should invite on a tramp. The artist with an eye for beauty, or the naturalist — to learn about nature.

Hikers are people who appreciate these things. But *I* give the beauties of changing seasons, glorious sunrises and sunsets, and long vistas over valley and river no more than a passing glance.

And in nature I see only essences. A tree is a tree is a tree. A flower is no more than a flower or a bird a bird. True, some are of different sizes and colors, but more than that I do not notice—or care. I come from a long line of writers who cannot distinguish one flower from another and have only a limited lexicon on birds and a restricted vocabulary in trees. Reading Thoreau's journal, you will find him walking deep in thought oblivious to his surroundings. But the great majority of his entries are those of a hiker. Thoreau's journals are filled with meticulous drawings and notations on what was occurring to flora and fauna, to flowers and squirrels. Only occasionally do these observations record the aphorisms we usually associate with his walks at Walden Pond.

Hikers are backpackers at heart. It is but one small step from a day trip immersed in nature to sleeping out under the stars. I personally prefer all the amenities our fight with nature has gained for us—central heating, a leakproof roof. I see no reason to turn my back on the human comforts found at the Hilton and the Sheraton, the Marriott and the Holiday Inn. It is enough that I sleep with the window open.

The truth is that hiking is a sport, very different from simply walking, and as with most sports, the more difficult the better. In running, this is true only in the race. My training runs are almost effortless, my body on automatic pilot requiring none of my attention. And while my body is running in one direction, my mind is sprinting in another. That means that I pick my runs to suit: free of obstacles, generally even, easy terrain. Hikers do it differently. The Adirondacks Mountain Club schedule not only lists the hikes for the week, but also the degree of difficulty. The hike is always a challenge, and the hiker selects the one best able to test his or her personal limits of ability.

One late afternoon, after being hopelessly lost, we met some hikers who showed us the trail that would get us back to our car. Then one of them pointed to a flat dirt road. "That will take you directly to the parking lot," he told us. My friend would have none of it. Getting out the easy way, walking on a level unchanging path where one can think and converse, is not the hiker's delight.

But it is, of course, the runner's delight. All I want is a safe unchanging surface, little or no traffic, and no interruptions of my train of thought. I want the world around to take a back seat and *let me think*.

21

BICYCLE BATTLES AND WATER WARS

And realizing that this is a game of inches, with disaster never more than a hand's span away, the rule is to ride scared—and I do that naturally.

EVERYTHING NEW IS NOT OLD

You never forget how to ride a bicycle. So goes the common wisdom. Anyone can learn, and once you have learned, you never forget. Get on a bike, regardless of age, and all the old skills will come back.

It is the common wisdom because it is also the common experience. Those who rode bicycles in childhood find returning to them no difficulty. The old mastery is still there. Riding a bike in senescence is as natural as it was in adolescence.

But.

I am now back to the bicycle, and I'm finding the common wisdom and the common experience only partially true. The bicycle I have come back to is not the sturdy Columbia I rode as a schoolboy in Brooklyn. It is a sleek Miyata Three-Ten, a finely designed machine built for speed and distance. It is as different from my old, heavy, thick-tired bike as my Honda Civic is from a Formula One racer. Riding a Miyata is like riding a thoroughbred hunter over brush when you've been trained on the kind of placid beast that stables provide for beginners.

Merely mounting this machine gives portents of dangerous things to come. The height, tailored to my own, makes it impossible for me to keep both feet on the ground when I'm on the saddle. Off the saddle, the center tube allows only one inch clearance when I straddle it: I have to be *quite* careful in coming to the at-ease position.

Just sitting on the Three-Ten's seat starts the adrenaline flowing. The hormonal surge hits even harder when I try to get my feet in the toe clips. Getting into toe clips is the real secret of riding this formidable machine. Once this skill is acquired, things get a lot more manageable. Riding a Miyata will never become easy, but mastering the toe clips makes it a good deal less difficult.

I begin every ride in the stationary position, and I do *not* make a move until I've gotten my left foot into the toe clip. I find this akin to threading a needle with my left hand—and I'm right-handed. I paw away at the clip. I flex my toes inside my shoe. The pedal spins and spins. Failure follows failure and then, quite suddenly, my shoe is in the clip.

My left foot secure, I push off, gathering speed. Next I coast, and engage in the second half of the project—getting the right shoe into the toe clip. This is like trying to thread a needle while running for a bus. I fail, and fail again. Then, suddenly—as if I could have done it easily all along—the toe is in the clip. I am ready for cycling.

This is not the cycling I did as a boy, however. Then, a bike ride was three blocks to get a soda or a couple of miles to play ball. The trips were leisurely, conversational affairs. Bikes were built for balance and easy handling, and very little was required of the cyclist.

But the cycling of my youth has very little to do with taking charge of a Miyata. One does not *meander* on this vehicle: There is an alarmingly high level of speed that is required just to maintain balance. Below that, the whole system of bicycle and rider becomes unstable. And to stop, I must get out of at least one toe clip. Otherwise I am *married* to this machine and its fate will be mine.

I go through this learning period in a large parking lot on Sandy Hook, a strip of land between bay and ocean. It is a beautiful seven-mile long peninsula maintained as a national park. Around me are dozens of cyclists doing the things cyclists do before they go on their training rides. And when I look at them, I know what I already suspected: This cycling is dangerous stuff. The panic I felt getting on the Miyata and then getting my shoes secured is only the beginning. There is clearly more panic to come.

First of all, they wear helmets and gloves. There was nary a single helmet among my schoolmates riding bikes back in the 1930s. Nor gloves, either.

"You need gloves," one rider told me, "because when you fall, your natural instinct is to put out your hand as you hit the ground."

Gloves, I was to learn, also help prevent ulnar nerve paralysis and carpal tunnel syndrome—cute little problems that plague many bicyclists. And the odd pants everyone wears—the ones with the built-in leather underwear—are insurance against a host of nerve and skin problems associated with the pressure from the seat.

This new and exciting and injury-filled world is all out there in front of me. But for now, I am learning to ride a Miyata within the confines of a parking lot.

I am once more a beginner. This is the same as my first day on a bicycle. I am reminded of Mark Twain's wonderfully funny essay on his initial attempt at cycling. He had, he wrote, absolutely no idea of where he was going, and consequently he completely befuddled a dog who was trying to get out of his way. Remaining upright required a series of reflex moves that surprised both victim and onlooker. The dog in the way of the struggling Twain had no more idea what writer was going to do than Twain himself.

It is all coming back, of course. But I will need new skills—and new caveats as well. Mostly those are a matter of caution—staying within my cycling capacity, for example, *anticipating* trouble. Keeping my head up, as the fighter pilots say, and my eyes moving. And realizing that this is a game of inches, with disaster never more than a hand's span away, the rule is to ride scared—and I do that naturally.

RESURRECTION OF A RUNNER

I ride my Miyata Three-Ten these fall days on Sandy Hook, with the ocean on one side, the bay on the other. As I cycle north, I can see the Verrazano Bridge and, beyond it, the Manhattan skyline. On very clear days, which tell me the rains will soon follow, the World Trade Center towers seem only a mile or so away.

On those clear days, the sky a deep blue and water on either side, the Hook is an Eden for cyclists. During my 3-mile reach into the wind on the smooth, flat asphalt road, only one or two cars pass me. Coming back in high gear with the wind now aiding me, perhaps a few more cars may pass. There is little reason for traffic. The sailors at a small Coast Guard station and a few fishermen are the only ones who will be using the Hook until summer comes again.

These bike rides have replaced some of my training runs. I still run races every weekend, but I have reduced my midweek distance running. This change came about for important physical and psychological reasons. One such reason: I was losing my *competence* in running, and with it the enjoyment of my solitary runs.

In the past, striding along at two minutes slower than my race pace, I felt virtuoso. I could dissociate myself from my body and get off into my head. The hour on the road would be a sensual pleasure, done with such little effort I would actually forget I was running.

That no longer happens. I've lost my bounce. Where running used to be noiseless, I can now hear my feet slapping the road. In the past, I could put my body on automatic pilot and all would be well. Now I am continually making corrections, making effort upon effort, never able to get away from the mechanics of running.

Making it even less enjoyable is the fact that I still remember when I was good at it. That is the worst part, knowing that running probably will never be like it was. As I age, and age precipitously, my one-hour run on the river road has become a chore, not a delight.

On the bike it is different. It is an entirely new relationship. There is no ghost of the past. My body has no memory of what it is like to be a competent cyclist. My body accepts my cycling as normal. This is the way everybody every age cycles, and whatever I lack in running does not seem to matter here.

I am no longer a has-been. Instead I am a child again given a bike for Christmas. I am learning how to be a good cyclist. And while I may well be no better at bicycling than I am at running, on the bike I have no memories to compete with.

The point here? When I run, I am an old man. When I bike, I am a child again. When I run, I am exquisitely aware of my loss of energy, of the deterioration of my form. But the bike is a new thing. My body thinks it is *good* at cycling, and getting better.

I am able to think on the bike, too, something I've stopped doing running the roads. I'm learning to shift gears to stabilize the effort. There is no need to hurt: I get into a rhythm and maintain it by altering gears. That odd heaviness of landing with each stride— deceleration, the running experts call it—has no place in cycling. And in that comfort, the mind floats free.

So cycling is a new thing, and a new thing is what I need. A new start, a new addiction, a new religious experience, but, overall, a new relationship. I need a place to go where I feel comfortable, do something well, and do it automatically, where I can observe and meditate and on occasions have a glimpse of Heaven.

CYCLING SCHISMS

If cycling were a religion, there would be two major sects: the tourists and the racers. The tourists take long rides to places at the periphery of their world. They bike to towns previously only accessible by car and rarely mentioned in conversation. These are day-long social affairs at an easy pace.

The racers, on the other hand, ride full-out at virtually maximal intensity. And their goal is not a place but a certain number of miles. Speed, not endurance, is at the center of their dogma. Their rides are flat-out competitive events with few of the social graces. The tourists go in packs by choice, the racers go in packs by necessity: Drafting (riding in someone else's slipstream) makes racing easier.

But both the tourist and the racer are true believers. Both have found that biking gives meaning to their lives—one in the lengthy communion with self and countryside, the other in the painful and concentrated challenge of competition. Each enters his own particular world, and cycling becomes the focal point of existence.

Now that I am biking on Sandy Hook, I have come to know these two groups. The tourists meet on Tuesday, the racers on Wednesday. Cursory observation would lead you to believe both are identical. Both nights there are dozens of bikers getting ready to ride. They wear the same gear, the same tight pants, the same gloves, and the same helmets. Even the bikes are the same—lean and light ten-speed marvels.

But there's a difference. The Tuesday group is relaxed. They stand around talking a good deal. Very few do any preliminary riding on a bike. They remind me of a bunch of joggers who meet every Saturday morning for a long, slow, conversational run. On Tuesday, there is no tension, no electricity, just a quietude and peace that match the approaching sunset.

But Wednesday? Well, Wednesday is—*not* the same. This crowd is in motion. Most are warming up on their bikes, waiting for the training to begin. There is a prerace feeling in the air. Everyone is attending to their shoes or their bikes, and very little talking is being done. On Wednesday night, biking becomes *serious* business.

The difference between the groups, however, is more than attitude.

My Tuesday friends give me one type of advice. On Wednesday, I am told the exact opposite.

The Tuesday bike, for example, is not the same as Wednesday's machine. When you tour, you must be prepared for the worst. I am advised to get a small bag for emergency equipment, a spare tube, a patch kit, a tire iron, wrenches. And, of course, I will need a pump to attach to the frame, and, finally, water bottles.

The Wednesday bike has none of these accessories. Wednesday is for racing, and the racing bike must be stripped down. Get rid of the reflectors, I am told. Remove the lock and chain. *Forget* about the pump and repair kit. Everything additional on the bike will hurt your time in the race.

At first I was not sure which of these services to attend—Tuesdays with the tourists or Wednesdays with the racers. Ultimately, the decision was easy. When I am a runner, I am a racer, and as a cyclist I want to be the same. And besides—I don't think I could *ever* learn how to change a tire.

HONORABLE CONTUSIONS: A RITE OF PASSAGE

Yesterday, I was a person who rode a bike. I had learned the basics: getting into the toe clip, cadence, cornering with prudence. I had taken long rides out on Sandy Hook. But I was not yet a biker.

That was yesterday. Today it all changed. Today I had my first fall. And not an ordinary fall, some run-of-the-mill everyday minor topple into the sand or the weeds. This was a legitimate crash—a *flip* that left me bruised and bleeding from scalp to ankle, and my Miyata several yards away.

It was not a novice fall, but it was a novice accident. I was coming back against the wind when I was passed by three cyclists. Automatically, in a carryover from my running, I tucked in behind them to take advantage of their draft. When running into the wind, I would always look for a broad back and follow close behind.

Even knowing how much easier this made running, I was unprepared for how much drafting increases bicycling speed. Before I realized it, my front tire was inches off the rear wheel of the bike ahead of me. On my trusty Columbia back in the 1930s, that would have posed no problem. Coaster brakes are simple to use. Not so the hand ones, and especially those on this high-performance thoroughbred.

Within a few seconds, contact was inevitable. And in less time than it takes to write this down, I found myself sprawled on the road and my bike some distance away. The whole thing happened so fast I could not recall what had happened between the time the wheels touched and I was lying in the roadway.

Several cyclists stopped to check my condition and one went to get my car at the parking lot. Then they left. I stood there holding my bike and assessing my injuries. Nothing broken, no major injuries, some minor pain. So I remounted the bike and, still bleeding, set out again on the course. Five minutes later the cyclist who had gotten my car caught up to me and yelled out the window, "You are a certified nut!"

Perhaps. But I had forgotten the fall and was enjoying the bike. I was pumping away at amazing speed and actually passing some other bikers. I had learned the cadence and was doing better with the gears. I was becoming part of this machine.

When I got back to the parking lot, sanity set in. A friend who is a physician surveyed my wounds. No stitches needed, he concluded, but I could do with a little first aid. So he took me to his home and tended to my cuts and abrasions.

By then I was beginning to feel like a hero. Picking myself up and continuing on the bike was a mark of something. I asked my friend about it. "At that moment," he said, "you became a biker." I believed him: His bike cost four times more than mine did, and he knows things about biking I will never know. I felt *knighted.* I had gone to the Hook a boy and come back a man.

Still, there was a small voice inside that was bothering me. I had to tell him.

"Perhaps it's a defect in my value system," I told him, "but when I found myself on the road I wasn't worried about myself. I was scared to death that my bike had been damaged."

I looked at him like the young Arthur looking up at Merlin awaiting his reply.

"This is what that means," he said. "You don't just like cycling, you love it."

WATER WARS

When I decided to train for the triathlon, a friend wrote me, "Swimming is the most difficult part of the triathlon and it *never* gets better." He was absolutely right. The swim has become *the* Herculean labor in my triathlon. I welcome the bike, and I even enjoy the last part of the run. But I have to force myself into the water—I dread the time I spend swimming.

I had expected swimming to be boring, but I had no idea that it would be so difficult. I have spent my summers at the beach since I was nine. I love the ocean and can handle myself in the roughest surf. The swimming part of the triathlon, I thought, would be no problem.

Now, I realize I am nothing more than a reasonably good body-surfer. I am not a swimmer. Bodysurfing is just a matter of catching a wave and then swimming out to catch another one. The swim takes little more than a minute or two, and it is not really a swim. It is more of a scramble during which I walk and dive and swim until I get past the breaking waves into still water.

Swimming for distance is an entirely different sport. It is a grueling, exhausting, and, at times (at least in the ocean), frightening activity. It is a mixture of pain and fatigue with moments of panic. Distance swimming is spending an interminable, arm-weary time trying to reach a goal that never seems any closer. It is no more like bodysurfing than a marathon is like a 100-yard dash.

This all became clear to me in my first triathlon practice. We gathered about 30 strong at the water's edge for a quarter-mile swim. Someone made the first move, and then all of us plunged in and began to swim parallel to the shore.

Until I hit the water, I had no idea how poor a swimmer I was. I flailed away at the water as more and more of the group passed. Things went from bad to worse. Although I tried to stay horizontal and high in the water, my arm strokes were too weak. At times, I was almost vertical. Periodically I would inhale what seemed like a quart of the Atlantic and come to a dead stop. Swimming, I learned, is like golf—it humbles you.

The truth is that I don't have the body of a swimmer. My muscle is in the wrong place. Swimming requires strength and stamina of both arms and the shoulders. I am an endurance animal, true, but only for *running*. My great, heavily muscled legs are of little use in the water.

The experience of a friend makes the point. He resumed his swimming after a 25-year break and gained 17 pounds. None of it was fat and *all* of it was in his arms and shoulders. I am shy 17 muscular pounds, and shy the ability that goes with them.

None of which means I'm going to give it up.

"You can swim," a friend told me, "so you will do well in your age group. Few people as old as you know how to swim or will take the time to learn." He was right. The older you are, the less likely you are to know how to swim or to bother to learn. But what neither he nor I realized was how difficult it can be to *return* to swimming.

Swimming is like many things that were part of our youth. It gradually becomes fantasy, only the good parts remaining in memory. I remembered myself as a water rat, an excellent swimmer who could handle any surf. In my mind's eye I was an undiscovered star with the potential of a Buster Crabbe or Johnny Weismuller. And as my friend talked on, I relived these dreams of glory. Forget about *people my age*, I thought as I listened. I can take on anyone in the field.

What I did *not* remember was that water was never my element. I was, then and now, an endurance animal who could not endure in the water. Low body fat does not suit the swimmer, nor are matchstick arms a natural advantage. In a matter of minutes, water left me not only cold but *exhausted*.

Unless there was a good surf, I never took more than a dip. Five minutes in the water and I would begin to pucker up. The skin on my fingers would wrinkle, and my temperature would drop. I spent most of my time on the beach while my friends spent hours in the water. I'd ride a few waves and then get warm lying in the sun.

All this came back to me. I was learning an old skill, swimming, but using it in a completely different way—I was swimming for distance, which had all of the bad parts and few of the good ones of the swimming I did when I was young.

I have seen polls showing that more people in this country swim for distance than any other form of exercise. I have friends who swim for play and relaxation. Their swims are periods of creativity and relaxation, their hours in the pool filled with mental as well as physical energy. For me, it is almost the exact opposite. I swim with no other goal than *finishing*, no other thought than how best to do it. Time, which is always relative, never passes more slowly; I swim for 30 minutes and when I look at my watch it has only been 5.

Swimming, therefore, can never become for me the sanctuary that running is—it simply demands too much effort. When I run, I retire within myself and think. But swimming affords no such time for mental gymnastics. It is a complicated physical performance that requires my undivided attention. I am consequently forced to put my mind and spirit on hold.

Nevertheless, swimming does get easier. Runner Frank Shorter once remarked on the time frames required to go back to alternate forms of training like swimming and cycling: two weeks to relearn the physical skill, and two months to develop the physiolog—the physical *structure* of muscle and wind—to do it. In swimming you reacquire the stroke, you restore the neural pathways, and the coordinated patterns again become reflex. Then you develop the strength and stamina needed to actually do it for long periods of time.

After two weeks in the water, I was no longer thrashing aimlessly about. I was able to do my quarter-mile in the ocean, although at a much slower pace than I had originally attempted. That, incidentally, is another attribute one acquires—realism. I found out how good (or bad) I really was.

With this improvement came the realization that I had not been an undiscovered Buster Crabbe or Johnny Weismuller in my youth. I had not been and never would be a good swimmer. Result: I now approach the water with zero enthusiasm. I do it because I must, even though I am already chilled to the bone and know the water will be even colder. I no longer wonder why Frank Shorter, a high school swimmer, has avoided the triathlon: With our ultra-low body fat (normal for runners), distance swimming is like being put in the freezer.

Swimming, however, does have its great moments. I have turned to interval training. I have found that flat-out, short-distance sprints are an exhilarating challenge, an experiment in how fast I can go and how much pain I can stand. When I finish, there is an uplift of mood and ego that provides a definite plus to the day. When I come out of the pool, I feel larger than life.

And for just a little while, I relive the glory days of my youth.

22

TEMPER, TEMPER— THE ANGST AND THE ECSTASY

Temper may be unsightly and a cloud on human intercourse, but there are occasions when a white-hot rage is the only weapon that will preserve us.

THE FIRE BELOW

"There is one phenomenon in daily living so degrading, so shocking, so miserable," wrote English novelist Arnold Bennett, "that I hesitate to mention it." He was alluding to losing one's temper. "This constitutes," said Bennett, "the most curious and humiliating spectacle that life offers."

Often that's an accurate description. The devil has broken his chains, civilization recedes a thousand years, and it's all because someone touched a tender point.

But oddly enough, getting angry is occasionally the right thing to do. There is a time *not* to be in a temper, but there is also a time to *be* in a temper. "Anger," said Greek philosopher Aristotle, "is a weapon for virtue and valor." At one time it was needed for survival. And frankly, I think it still is. It's just that now the threats to survival are more likely

129

to be psychological than physical—verbal assaults instead of saber-toothed tiger attacks.

My youngest son put it this way when we were discussing anger at the dinner table recently: "You should only lose your temper when you are violated."

The rest of the family was silenced by the strength of that word *violated.* Until he spoke, we had been talking about ways to manage rage, not justify it. Temper, in our view, was just another of man's weaknesses. "To seek to extinguish anger utterly is but a boast of Stoics," said thirteenth century English philosopher Roger Bacon. The best most of us can aspire to, then, is to minimize the damage, diminish the number of casualties and the consequences of our episodes of anger.

"Internalize it," another son (the new doctor) advised. "I like people who internalize their anger. I want no part of those people who rant and rave. I avoid them then *and* later."

But a third son disagreed. "Externalize it," he advised, "or things just get worse. If you internalize, you become the victim: You get ulcers, hypertension, or a heart attack as a reaction to unexpressed anger. Let it all come out," he said, "and you will be saved."

But it was not until my youngest son made his observation that we could see temper in the right perspective. He repeated St. Paul's message to the Ephesians: "Be angry, but sin not. Let not the sun go down on your wrath." There are times, in other words, when righteous rage is the right response. Temper may be unsightly and a cloud on human intercourse, but there are occasions when a white-hot rage is the only weapon that will preserve us.

When? As my youngest put it—when we are violated, when we have been made less than human by others or even by ourselves. "Anger," wrote sociologist Ernest Becker, "is a reaction, a way of reasserting ourselves, a setting things in balance again and preventing a person's body from being flooded by the environment."

Temper, then, becomes life-enhancing.

"Some people," stated Becker, "never learn that their organism has a right to take up space without shrinking, to assert itself without feeling guilt, to emit odors and digestive noise without shame, to scream in affront and pain when they are attacked."

The truth of the matter: There can be no *last* angry man. When there is, the world will have given up. Great deeds need hot blood, and great lives require great emotion. The fire down below, that smoldering source of energy, is what lifts us over obstacles, and keeps us moving when further motion seems impossible.

THE IRISH IN ME

When I get my Irish up, few things are safe. I've torn telephones out of the wall, smashed china, and, on one occasion when our third son would not get up for school, I threw a chair through a window. When I lose my temper, I am an anarchist: *Anything* that suggests order and stability is in danger.

Writer Arnold Bennett described this dreadful spectacle well. "Temper," he wrote, "is an insurrection, a boiling over, a sweeping storm. Dignity, common sense, justice are shriveled up."

At such times, it is best to exhaust the storm with some vigorous but essentially harmless action. Sanity can easily be restored if only you have an alternative way to work off your wrath.

My father, who was subject to similar explosions of Irish ire, would dissipate his anger with a bar of soap. He would burst from his office in the basement of our house, displaying all the storm flags of an Irishman in a righteous rage, and ascend to his room. Once there, he would proceed to throw a large bar of soap against the wall for five minutes or so. Composure restored, he would then discard the soap, descend the stairs, and resume his office routine.

He had an Irish temper and so do I—I inherited it from him. I realize, of course, that it's not fashionable nowadays to think so ethnically. Of current writers, only Michael Novak seems to take one's country of national origin seriously. And temper is certainly universal: Irish or Polish, black or white, Scandinavian or South American, you are certain to have a temper. The sun never sets on anger in some form, including the Irish variety.

Yet we common folk know that anger is a *cultural* trait, a feeling flavored by locale: Each one of us is a survivor of generations of people exposed to a specific experience, each one of us formed from the unique stresses of a special geographic and political and social environment. In my case, that special place was Ireland.

My body is made up of the cells that enabled people to endure through centuries of what the Irish called the Troubles: war, famine, and general all-around hard time. I am the reaction, the final product, and I include among the necessary qualities that helped my ancestors survive my uniquely Irish temper—a temper distinct to the people of Ireland and the human experiment that occurred on that island.

I have inherited a Celtic approach to living and the temper that goes with it—a special kind of anger best compared with the steam held in by a pressure cooker. The history of the Irish is a story of frustration, of anger concealed. They inhabited an island that made them insular, had a church that made them parochial, and a foreign rule that led to a consuming inner rage. Their only freedom was of the mind.

But only those with great gifts rebelled. The rest of us managed in different ways—with humor, with stealth, with madness. And all the while, boiling away inside was a temper whose volcanic possibilities were rarely revealed. The Irish temper erupts *only* when the barriers of self-restraint and the acceptance of frustrations are finally breached. It is therefore an awesome display and, when abetted by alcohol, little short of terrifying. Consider: In New York of the 1880s when the Irish were working off their rage, the police would simply cordon off the Irish section and let them go at it.

The secret of the Irish temper (and remember, this is an Irishman speaking)? It is the only time, save being drunk or joking, when we can tell the truth.

GETTING A HANDLE ON HOT TEMPERS

I have reached a stage where temper is no longer a necessity, but a sign of malfunction.

Arnold Bennett, a follower of the Stoics, saw it in that way, too: Temper, he said, was a sure indication that one's human machine had gone awry. One must get the machine back on the track, stop conferring blame, accept the universe, realize that the only thing you can control is your own brain.

But should temper intervene—and Bennett being a realist knew that it would—then he took a different tack. Here he was pure English: "See yourself as a fool, behaving like a grown-up baby. Say to yourself, 'I am a dunce.'" It was his contention that reason would not prevail in such instances. Use instead, Bennett advised, the horror of looking ridiculous.

Given the fact that you wish to control your temper, there are better ways to do it.

"Hesitation," said Seneca, "is the best cure for anger." That ancient advice still holds. American thinker William James also ascribed to it. "Refuse to express a passion," he said, "and it dies. Count to ten before venting your anger, and its occasion seems ridiculous."

James also believed that to *be* calm, we should *act* calm. "If we wish to conquer undesirable emotional tendencies in ourselves, we must assiduously—and in the first instance, cold-bloodedly—go through the outward movement of those dispositions which we prefer to cultivate."

Easier said than done, though—and unfortunately, when we do get angry, it is sometimes the weak and even the innocent who pay. My father, who was a doctor, said it was not the patient who got him mad who felt the wrath. It was his *next* patient.

Once, when that happened to me, the next patient was an elderly Russian lady I had taken care of for years. When she sat down and began to recite her usual litany of complaints, I interrupted her and shouted, "Why do you come here? I have not helped you and never will. You have the same complaints as the first day I saw you."

She looked at me and then said, "Where is my Dr. Sheehan? You are not my Dr. Sheehan. Where is my Dr. Sheehan?" She was, of course, seeing her real Dr. Sheehan—and seeing my ancestors as well.

CHAPTER

23

A FEW WORDS ON HAPPINESS

Happiness *we receive from ourselves is greater than that we receive from our surroundings.*

WISDOM OF THE AGES

German philosopher Arthur Schopenhauer called it *eudaemonology* and wrote a book about it—the study of the happy life, the art and science of ordering our lives to obtain the greatest amount of pleasure.

He described his book, *The Wisdom of Life,* as a collection of his own aphorisms. Nevertheless, he admitted he was following the thoughts expressed by many others. "In general, the wise of all ages have always said the same thing."

The basic rule for the happy life, according to that consensus, is: Develop the self. The rule's application obviously varies from one individual to another—each life becomes a unique manifestation of the principle in action—but the role stays the same: To be happy, grow.

In Schopenhauer's view, there are three distinct categories of the self: (1) What a man is; (2) what a man has; (3) how a man stands in the estimation of others. Many thinkers have said much the same thing but perhaps not quite as clearly and dramatically. In three short sentences, Schopenhauer set the stage for all that follows. The happy life depends on how we deal with these three faces of the self.

What is obvious to the wise, and indeed to most of us if we live long enough, is that the first heading is the most important one. Psychoanalyst Erich Fromm put it succinctly: "Modern man *has* everything. He *is* nothing." The ancients, notably the Stoics, made the point centuries ago. "Happiness we receive from ourselves," wrote a disciple of Stoic philosopher Epictetus, "is greater than that we receive from our surroundings."

For Schopenhauer, what a man is in himself, what accompanies him when alone, is essential. What a man is, in a word, is *everything*. The becoming of that self is one of the few things a man can achieve. Possessions and the good opinion of others are elusive prey and may well escape our greatest efforts. Frequently, they are a matter of chance. And once acquired, they distract us from the true joy and happiness that lie within our grasp.

Becoming *who one is* requires, above all, health. "Health," wrote Schopenhauer, "outweighs all other blessings." Health, as he saw it, depends upon exercise. "Without proper exercise," he warned, "no one can remain healthy; all the processes of life demand exercise; exercise not only of the parts more immediately concerned but the whole body."

Like American philosopher William James in his *Gospel of Relaxation*, Schopenhauer stressed exercise as the basis of mental as well as physical health. "When people get no exercise," he declared, "there is glaring and fatal disproportion between our outward activity and inner tumult."

What results from exercise is total health, which Schopenhauer defined as "a quiet and cheerful temperament, a sound physique, lively and penetrating intellect, a moderate will, and a clear conscience."

In *The Wisdom of Life*, we see once more that it is the thinkers who give us the strongest arguments for fitness. If we wish to live the happy life, we have no choice but to exercise and become fit.

"Nine-tenths of happiness," Schopenhauer concluded, "depends upon health alone." He's right: Health is the science of the happy life. But the art lies in how we use it.

THE LOVE CONNECTION

"Hurray for love." So goes the song. We echo the sentiment. Love is a grand passion. It can move mountains, it can bring peace. Love is a fusion with another that creates joy—but is it necessary to happiness?

There is no gainsaying the detrimental effects of loneliness—being without someone to love—on our enjoyment of life. But of the lonely, one spokeswoman wrote, "It is intimacy, not love, we long for most." Intimacy is being there for another person. It is friendship, and the respect that goes with friendship. And intimacy is quite possible without love, or at least without those uncontrollable and often unexpected emotions we experience as love.

The struggle to achieve intimacy may result in what psychoanalyst Erik Erikson called the psychosocial strength of love. More realistically, it can—and should if we are to be successful human beings—result in respect for ourselves and for others, thus allowing the privilege of accepting not only our selves, but also the previously dangerous Other Person.

Love is in many ways a talent. And trying to love may be as difficult for some people as trying to sing the scales when you're tone-deaf. Yet all of us are capable of happiness. Philosophers who would teach us how to live largely avoid the topic of love, and, indeed, love does not even enter most discussions on happiness. In Schopenhauer's treatise, he assures us that he has nothing much to say on happiness that hasn't been said over the centuries, and leaves love completely out of his dissertation.

Personally, my life works a good deal better when I *don't* feel an obligation to love a particular person. Love is too frequently an emotion I do not have nor could in any way develop. There is, of course, an ersatz form of love, a feeling that may overwhelm one in the absence of the love object. But it rarely holds up when the person is within range.

Love is indeed an elusive butterfly. Love can be here and beautiful one minute and then gone forever. We cannot control it. Should we try, it becomes lifeless. It dies in the hand of the collector. It becomes a memory pressed between the pages of a book.

Love can fill a life permanently, but more often it provides a transient and insecure happiness. A critic of a recently published book noted, "It details unsparingly the fragility of modern human relationships." Most of us have experienced that fragility. Relationships built on love have no solid foundations. On the other hand, relationships built on respect need never collapse.

REGENERATION: THE PATH TO HAPPINESS

I have in front of me letters from two women runners both disabled with chronic viral diseases. Neither one is able to run as fast or as long as they did before illness struck. And the prospects for complete recovery for both runners are quite dim. Their unhappiness is evident in the letters, and it makes a point.

Until misfortune struck, these women did not realize how happy they already were. No doubt in their disease-free days they thought themselves reaching for happiness, not knowing they already had it.

There is something to be learned from this longing for yesterday. Today is tomorrow's yesterday. And looking at it we should be able to see what will become important when we lose it. Here in this very day, should we strip it of accidentals, is our happiness. We already have in our possession, if we look closely enough, the elements of happiness. We have to become conscious of their presence and the opportunities they present. If we are unhappy, it is our own fault.

British philosopher and social reformer Bertrand Russell has written on this problem in *The Conquest of Happiness.* First, he asks the question: "What can a man or woman, here and now, do to achieve happiness for himself or herself?" Note that he makes no exceptions. He assumes that every common garden-variety, run-of-the-mill human being, regardless of what is going on in his or her life, can achieve happiness.

"This book," he wrote, "is not for highbrows." Critics felt that Russell had largely succeeded. One called it a primer for self-regeneration. Another pronounced it "beautifully simple, immediate to everyone in its outlook and suggestion."

I like the idea of self-regeneration. Happiness, it seems to me, does require a new birth. A new attitude, a return to fundamentals. When we think of happiness, we should not focus on our needs so much as our possibilities. We are unhappy not because of things we lack but because we have potentialities that have not been realized.

Russell, the scientist, saw happiness as the logical outcome of correct living. Happiness is not some will-o'-the-wisp with unpredictable appearances and disappearances. It is there for the taking.

"All happy families resemble each other. Each unhappy family is unhappy in its own way." Those famous lines of Tolstoy's apply to individuals as well as families. We are each of us unhappy in our own way—and specifically because each one of us is a unique never-to-be-repeated event.

"I am myself and my circumstances," wrote Spanish thinker José Ortega y Gasset. But despite the fact that I am identical to no other person in this entire world, I do have some common tendencies in which I resemble Russell's portrait of the unhappy man.

What makes the unhappy man unhappy? Any number of things,

according to Russell. Among them: competition, boredom, worry, envy, and a sense of sin. Most of these enemies are generated by a preoccupation with the self. There are other causes, of course, but being a sinner, a narcissist, or a megalomaniac are forms of self-absorption that generally lead to unhappiness.

"I was not born happy," admitted Russell. "As a child my favorite hymn was 'Weary of Earth and Laden with Sin.'" In his adolescence, he confessed, he hated life and was continually on the verge of suicide. It is instructive that even William James, one of the most optimistic of men, wrote that grappling with the thought of suicide was the turning point in his life.

"Now I enjoy life," wrote Russell. "I might say that with every year that passes I enjoy it more." He ascribes this to three things: (1) Discovering what were the things he most desired; (2) dismissing certain objects of desire as essentially unattainable; and (3) the most important element, a diminishing preoccupation with himself.

Happiness is more than a large subject. It is the subject. It is the purpose of our lives. I think we can take it as a general principle that life is worth living, and its goal is happiness. Our pursuit of that happiness all too often reflects the narrowness of our vision and our difficulty in handling misfortune.

The message to these two runners? In the race for happiness, there are no handicaps. We start each day as equals.

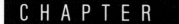

CHAPTER

24

WHEN LOVE
GOES WRONG

M*en and women are here to do heroic deeds.*
Love is one of them.

LONELY HEROES

As the days become weeks and the weeks become months, the dominant emotion is loneliness. After she left, I had a cascade of reactions, one on the heels of the other. That white water of feelings, that inner turbulence, has subsided. Now I am alone, and alone in a way I have never been before in my life.

I have always been a loner. I was cast in that mold. I am brother to Hawthorne and Thoreau and Emerson. At heart, I am a transcendentalist, one removed from people. Ideas are my companions. I sit now early in the morning, the newsroom deserted, alone at my typewriter. When the people arrive, I may not even notice. If I do, it will be a terse greeting that will have to do for conversation until I depart.

I am a loner, but I am rarely lonely. Being alone is my natural state. I seek solitude to think, I isolate myself to write. In this pursuit of ideas, I need no company. I retreat into my mind and there I do what I do best. Then, I am content—never less alone than when alone.

But now that she's gone, all has changed. I cannot stand the solitude, I cannot cope with the isolation. I have a desperate need for company. The retreat into my mind is now a painful journey from which I want only escape. I no longer seek privacy, I no longer want to think. I have never been so lonely in my life.

Not that I need people. I need a specific person. Not friends, but a lover. When loneliness came, it was not that I was friendless—I was *loveless.* I once read of Emerson's "impenetrable agonies of loneliness," without understanding them. Now I've penetrated them and know their cause—a lack of love.

Emerson recaptured some measure of his ability to function by marrying again, but I have no one. I have lost the love that gave me the freedom to live the loner's life. In the past, there was always a person I loved and who loved me back. No matter how far I went on my solitary journey, she was within reach. When I returned, she was there to hold me. Her strength was my strength. Her ability to handle the world shielded me from my ineptitude and incompetence. She rid me of the need to do things I never learned to do. And she loved me no matter what: She gave me the security and intimacy I could get from no other.

It was she and I, not so much against the world, but becoming the world. In her I found myself completed. She was everything I needed from my fellows on this earth. I could then seek everything I needed from myself. The physical, the mental, the spiritual. I could devote myself to the heroic life—push myself through depression and fatigue, through guilt and exhaustion, through failure and past success—because she saw me as a hero, and, in her own way, had become a heroine.

We are born to be heroes. Both men and women are here to do heroic deeds. Love is one of them. The marital virtues are not much different from the martial ones. Peace and contentment at home come from winning the war with yourself.

For both of us, that struggle was a lonely one. One friend said of me, "George is continually out on a tightrope." And on a tightrope, there's room for only one. There I can have no thought for anyone else. The woman who loves me must therefore stand and wait. That can be even lonelier—and it is something *beyond* what I can ask.

She can only ask it of herself.

LIKE BURIAL AT SEA

When your life is going nowhere in particular, there is nothing better than being knocked on your ass. Mindless mediocrity needs a hard right to the solar plexus. When you are in a permanent holding pattern, getting hit from the blind side may well be the best thing that can happen.

When the woman I had lived with for two years told me to leave, I felt as if all three events had happened simultaneously. I had no hint then that I would be able to pick myself up and make a fresh start, that eventually I would look back and see it as a necessary and good thing to happen. I was injured—and for the moment—mortally.

English author G. K. Chesterton once wrote of his experience in a runaway hansom cab. In the matter of seconds, he said, he went through five different religions. In a matter of days, I went through a similar number of philosophies. My nadir was on the fourth day, when I experienced a counterpart of what is called "the four day blues" on the obstetric floor. That day, I collected every reminder of her—letters, photos, and gifts—put them in her final (and prophetic?) gift, a suitcase, and left them on her porch.

But first came the keening. There is nothing more piteous than the wail of a man who has been told to pack up and go. It is the beginning of the mourning period. I mourned for the end of a future, the beginning of the past. I cried then and cried still. In a moment, in a single sentence, my life vanished before my eyes: My love became a stranger.

It was like a burial at sea. This living together, this individual we had jointly become, was now in a box and sliding down the ways. Nothing could stop it. It was dead and done with, with a splash gone irrevocably and forever.

Friends were helpful. They made the event commonplace. Join the crowd, they said—it's happening every day. Tough for a while, very tough. But time heals. I heard the chorus: Hunker down, they advised. Wait it out, they recommended.

The reflex, of course, is not to think about it. The wounded animal's one thought is escape. Only later does it put into practice what is learned from that near-fatal encounter. If one survives, there are no bad experiences. Whatever does not destroy you makes you strong.

I'm getting *very* strong. Being knocked on my butt and kicked in the stomach has been good for me. In one week, I learned more about myself than in the past two years. I have changed in ways I would not have believed possible or necessary, and explored areas of my mind never before penetrated.

And since my writing is really just me speaking to myself, that week gave me enough new insights to fill pages and pages of my journal. I have discovered new and exciting and interesting things to say to myself. I have once again been through a human experience that has led to unimagined heights of self-revelation. The death of this love has given new life to my heart and mind; my dismissal as a man has given me rebirth as a person. I have resumed a growth interrupted by my own hand.

One good friend had said, "Look inside, George, there is a reason for this, but you alone will know it." I know now that there *is* a reason, and I see it, clearly enough to make out the major features: the failure to live up to my own beliefs. The failure to develop them further. And the failure to see that my concentration on the mind and the body had atrophied my life with others.

In seeking the sound mind in the sound body, I neglected my soul.

THE GREEN DEMON

"What finally cured me of jealousy," said a friend, "was realizing I wasn't willing to pay the price."

What price? Why was he no longer jealous of the man who had replaced him in a woman's affection?

The answer surprised me. The true cost, he said, was not the anger and frustration and depression that accompanied the loss of his lover. The price would be to become that new man she now loved.

And that price, becoming someone else, he refused to pay. The thought of living someone else's life repelled him. If he had an absolute, it was to be himself.

I suggested he might have a hero or two that would change his mind. Didn't he want to step into the shoes of a great athlete, take the place of an outstanding scientist, live the life of a celebrated writer? His answer surprised me: No.

"What I was, am, and shall be—*that* is my life's work."

It suddenly made sense. I rarely feel envy, but when I do it concerns what a person has or does. I have no desire to become that person. Indeed, the thought is repugnant. I want to remain myself and yet have what this person possesses. But that is impossible, and my friend is right: Being one's self takes precedence over all the other wants and satisfactions in life.

This is even more true in regard to a strong emotion like jealousy. There are few more wrenching events than the loss of your lover to another person. The mind cannot think of anything but this individual enjoying a relationship that was once exclusively yours. And this anguish feeds on hope.

"Hope should be avoided at all costs," my friend said. "It allows jealousy to live, grow, and take over your life."

The reality is that what has occurred is a *fait accompli,* and beyond your control. Love, which is in any case a gift, has been taken away and can never return.

"Give up hope," said my friend, "and you can look this fact in the face. See that only this man and no one else can take part in your lover's life.

"Now ask yourself," he went on, "if a miracle could take place, would you be agreeable to switching identities with him?"

Few people would answer in the affirmative. And there is not one philosopher I've ever read who would. You might argue that poets, who are at times maudlin in their poems of unrequited love, would make this sacrifice. I doubt, however, that these literate outcries of broken hearts survived too many dawns. No true poet would prefer to be anyone else.

And that is true of most people. Those who are jealous of other people have not thought hard and long enough about the life they envy. Some years back, a book was published on how not to succeed at almost everything, including love, golf, business, and politics. For those unhappy with their lot and envious of others, the author suggested putting yourself in the other's place. Our major effort, he said, should be to take an objective and dispassionate look at what the desired state entails. One day spent enduring what goes with another person's success is usually enough to make you content with your lot.

We can look—again—to Emerson on this matter. "Why should my happiness," he wrote, "depend upon the thoughts in someone else's head?" And especially when those thoughts are controlled by something as volatile and unpredictable as love.

Happiness ultimately depends upon the extent to which all our needs are within the self or under our control. Jealousy can then be seen as a senseless display of another human trait—stupidity.

"Thousands of thinkers have told us to look ahead, not back," said my friend. "And none better than Emerson: 'Heartily know/When half-gods go,/The gods arrive.'"

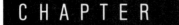
25

FURTHER REFLECTIONS ON RELATIONSHIPS

The day-to-day reality of living requires strong, durable, and rust-resistant joinings of mind and heart and body. Given these, we can then seek to join with others and the world about us in pure joy.

MEDITATIONS ON MEN, WOMEN, AND MELDING

People are strong. Relationships are fragile. The more complicated the system, the more vulnerable it is. I am myself a relationship, a composite of body, mind, will, and spirit. I am at every minute in the process of forming a personality. I am a product of my strengths and weaknesses. I am shaped by the stresses, the strains, the tensions, and the forces within me and about me. Result? The only constant is change. Greek philosopher Heracleitus wrote that one never bathes in the same river. Our circumstances are never quite the same. But it is also true that one is never the same bather. The *self* changes as much as its surroundings.

I would not describe the relationship I am in as particularly strong. It is, however, infinitely stronger than any relationship that includes another human being. And that is important: The day-to-day reality of

144

living requires strong, durable, and rust-resistant joinings of mind and heart and body. Given these, we can then seek to join with others and the world about us in pure joy.

The more basic the union of two people, the closer it becomes. When *survival* is at stake we can join together as one. Relationships based on fundamental animal drives—sex and hunger—are limited but usually successful. However, as we go up the ladder to higher needs—love and companionship, to name two—maintaining a relationship becomes increasingly difficult. When communication of minds and then souls is required, when language must express the person I am to the person I would have enter my galaxy—well, let's just say that things get sticky.

Relationships hold out the promise of happiness. They are also the greatest *threat* to that happiness.

"The supreme law of life is this," wrote Austrian psychologist Alfred Adler, "the sense of worth of self shall not be allowed to diminish."

When one enters a relationship, that sense of worth is at stake. Self-esteem is basic, of course, to the good life. But just below the surface we have on record that we really feel worthless, helpless, dependent, mediocre, inadequate, and finite. We do not need Freud to tell us that. Our life is a battle to fill our subconscious with good news instead of bad.

Relationships risk our self-esteem because they're capable of taking us in either direction. They're kind of like *us* in that regard. And to make sure they take us in a direction we like, we have to put our own house in order before inviting someone else in.

When a relationship breaks up it is due to a conflict between two personalities. It is also caused by the eternal conflict between the one and the many. There are two struggles—the self attempting to adapt to another self, and also to a new whole which they now form.

One would think this adaptation would come about naturally without effort. But it proves to be the most difficult thing you can attempt in life. To accomplish it, you must go back to the ancient injunction, "Know thyself." If you have the attitude, "Take me as I am," you are bound to fail. To believe the self is complete and unalterable is to assure failure with other people.

I learned that the hard way. In the past, despite faults galore, I had no apology other than, "That's the way I am." I had asked myself, Who am I? and was satisfied with the answer. This was the real and eternal me; I had discovered my strengths and I reveled in them.

But my faults? Well, they were eternal and unchanging, so why think about them?

A relationship attempts to reconcile the "I" and the "we." The we in me is a very small voice. I am a loner. I want to be hugged and held and loved, but I also want to remain the self-centered person I am naturally. I want to be part of a we, but without making the necessary sacrifices in return.

Each of us needs and wants his or her own life. But one person's life can never be a common project, so the I can never be the overriding concern of the we. Love is indeed a positive sum game where both sides can and should win. But winning comes about through mutual giving and receiving as the I's join to become we. There has to be growth and change and movement toward a higher, common goal than each one's individual existence.

Being the self I am is easy. Being the self I could be is quite difficult. It is a task I have never fully attempted. I have honed my talents, perhaps, but I have done nothing to eliminate my weaknesses—my lack of sensitivity to the feelings of others. I have not used my self-knowledge to create a self that can sustain a relationship with a fellow human being.

VYING WITH EACH OTHER

In relationships, opposites fail and absolute opposites fail absolutely. At times this is not obvious to observers. Couples adapt to failure. They live together but on parallel courses, in reality totally independent of each other. On every plane of existence they coexist without coming together. They remain I's; there is no we.

At best, living together is difficult. Nor does it get better by adding numbers. The proper word for the family, said Spanish thinker José Ortega y Gasset, is strife. Adding more egos compounds problems, it does not alleviate them. And that's chiefly because our normal instinct is to be number one. Consider the man beaten in the fight for the heavyweight championship of the world. For him it is not enough to be the second-best fighter in the world. He will try again and again, if possible, to dethrone the man ahead of him.

Perhaps better than anyone else, the athlete is an example of our internal drive toward excellence. That same drive is present in every other sphere, albeit not so visibly. When I was a young doctor in practice, for example, I took umbrage when a patient left me for another doctor. And I knew surgeons who felt they should be the choice of everyone in town who required operations. They were confident they were without equal.

Living with someone who is constantly involved in being number one is difficult. Yet overtly or not, each of us is engaged in that struggle. With some, however, life is an hour-to-hour struggle to reach or maintain that position. Being a companion to such a person is an almost impossible task. It becomes achievable only if that becomes the goal of one's life—to aid and assist another person in becoming the best.

At this point, I am talking about the creation of a team. This is the way to change "I against you" to "we against them," to use our drive in a healthy way. In life, any*one* can be a winner. What is difficult is having any *two* be winners.

A team has a goal above and beyond the aspirations of the individual player. And a league of teams may have a goal above and beyond the individual team. It is the idea of this transcendent, overridingly important goal that gives hope to people vying with each other inside relationships. The pursuit of being number one must somehow be reconciled with a mutual goal even more demanding and therefore more heroic—the creation of a family, perhaps.

It is indeed difficult for a man and a woman to be friends without being lovers. The animal instincts supersede the social ones. Sexual attraction dominates any relationships between men and women. Only work on a common and important interest could bring a man and woman together on a higher level.

That observation is an important one. No lasting relationship can be built on sexual attraction alone. No lasting relationship can survive without it, either, but this means couples *need* the higher goals. Each one must work for more than his or her individual needs and wants. The success of the other must be equally important. And above that the pursuit of a common purpose of much greater significance—perhaps a family, a political goal, or a professional aspiration.

Relationships recapitulate psychoanalyst Erik Erikson's stages of an individual's life. Relationships are born in hope and arrive at fidelity and reach the summit of charity. Relationships fail at individual stages just as individuals do. But a person who does not attain intimacy or generosity can try again and again. Relationships, on the other hand, often do not afford us a real second chance. Fixing a relationship that's gone awry means fixing three things—you, me, *and* the relationship. When we must reverse the past, it is difficult to have a constant reminder of that past—and that's exactly what the relationship frequently is, a nagging reminder. Repentance and a firm resolve to change are often not enough.

Nevertheless, relationships are worth all the effort and anguish and suffering they entail. English novelist D. H. Lawrence, using the word relationship in a larger sense, said that the root of all happiness was a perfect relationship, either with ourselves, with nature, or with another. And most of us know from our own experiences that Lawrence was correct. Those moments of happiness with another human being make everything that led up to them worthwhile.

LOVING OTHERS, LOVING OURSELVES

"Even in our intimate lives, our friendships, and our marriages," reads a passage in my notebook, "we are thrown against people who have very unique ways of deriving self-esteem and we never quite understand what they really want."

I am not sure where I found that sentence. I know it must have struck me as true. Otherwise I would not have recorded it in my journal. But only now, as I ponder on the dissolution of a serious love affair, does the full import of those words become evident.

A dispassionate study of such a parting is not immediately possible. The initial reactions are quite similar to those of a person having a heart attack. The physical breaking of one's heart is, in many respects, identical with the emotional breaking when the loved one is lost. It follows a day-by-day sequence: first panic, then denial, followed by depression, and then an exaggerated expression of one's underlying personality. And, somewhere, at all times—elements of hostility and anger and frustration.

Only later, after these concomitants of injury have run their course and the healing has begun, does heartbreak metamorphose into a learning experience—something that will prove valuable when I am able to live and love again. And, because hope dies hard, something that will be useful should my one true love return.

Love is not blind. I saw all the blemishes, all the warts. I saw them and accepted. No one is perfect, and we shouldn't expect another to be. What is necessary in love is a sense of humor—the ability to see as trivial what might otherwise cause tension and argument and needless displays of temper. I found this not at all difficult.

Love actually has excellent vision. I saw things invisible to others. If people would ask what I saw in her, I could reply with a litany of wonderful things. And in fact, *everyone* has more than enough to be cause for love by another person.

I recall hearing actress Liv Ullman, being interviewed by Dick Cavett, say how easy it is to love someone. Cavett had remarked on her ability to convey an impression of deep feeling for the men in her films.

This is especially evident in her films with Swedish director Ingmar Bergman, where virtually all the acting is done by facial expression.

"If I had dinner with you," Ullman said, "and we spent an hour or two talking over the candlelight, I could believe I loved you." Cavett was shaken by that answer and quickly changed the subject. But it is quite true. The human condition is such that we can indeed love almost anyone if we try.

This does not mean the love *affair* arising from that love will last. The love itself may last. I still love her and my lover still loves me, but we are now apart. In being with me, she had to give up something more important. Loving me meant no less than giving her whole self to love. That is a bargain that should seldom be made.

The self must first be whole and strong before a person can offer a true and lasting love. That task of developing the self is our real priority as human beings. When love interferes, it must be set aside. It must wait until the person is complete, until the individual has attained an unassailable sense of self, and an invulnerable self-esteem. Only when I love myself can I totally love another.

It is here that love is blind—or deaf—or inarticulate. I never understood and she could not put into words what this self locked in her subconscious needed so desperately. There is a line between every one of us we cannot cross. We can never feel another's pain or exactly know another's needs or emotions. All we can and should do is listen and listen well. Listen to what is said and unsaid. Listen to every gesture, every movement. Every action, every inaction.

The Greeks said, "Know thyself." If you love another and would have that love affair survive, know the other as well.

CHAPTER

26

THE WELL-ORDERED MIND

It is the quality of our ideas, the self they create, the life they generate, that should alert us and impel us to action.

THOUGHTS ON THOUGHT

My track coach in school was also my Latin teacher. He had an intimate working knowledge of both the body and mind. On one occasion, he had difficulty teaching a sprinter how to come out of the starting blocks. Time and again there was a perceptible delay before the runner, who was also a very bright student, would respond to the gun. Finally the coach yelled at him: "Don't think, dummy! *React!*"

Thought delays the reflex to act. The sprinter's response to the sound of the starting gun must be automatic. The usual sequence—observe, judge, and act—must be suspended. It is unnecessary and self-defeating. When the gun sounds, the athlete must be an unthinking animal.

For most of our waking day, however, we are more than animals. We must reverse the coach's command. It becomes, "Don't react, dummy! *Think!*" When we merely react, we become members of the herd. We lose individuality, and we do not become the unique self each of us is.

But learning to think isn't easy, and, in fact, most of us wander through life without ever even *considering* how that part of the human machine works. We no more study the science of the mind than we study the science of the body. We do not take these great gifts and make the most of them. Again—we lead lives inferior to ourselves.

But thinking gives rise to the actions that determine our lives—and the kinds of lives we lead depend upon how well we think. English writer G. K. Chesterton once said that the most important thing about a man is his view of the universe. When I read that, I realized I did not truly *know* my view of the universe. Even more upsetting was the fact that I was uncertain how to develop such a view, and then how to use it as a basis for making the ever-present choices of life. This I do know, though: No one else can do it for me.

"Man, everyman," wrote José Ortega y Gasset, "must at every moment be deciding for the next moment what he is going to do, what he is going to be. This decision only he can make; it is nontransferable."

Man's destiny, Ortega y Gasset said, is primarily *action*. We do not live to think, we live to act. It's necessary for survival, but thought is not easy. It is, Ortega wrote, a laborious, precarious, volatile acquisition—but acquire it we must. In this we have no choice. Without thought, a truly human life—a life of direction and purpose—is impossible.

Ortega y Gasset saw three steps in the process of learning to think. First, you feel yourself lost—shipwrecked among things. He uses the Spanish word *alteración*, which is almost untranslatable but implies possession by everything that is outside of you. You are agitated, beside yourself.

Second, you withdraw into yourself, and there form ideas about your circumstances and how to dominate them.

And third, you return to the world to act—to execute a plan of action. Action, therefore, is the result of contemplation; and contemplation is the planning of future action. The message: Your life is not given to you ready-made, you must make it for yourself.

I must decide what I am going to do and what I am going to be. To do that, I must come to terms with myself and define what I believe, what I esteem, and what I truly and rightly detest.

It is time I stopped reacting and went back to thinking.

GETTING STARTED

In 1929, a Frenchman, Ernest Dimnet, wrote a best-selling book *The Art of Thinking*. Dimnet's theme was that thinking was self-expression, that it was best exemplified in the child, and that the best way to think was to write.

Dimnet felt his book would provide the necessary conditions to bring a motivated person to maturity. "What is wanted is a beginning and a method. The beginning belongs to God, but the method belongs to us and it can be learned in a few hours even from such a book as this."

It is not superior beings Dimnet would instruct, either. "The most ordinary of us know moments," he said, "during which we glimpse the very states of mind which make for brilliant conversation." All we lack? The words, or the confidence: Many of us are loath to speak of our innermost lives.

Thought, in his view, was self-expression, and that self-expression, is our individuality. Thought takes us out of the herd. It removes us from the temptation to imitate. "To sum up," he stated, "everyone of us can be personal, and in so doing become interesting to ourselves as well as *becoming* ourselves."

It sounds simple, and, in fact, it is simple. The truth is always simple. Nothing is simpler than the formula for a sound body. All the science of exercise can be contained in a single sentence—exercise is good for you and you should do it—but people and events and circumstances make its practice extremely difficult.

So it is with this fitness of the mind—simple in principle, but difficult to achieve. Dimnet points out, for example, that all children under nine to ten years of age are poets and philosophers. And this true superiority of intellect persists until they begin to imitate the outside world. For the adult to rediscover that childlike ability is arduous. "It takes a long time to become young," the aging Picasso said.

"It does not occur to one in a thousand," said Dimnet, "that he was more intelligent when he was 8, than now when he is 50." But admit this, he recommended, admit that your mental wealth at that age was extraordinary, and you are on your way to truth and salvation.

Part of the problem is that we *know* when our bodies are unfit, but we are rarely aware that our minds have gone to seed. They *seem* to be functioning correctly. Ideas continue to flow through them at a great rate. But it is the quality of our ideas, the self they create, the life they generate, that should alert us and impel us to action.

English writer Arnold Bennett was not even sure of the quantity of our ideas. "Think, for God's sake and your own, think," he says to his readers in *How to Live on 24 Hours a Day.*

Dimnet was of the same mind. He believed that 19 out of 20 people do not think. They live like automatons, he said, and consist merely of clothes, fashions, mannerisms, and formula. Their lives are alike.

Times have changed since then. Such generalizations are no longer valid. There is a renaissance in this country. People are mastering the art of thinking and the art of living. Still, the bill of particulars pertains to all of us: Fit or unfit, we all could do better.

AN HOUR OF SOLITUDE

"I believe that in our good days," wrote Emerson, "a well-ordered mind has a new thought awaiting it each morning. And hence, eminently thoughtful, from the time of Pythagorus down, have insisted on an hour of solitude every day, to meet their own mind and learn what oracle it has to impart." This one passage contains the ways to remove the inner and outer obstacles to thought.

The first important word in the passage is order. In thinking, order is the order of the day. We must know what we know. We must understand what we understand. We must remember what it is we remember. We take these things for granted, but we should not. Our ideas on most subjects are vague. We rarely think through the topic before us.

The two major hurdles to mastering the art of thinking and attaining the well-ordered mind are feelings of inadequacy and inferiority. The decision is made: "I can't do it. It can't be done." Emerson's passage, we think, is not for us—it is for professional thinkers. Thinkers, after all, are *supposed* to think. That is what they are paid to do. How can we common folk hope to do well in this difficult business? Let Emerson and his fellow thinkers consult their oracle and then report to us. This should be sufficient.

For most of us, it is. We go to school to learn what others have thought. After we graduate, we continue that practice. We allow other people to do our thinking for us. We believe we have well-founded opinions, but on close inspection our ideas are vague and of little substance. We make decisions based on impulse or prejudice. We are bored. We are lazy. We are copycats. We are most certainly *not* thinkers, but rather *mirrors* of those who work at thinking.

Dimnet suggested a way to get back on track: "If we sit down before a blank sheet of paper and write in two columns the arguments pro and con of an idea that occurs to us, the truth will flash on us." If the evidence is not compelling, then we can proceed to another sheet on the pros and cons of getting good advice. When we want to be clear and definite about anything, in fact, a sheet of paper and a pen become essential.

Bennett also thought we should use our minds on things that attract us. It is all right, in other words, for me to confess boredom or incompetence in art, music, or poetry. The important thing is to think about the stuff that makes living a joy.

Finding the hour to do all this remains the main stumbling block. I may have a well-ordered mind and something I'd like to think about, but I still must find that hour to do my thinking.

Dimnet suggested early rising: "An hour in the morning is worth two in the evening." Only, however, if you actually *use* it. My personal cardinal sin is procrastination. I cannot make decisions. This condition is called *abulia,* and I have a malignant form of the disease. The morning works best if the only decision to be made is to think. I then win the battle over my innate tendency to hesitate and delay.

In thinking, then, that's the final lesson: The beginning is the whole thing.

THE DISCIPLINE TO CONCENTRATE

Arnold Bennett's treatise on the correct intellectual use of the 24 hours in a day is based on one simple principle—the conscious discipline of the brain by selected habits of thought. The principle is simple, but the application is as complicated as anything can get. "Advanced golf," wrote Bennett, "is child's play compared to it."

A few minutes' time trying to control this willful instrument will convince you of that truth. Comparisons leap to mind immediately: riding a Brahma bull, baby-sitting a two-year-old child in a room full of bric-a-brac. No matter how alert you are, the mind escapes. Undisciplined, unmotivated—uninhabited?—it dallies, then dances, then slows to a crawl or refuses to move. No matter what it is you want to do, the mind wants to do the opposite.

And even when you succeed, the fruits of that victory don't endure. Every day is a new beginning. The simplicity arrived at the night before becomes an even greater complexity. "The history of any art, and this [thinking] is an art," wrote Bennett, "is the history of recommencements, of the dispersal and reforming of doubts, of an ever-increasing conception of the territory conquered."

The chief danger, therefore, is the conviction that a great effort has been made but no progress achieved. You will note that this is a common danger with all such enterprises: All good goals demand *persistence.*

Persistence in the mind is concentration, the power to dictate to our own brain. Concentration is mind control, and through it we can tyrannize the brain. It does not matter what we force the brain to do, it is the discipline that counts. Perseverance in concentration will get our mind in hand. And if we do that alone, Bennett assures us we will cure half the evils in life.

And it doesn't really matter what we concentrate on. It is the repeated performance that leads to mastery. But there's nothing better, in Bennett's opinion, for practicing these abilities than the works of the Stoics, Marcus Aurelius Antoninus and Epictetus. Their simplicity makes concentration easier since any attempt by the mind to escape is immediate obvious.

For the present, however—and Bennett continually brings us back to the present—we must bend every effort to the development of the *habit* of thinking. When is success assured? When one becomes a fanatic in its pursuit, when a true conversion occurs and one goal becomes paramount. When a person knows that failure in this action is preferable to the good life elsewhere, then he *cannot* fail. We may run out of time, as football coach Vince Lombardi was wont to say, but we cannot lose.

Until then we are dealing with mere wishes, not wants; with sentimentality instead of sentiment. We are spectators leading a vicarious existence.

The first requisite for escape to reality? Knowledge. Know that it can be done. Next, create the opportunity to put these powers into practice. This is the essential clearing out of enough free time for the mind, and body, to go to work.

Eventually we break free. And with this new consciousness and the opportunity to act on it, we discover the most important fact of all—that *we* are the only obstacles to our success.

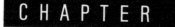

27

RUMINATION ON READING

Wisdom comes after *information and knowledge. And books provide the scaffolding that allows us to build our own systems of thought.*

THE GOLDEN SENTENCE

"We are too civil to books," wrote Emerson. "For a few golden sentences we read 400 to 500 pages."

Still he opened every new book with anticipation. He spent his life searching for sentences. Most, of course, came from within—the original thoughts of an original thinker. But he was always ready for any person or book or lecture that offered to open his mind to a new perception.

Not novels, though. Emerson had a low estimate even of those considered the best. His chief criticism: terrible dialogue. Again, it was his search for fine words that led him to discard the novel. He preached the infinitude of the common man, and while the good novelist may depict this, the characters cannot *say* it. We find memorable people in these books but few memorable thoughts.

Even the truly great books, Emerson said, fail to deliver on their

156

promise. Come, they say, we will give you the key to the world. Then they do not, of course. And in the end we must draw on our own experiences, write our own sentences. And read Emerson.

"You cannot find Emerson's equal in any age or country," stated the foreword to his collected works. "He says so much, so briefly." And that is true. In Emerson, every sentence matters. It is said that he spent 15 years collecting the sentences that went into his famous essay *Self-Reliance.*

To open Emerson is to plunge into a raging surf of ideas. One must stop to get one's breath, to restore the points of the compass. The ideas come like huge powerful waves that threaten your previous placid existence. You must stretch yourself mentally to stay afloat, you must be at the top of your powers just to survive.

"Books are for nothing but to inspire," someone said. Emerson's do that. His main message: Make the most of ourselves, trust ourselves, and *be* ourselves to the uttermost. And while Emerson looked for inspiration in Shakespeare, Plato, Plutarch, Montaigne, his thoughts were ultimately his own.

And so it should be. The golden sentences in Emerson inspire us. They help us understand our own experiences. And they may even express it better than we ever will. But we *must* have our *own* thoughts, make our *own* sentences.

"These *novels*," Emerson writes, "will give way to diaries and autobiographies—captivating books if only a man knew how to choose among what he *calls* his experiences and that which is really his experience."

This is why writers have a love/hate relationship with books. We read books looking for that sudden revelation of truth, but, by doing so, delay finding our own. "To put away one's original thought in order to take up a book," the German philosopher Arthur Schopenhauer wrote, "is a sin against the Holy Ghost."

Fine for Schopenhauer, whose mind apparently teemed with thoughts and had the talent to express them. But what about the rest of us? Some of us doubt that we have *any* original ideas, and in any case, lack the skills to set them down. Isn't reading, then, our salvation?

The answer, of course, is yes—and no. We need books. First, to be educated. Emerson knew Shakespeare by heart, and read widely in the classics and Eastern philosophers. He knew his world and the principles that governed it. The great thinkers begin by knowing what others think. Wisdom comes *after* information and knowledge. And books provide the scaffolding that allows us to build our own systems of thought.

But in the end, we must think for ourselves. There is no precedent for you or me, because each of us is different from anyone else. Others can tell us what works for them, but we must find what works for us.

Emerson himself expressed that inevitable ambivalence. In one essay, he told us we must read. He even gave us a list of the books he found most valuable. Then—in an equally convincing essay—he told us there is *no* need to read. In one piece, he quoted from other thinkers in virtually every paragraph. In the next, he said, "I hate quotations. Tell me what you think."

That is what writing is: telling what you think. Telling other people certainly, but primarily telling yourself. And that is why we must write—to find out what we think, to discover what we believe. Because until we write it down, we don't know what is actually at the root of our lives.

But still we must be civil to books—because it is *worth* reading 400 to 500 pages to find that golden sentence that changes our lives.

VITAL ESSENCES

"Literature exists," English writer Arnold Bennett affirmed, "so that where one man has lived finely, ten thousand may afterward live finely." Bennett acknowledged that getting the most out of literature is not easy. We fail to assimilate the vital essences in these books; do not acquire the insights the author supplies; do not accept the chance of living fully.

Literature does not provide answers. It gives us another's experience of the human condition. And it does it again and again, filling in the voids of our own experience. "Man is a machine by birth," wrote a historian, "but a self by experience." And he learns how to be that self through the experience of others best of all in literature. Every work in literature, according to the historian, hides within it the human predicament—the unresolved choice between two directions of action. We therefore need *both* reading and writing. But timing is important: There is a right time to read, and a time not to read. There is a proper time to write, and a time not to write.

Emerson made the point. He wandered through history as if he lived in every century. He was familiar with Eastern as well as Western philosophy, and had conversations with the greats of all ages. But he was no man's disciple. His writing came out of centuries of writing, his thinking was preceded by centuries of similar thoughts. But Emerson's thoughts were his *own*.

The reason? Emerson's reading was not passive. His reading was always accompanied by thought; so, too, his walks.

The bottom line is clear: What you get out of a book depends on what you bring to it. That is true of every book. A book can be read on various levels: factual, allegorical, metaphorical. One person reads a novel and has a completely different emotional or intellectual experience from another. Catholics read a Graham Greene novel with Catholic themes, for example, and are affected in ways non-Catholics would never be. What the reader brings to the book determines the outcome of the undertaking.

MY PERSONAL FAVORITES

Because I use numerous quotations in my columns and my lectures, people frequently come up and comment, "You must do a lot of reading." I don't. Not, at least, by the standards of days past. I read few authors, but those I do, I return to again and again. I read them thoroughly and *seize* upon their insights to make mine more forceful. But my library is limited and I rarely consult a wider one.

In ancient Athens, people were either students or slaves. Those first aristocrats spent their lives reading and writing and in conversation. In Florence during the Renaissance, there were no distractions: Every individual was an artist. And in our own Athens, the Boston of the 1800s, the citizenry knew the classics and could quote from them. Yet when poet Robert Penn Warren was teaching at Yale, he found a completely different situation. He asked the seniors how many had read Hardy, or Melville, or Shakespeare, and who could quote from them. "Practically nobody," he reported.

I am in my sixties and cannot do it either. My readers and listeners take me for a great reader only because they do so little reading themselves. And what they do read is of little substance with no lasting value—authors with little grasp of the complexity of life and *less* ability to express it.

I have my personal favorites, like William James, and I join them as some others might go to the corner bar for good talk and companionship. I prefer my limited circle the way others prefer their own friends, or one particular pub. And not one visit goes by that I don't find a phrase or a sentence that echoes down the ages. Since most of these writers are great quoters themselves, they pass along everything *they* have read as well: I share in an education unequaled today.

Not all the writers I read are worth the time. They can be as garrulous and boring as some of the people at the local bar. Amos Bronson Alcott is one. In a town where geniuses lived cheek-by-jowl— Concord, Massachusetts, home to Emerson and Thoreau—Alcott was tolerated as a friend and avoided as a thinker. No one read his books. I have tried, because he was a contemporary of two of my favorites, but the spark is not there. Whatever Concord gave to the masters who lived there, it kept it secret from Alcott.

Such excursions, however, are rare and generally restricted to writers that my favorite authors recommend. I excuse this limited reading as I do my limited friends. One or two companions in life are all a man can expect. So I read deep in a few and let the others go.

But I'm not alone in this practice. Eric Hoffer, in his days with the Civilian Conservation Corps, bought a volume by French essayist Montaigne because it had the fewest pictures and the most print of any book he could buy with his money. For a year or more he read nothing but Montaigne, annotating him on every subject. When a topic would come up in conversation, someone would invariably turn to Hoffer and ask, "What has Montaigne got to say about that?"

Hoffer saw no need to look further. And he could have done a lot worse. "If people realized," wrote American author Christopher Morley, "that almost everything conceivably sayable has been said by Montaigne, why should they ever buy another book?"

But becoming a one-book man won't happen to me. "Be no man's satellite," said Emerson. Nevertheless, I am. I continue to scan the skies looking for those sentences, those incredibly right words, that he and those others left trailing behind them. And when I find them, I store them up against the occasion of need.

When that occasion arises, I know exactly where Emerson said such and such, or where Thoreau wrote the appropriate line. I can pick up a volume of Ortega and immediately find what I am desperately trying to say.

My ideas are still my own. They come unbidden during my runs or at other times when I am alone and thinking of nothing. Their development is also mine—I follow the trail hoping to sight my game and bring it down.

But when I try to articulate them in my own words, I am usually unhappy with the results. Then I seek out my published friends from the past and seek help. They have been there and already know. When I can't say exactly what I mean, I let them say it for me. And when I lecture and am at a loss for words, it is their words, not mine, that save the day.

What else are friends for?

ALL THOSE BOOKS

All those books out there—the impulse is to say, "There's too much to know." The proper response to that statement is that knowledge is a process. We are always in the process of knowing. Knowledge is never ultimately acquired or achieved. But what we have truly learned becomes a part of us, body and mind. "A thing known," wrote American poet and physician William Carlos Williams, "passes out of the mind into the muscles."

Learning, however, is of little use and no profit if we do not know who we are and where we are going. "No reading of books," stated Bennett, "will take the place of a daily candid honest examination of what one has recently done and what one is about to do—a steady looking at one's self in the face."

We do this so we can act as we think. Our conduct will then correspond to our principles. The difference between what we value and how we actually live introduces discord into our lives. When harmony exists, we can get on with a 24-hour day that is filled with discovery and delight, a day overflowing with curiosity about ourselves and the world around us.

But it's impossible to learn, to discover, without reading. I have difficulty initiating a new thought, but find it easy to react to an old one. I am like a fighter who is primarily a counterpuncher. If I am first challenged, I can then respond in my individual way with my own individual thoughts. So I read the geniuses of the the past and then am able to clearly see my own personal experience in perspective.

But to get the most out of your reading, you have to go about it in the right way. Bennett had two general suggestions. First, define the direction and scope of your effort. Choose a specific period in history, a limited subject, or a single author. I do that as a general rule, and have consequently discovered another general rule—everything is connected to everything else. No matter how circumscribed the subject, eventually it involves the whole individual, the principles of the universe, and life itself.

The second suggestion is to think as well as read. "I know people," wrote Bennett, "who read and read, and for all the good it does them they might as well cut bread and butter. Unless you give at least 45 minutes of careful, fatiguing reflection upon what you are reading, your minutes are chiefly wasted."

The walker and the runner find this no problem. The mind gladly turns to reflection once the body is put in motion. Thoreau spoke frequently of the effect of walking on his thoughts: "The moment my legs begin to move, my thoughts begin to flow." Then, later in his journal, "I suppose this value, in my case, is equivalent to what others get by churchgoing and prayer."

Thoreau also touched on the idea of narrowing one's focus. "No subject," he wrote, "is too trivial for me; for, ye fools, the theme is nothing, the life is everything. All that interests the reader is the depth and intensity of the life excited."

So let this excitement of your mind and body begin. It is now time to know thyself—and make the most of who you are. William Carlos Williams, in his essays on education and knowledge, comes to this conclusion: "So life then is to do where I am, to the fullest of my power, with clear eyes that tell me plainly that it is neither possible nor desirable to do all, but that my best is all I can do."

Start reading.

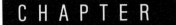

28

THE WISDOM OF WRITING

Enough will happen to me this day alone to fill a novel, if I were only to attend to it.

TELLING STORIES, FINDING MEANING

"If you can't tell a story about what happened to you," wrote John Carse, "then nothing happened." If you cannot find the meaning in an experience, there has been no experience. If you cannot find a tale in an event in your life, that event never occurred.

Carse is a professor of theology at New York University. He knows intimately the world of story and myth and parable. And what Carse implied is the vital difference between a diary and a journal. A diary is a recording of events. A journal is an unfolding of the meaning inside those events. A journal is biography. And writing one is the seeking of the innermost self, the art of thinking seriously.

A life without a journal of some kind, whether biography, letters, or *Pensées*, is a life gone unexamined. It is as if a sailor had set out without charts or sextant and had no idea where he was, where he was headed, or where he had been. "What is the meaning of this?" demands the teacher entering a skirmish of students. So should we demand when we enter any of life's many skirmishes.

The poets have tried to tell us this for centuries. The marvelous and the miraculous are all around us. Enough will happen to me this day alone to fill a novel, if I were only to attend to it. Enough is present in this very moment to make a poem, if I were only aware of it. Something will occur before sundown that could change my life, if I could only recognize it.

This is a world of facts and data and scientific method—precise little scribblings we make in an effort to define the world. But scientific method *always* falls short. "The secret is simply this," wrote American novelist Walker Percy, "the scientist in practicing the scientific method, cannot utter a single word about an individual creature insofar as it is an individual, but only insofar as it resembles other individuals."

Which is why storytelling—and the stories we make from our own lives—are important. We see our personal situations *best* in myths and parables and stories. The novel, English author D. H. Lawrence said, is the only place where we see man, "the whole hog." And Michael Korda, editor-in-chief at Simon & Schuster, is of much the same mind. "The works of self-help gurus," he wrote, "are thin fodder compared to Tolstoy, Dickens, and Balzac."

And so we see ourselves best revealed in our own fables. True—our listeners may learn more about us from our stories than we do ourselves in the beginning. We may in fact even *miss* the point of what happened to us. But as we become more aware of our inner and outer lives, our stories will reflect that growth: Understanding will evolve.

I was driving with a friend through the Berkshires in early summer. "When I took up painting," she said, "my teacher taught me to see all the different greens in a setting like this." I looked at what had been until then simply a green expanse of trees and grass and foliage. And in an instant I became aware of the infinite variety of greens that had previously been invisible to me.

If you look, you see. If you don't look, you will miss more than the greens on the hills around you.

OLD ACQUAINTANCES OFT FORGOT

When I was in Dublin, I heard a tape of a popular Irish comedian. Every once in a while, he would make a very clever remark and get a tremendous reaction from the audience. Then he would say, "Write that down! Write that down!" No need, I would say to myself, and then promptly forget the joke.

I'm the same way with new ideas. Every once in a while, a new one well-expressed will suddenly emerge. No need to write it down, I say to myself, I'll remember—and then the new thought or absolutely right words framing an old thought are lost forever.

Ideas are the most elusive things in the world. I can't tell you how many times I've had an interesting idea out on the road only to lose it in the next hundred yards.

So what to do? How *do* we hang on to good ideas? Jotting such thoughts down immediately is the best solution, but not possible on the road. And sometimes an idea escapes no matter how quick you are. "I had one escape me while rushing to the library to get it down on paper," an advertising man told me.

Max Schuster, the book publisher, had another solution: He saved his ideas on slips of paper. He would start the day with a solid supply of them in the left-hand pocket of his jacket. All day long, he would jot down anything of interest in his mind or reading or conversation and then put the note in his right-hand pocket.

Most ideas still fall through the cracks, though. In part, that's simply because that's just the way ideas *are*. But thought is a bit like a lightning bug: It ignites in the dark, goes out, and then cannot be found. It must be caught when it burns brightly or perhaps it will never be found.

Pursuing a lost idea is usually a lost cause. *Remembering* almost always fails. Nevertheless, I sometimes try to repeat the string of associations that led to the sudden insight. I begin with the original thought and seek the final product. Almost always, however, I resign myself to the loss, and get on with life in hope that the grand concept will return again. Or in hope that a newer, better, grand concept will storm into my brain.

You never know *when* one will come. One thing's for sure, though —it will not come when a trap is set. If you prepare yourself with pen and paper or a tape recorder, your mind will become a blank and stay that way.

The mind must be allowed to *play* for ideas to flow. You can, however, insist that it play in a certain area. We can have it explore a subject the way a dog would investigate a plot of land. Let the mind slip the leash but stay on a given scent—let it move about following leads, investigating the trails of other thinkers, dreaming up new possibilities.

In play, there should be some focus, some area of concentration, because thinking is work as well as play. There are rules and effort and system. There is discipline, there is process and product. But play is the catalyst. Work comes before, in the preparation, and it follows in the aftermath. But play is where we actually experience the thought.

The nice thing about all this is that thinking is where we are most likely to be happy. It is the source of our most joyful experiences. I think, therefore I am happy. But I will never know *why* unless I write it down.

JOURNALS: THE THINKING PERSON'S WORKOUT

Writing is the first form of thinking. It is rational, logical, systematic—a matter of bringing to the surface data and observations, reading, and experience, and then synthesizing them. This is the preliminary, often a long and protracted one, for the illumination that should follow hard thought.

When I run, I take with me the ideas I have acquired on the typewriter. I hope to find in the run the *meaning* of this accumulated thought. This process of understanding cannot be forced. What I did at the typewriter was work, but *this* must be play. That is the paradox. The best thinking is done *without* thinking. Those moments, however, come only as a reward for the onerous and difficult work that has gone before. Such treasures do not occur unless I have earned them.

The final result—my magazine column—is actually my journal. Writing a journal is something we should all do. The practice goes back to the Greeks in Plato's time. Their *hypomnemata* were copy books that contained things they considered useful in the conduct of one's life— quotations, scraps of conversations, events, and readings. These books were a material memory of things read or thought.

Emerson said his own journal was his most valuable possession. He indexed his thoughts and used them later in his essays. In many respects, his essays were more or less compilations of these individual thoughts. One result: He took 15 years to write *Self-Reliance.*

Our journals can become, as did Emerson's and others, a history of our evolution. Our development will become evident on every page. "What one is," wrote Emerson, "only that can we perceive." As we become more, we perceive more. We see more and more meaning in the things around us.

Our journals can help us do that—*if* we create them. Most of us don't, because we hate to write—and for that we have our schools to thank. Recall those blank pages and the prescribed number of words on a subject of no interest. Remember the rule of not using the first person singular. It's no wonder we approach such a task with reluctance.

Nevertheless, writing is the method that perfects the art of thinking.

"Every day you waste a chance—many chances in fact," wrote Ernest Dimnet, "of getting to your innermost consciousness by expressing yourself as you see yourself."

The pure journal is a dialogue with the self. Thoreau in the foreword of his own journal said that it could be subtitled *Says I to Myself.* And that's true. Note, however, that journals differ from diaries. You can immediately tell the one from the other although you may be at a loss to say why. The real difference? Diaries are factual and boring. They reveal little of the writer and rarely contain a phrase or sentence with the ring of universal truth.

Journals, on the other hand, give the inside story. In a journal, *thought*—not action—is paramount; not experience but our intellectual and emotional reaction to it.

The purpose of a journal is very different, too. The diary records events. In the journal, the goal is truth. In writing a journal, then, one necessarily must become a philosopher, and draw conclusions on how to live life. The journal presents the fruits of this meditation and contemplation.

A journal is a record of a conversation with the *self.* Like good conversations, it is a learning experience. This dialogue with yourself reveals what you already knew but had not put into words. The journal tells you where you are and indicates how you arrived there.

But it also serves to show you if there has been no movement, if your thoughts are no more perceptive, no better expressed than years ago. This can be a danger signal that you are preoccupied with *things,* not ideas—that your life is now a matter of what you have rather than who you are, that you are concerned with what people think about you rather than who you are trying to be.

There is an equal and opposite danger of *straining* for significant ideas. Rather than using the journal to record good ideas, a person tries to think of good ideas to record in the journal.

The correct sequence is obvious: I come upon a thought or insight that I must store away. I then place it in the journal. But almost inevitably, this procedure is reversed. I sit down with my journal and try to come up with a thought or insight worth saving. Irish poet William Butler Yeats described this as the incorrect approach to poetry, "trying to make the will do the work of the imagination."

Trying to will what cannot be willed may well be the basic cause of all our unhappiness, but it is *truly* the basic cause of a bad journal. What I write in my journal should be spontaneous, arising unexpectedly in my mind. It should be a surprising statement surfacing from my subconscious, and therefore under no control. I remember things, as Robert Frost says, I never knew.

When that happens, truth—*my* truth—radiates out of every word.

The phrase—or the sentence or the paragraph—sparkles on the page like a jewel. This ever-so-right expression of my personality has been caught and landed like some magnificent fish until that moment swimming unknown in the depths of the sea.

But this spilling out of my subconscious, like the fish, often needs some bait. There is some word or scene or event that causes the subconscious to go into action. Contemplation is preceded by an experience, thoughts are provoked by change. And that change is brought about by the books and people and events that fill my consciousness each day.

When I allow this conscious world and subconscious treasury to come together, what follows may be a creative statement about myself, or others, or life in general. It should be the truth, as I see it, that particular day. If I am fortunate, I will continue to see in it my basic philosophy of life. If I am even more fortunate, it will apply to all men.

Of necessity, such entries are infrequent. I can, nevertheless, write something every day. One look at Thoreau's journals will disclose the probable result. Days of observations on his external world. Weeks of entries describing flowers and animals about him. But only occasionally and perhaps even a month apart, those incisive statements about the great questions in life that made the man of Walden Pond so famous.

My journal should be me. It should disclose the person I am. Because more than anything else, a journal is a record of the search for one's essential truth. It is the study of the self. And in this, as with all treasures, we must glory in the pursuit, not the victory.

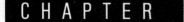

CHAPTER

29

STRAIGHT TALK ON SPEAKING

On occasion, I schedule two talks — my "right brain speech," which is mainly inspirational and motivational, and my "left brain speech," which is an outline of the basic facts on exercise.

MUTTERINGS OF MOMENT

I came of age as a public speaker one night in Staten Island, doing a runners' clinic at a local YMCA. I arrived that night like an untested draftee entering basic training and left with the courage and confidence of a marine commando.

My host at this initiation was a short, slightly overweight Irishman whose cherubic face wore a perpetual grin. As things that evening went from bad to worse, he never lost his smile. That was my first lesson: I was on the line, not my host. My ego was in peril, not his. My self-esteem was at risk, not anyone else's. My self-confidence was at hazard, while everyone around me kept theirs safe and secure.

Public speaking is a lonely pursuit.

Adversity was waiting for me with open arms that night. My host strode to the podium, picked up the microphone and introduced

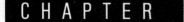

169

me—or attempted to. The microphone was dead. The sound system was inoperative. I sat there shaken. Cold sweat enveloped my body. My cheerful Irish friend, however, ignored the failure and continued to talk into the microphone, holding it tightly in his hand. When he finished what he had to say, he smiled and handed the dead mike to me.

Completely unnerved by this calamity, I decided to go immediately into my slide presentation. Slides make for an easy, relaxed lecture. For this reason they are used almost universally by those of us who spend time telling people what's good for them. Some lecturers even reduce their talks to commentaries on the slides. It makes for an effortless, no-notes presentation when it goes well.

That night, it didn't. The slide carousel jammed almost immediately. Once again bathed in a cold sweat, wondering whether I was going to survive the evening, and needing time to regroup, I called for my movie. This short film makes many of the points I use in my talk. I usually run it at the end to summarize my presentation. But now I was desperate and decided to use this ace in the hole immediately, confident that, as always, it would prove a winner.

But not that night. When the movie came on, we could *see* everything. We just couldn't *hear* it. The audience and I sat there silently watching this silent movie, and nothing anyone could do would make the projector emit a single word. By then, I was reeling under this series of misfortunes—and learning the first rule of public speaking: He who lives by audiovisual aids will die by audiovisual aids.

I took a deep breath and began at the beginning. Whatever devices we speakers use, we are still trying to do the same thing: communicate what is until then an unrecognized common experience, and communicate it in such a way it never will be forgotten. There is no substitute for this meeting of the minds, and the basics are the same today as in Plato's time. Before microphones, before slide projectors, before movie projectors, men inflamed with ideas were able to inflame others with those same ideas.

So I rallied, gradually warming up to the task, gradually regaining my confidence. If you would instigate, as Emerson said, you must first be instigated. My adrenaline was flowing, so I was good and getting better.

Forty-five minutes into the talk, I could see that I had captured the audience. Every eye was on me. I also could see that the YMCA director was smiling even more broadly. Then I happened to look down and saw why.

My zipper was open.

TIPS FOR THE TERRIFIED

"You are one of the best speakers I've ever heard," a man told me in Portland, Oregon. "You're a natural, but the reason you're *good* is that you believe what you're saying."

Well—what can I say? I doubt that I'm a natural. In college I received a D in public speaking, and for years I was reluctant even to ask a question at medical meetings because I'd get heart palpitations when I did. But I do believe in what I'm saying. And I believe with the passion that comes from the belief that I alone possess the truth. When I work myself up to that pitch, the audience believes it, too.

Until recent years, I shared the common dread of public speaking. Now, lecturing is what I do best. Losing the fear won the battle. My belief became the message, not myself. And when I shifted the focus from what my audience would think of me to what I could do for them, I no longer worried about being stupid or foolish or boring. And—gradually—I learned how to make them laugh and think and even cry, so they would take my thoughts into head and heart.

Good or bad, every speaker is vulnerable to the audience. No matter how experienced the lecturer, an unresponsive audience can interrupt the thought, alter the delivery, destroy the timing. When that happens to me, I look for the person whose face is saying, Yes. And when I find him or her, those approving eyes are enough to carry me through to the finish.

How do you know when you're facing a tough audience? We all acquire our own warning flags.

As an introduction to my own talks, for example, I often run a short film called *Thoughts on the Run*. Most of the thoughts are mine, uttered as I run through a Florida game preserve, a New Jersey horse farm, and in the Boston Marathon. With Bach in the background, the film establishes a simple and humorous tone that usually makes the subsequent talk a lot easier.

But there are times it doesn't. The audience does not react with the usual laughter, the usual smiles. I know then that I am going to have to work hard: I am facing a resistant show-me group who will respond to facts but not to rhetoric.

How do I handle it? The best answer is simply to be flexible. When I am talking to a specific group, salesmen on one hand or researchers on the other, I change my approach to adapt to the different personalities. In fact, if I *don't* make that accommodation, I am likely to fail at *any* time. It is a simplification to divide people into right-brained, creative and spontaneous individuals, or left-brained, logical and organized individuals. But like most simple solutions, it proves to be quite practical.

Most audiences I speak to are not homogeneous, however. They contain all *sorts* of people with different personalities, interests, and mental processes. One result is that, on occasion, I schedule *two* talks—my "right brain speech," which is mainly inspiration and motivational, and my "left brain speech," which is an outline of the basic facts on exercise.

I dodge the alternative of giving a schizophrenic mixture of both. No one is happy with that, least of all me. When in doubt, I go for the ABC's and insert just enough humor to make it palatable to the right-brainers who happen to be listening to me.

Getting motivated yourself helps, too. I have always felt the need to work myself up for a speech, to get the juices flowing ahead of time. I really want to feel the way I do on the starting line of a race—alert, ready, feeling that tension about what's to come but anxious to get going. But there are times, however, when I wonder if such preparation is unnecessary and no more than a superstition. I just don't seem to faze as easily anymore.

On my way to speak at the Twin Cities Marathon in Minneapolis, for example, my plane made an unscheduled stop and arrived 20 minutes late. I entered the ballroom at the St. Paul Radisson, dropped my bags, shed my jacket, and took the microphone. I spoke as well as I can speak, and one hour later received a standing ovation. So much for mental preparation.

But the most important point of all is to try to make it fun. When I lecture, I hope to fulfill the aims of Cicero: *Ut doceat, ut moveat, ut delectet.* To teach, to stir the mind, to provide enjoyment. Many times, I settle for the last. If my audience is about to waste an hour listening to me, I should at least make it fun. One time when I spoke at Trinity College, Dublin, a gentleman seated next to my wife leaned over and said to her, "He does make the time pass, doesn't he."

But I can do too much of that. It is an ego trip to milk the audience for laughs. That is not the basic purpose of my talk. A friend who counseled me on my performances told me, "Don't play for the laughs, get your message across." Good advice, but laughter is a rare commodity. And, besides, it feels good: Getting people to laugh makes me feel as if I am in a state of grace.

Another tip: Good writing is rarely, if ever, good speaking. Speeches that are barnburners in front of an audience are frequently not impressive in print. Stephen Jay Gould, the Harvard paleontologist, who speaks without a prepared text, writes the outline in detail. "But the words—you have to find them inside yourself if it's going to be any good."

The unique timing, the pauses, the body language, and verbal digressions I indulge in on stage would also never work in print. Yet all contribute to the unique quality of the communication between speaker and audience.

Telling stories helps, too. Christ spoke in parables for a reason. Every listener understands a parable at his or her own level. Parables call for understanding, and they cause no arguments. I lean heavily on generic anecdotes that allow everyone in the audience their own interpretations.

And a sense of humor is invaluable. I once spoke at a Heart Association meeting in Baltimore for an hour without once citing a single statistic or research report. Afterward, a professor from Johns Hopkins told me, "I don't know how that speech could have been any better. I don't remember what you said exactly but it was quite marvelous."

That can make it tempting to try to repeat yourself, exactly—but that's a fatal error, because it can't be done. Austrian philosopher Ludwig Wittgenstein, a thoroughgoing eccentric as a teacher, always gave his lectures *without* notes. As one friend described it, "He thought *before* the class." Once, when he tried to lecture from notes, he was disgusted with the result. The thoughts that came out were stale or, as he put it, the words looked like "corpses" when he began to read them.

"I remember how awful I was when I had to repeat my lectures on Freud and Gandhi," reported a religious scholar. His original talks had been so successful that the several hundred people who hadn't been able to get into the hall induced him to give them again several days later.

"During the first talks," the scholor said, "I was inspired, and I spoke with enormous success. The second and third times, I'd lost my fire. I had the feeling I was repeating myself, that I was no longer authentic. Only the few fragments I improvised, thoughts that I hadn't had time to develop in the first series, saved me."

Bringing the same words to a speech is a mistake, but bringing the same emotion—enthusiam, fervor, what have you—isn't. Extemporaneous speaking *depends* to a great extent on emotion. That being so, the more emotional the setting or the event, the more likely the outcome will be memorable. I have spoken four or five times on the eve of the Boston Marathon. On all but one occasion, I was to run in the race the next day. I count those talks among the best I have ever given.

But the emotion has to be real. There is a fine line between sentiment and sentimentality. A distinction has to be made between those feelings we simply enjoy having and that cost us nothing, and those we've *paid* for with pain and sacrifice. Your audience will know the difference. When I face an audience of marathon runners, for example, I feel free to talk to them as saints and heroes. I can point out the deeper meanings and the eternal values in our athletic experience. "In the race, I can die and be born again," I tell them. And they, having experienced whatever it is I am trying to put into words, show their belief in their faces. They hear the truth in my voice, and that's the final lesson.

You can't fake sincerity.

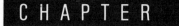
30

THE
GREAT
CONVERSATION

Whenever we achieve new heights as persons, whenever we move toward a deeper knowledge of our true selves, we almost always find that there is a writer there who has been waiting to speak to us.

SHARING EMERSON

One proof of the existence of God, said Buckminster Fuller, is the fact that whenever we need anything, it is there. Whatever is necessary for the advance of mankind, essential for our technology, or required for our progress toward the millenium, has been stockpiled for all time.

And the same thing applies to thinkers. Whenever we achieve new heights as persons, whenever we move toward a deeper knowledge of our true selves, we almost always find that there is a writer there who has been waiting to speak to us.

When I became a runner, I found these new friends, those whose hearts and souls and intellects and, yes, even faces and bodies somehow resembled mine. Friends who had felt what I was now feeling, known what I was coming to know, and written in words that rang with *my* truth.

One such person was Ralph Waldo Emerson. At 60, Emerson was 6 feet tall and 130 pounds. He was a person of squirrel-like shyness, with a rapid and tireless body, but completely inept with horses and cows and garden tools. He wore a 6⅞ hat and had a face that was lean and bony and all angles. And when he wrote he was that person — a person with a remarkable resemblance to a distance runner, not only in body but in mind. Below are some thoughts from his essays and journal.

- My doom and my strength is to be solitary.
- I like Man but not men.
- Who so walks alone accuses the whole world; he declares all to be unfit to be his companions; it is very uncivil, nay insulting; society will retaliate.
- The isolation of men of thought to society is always the same. They refuse the necessity of mediocre men, to take sides.
- Dante was bad company and was never invited to dinner. Michelangelo had a sour time of it. Columbus never discovered an isle or key as lonely as himself.
- I, cold because I am hot — cold at the surface only as a guard and compensation for the blind tenderness here, have much more experience than I have written, more than I will ever write.
- It is a peculiarity of humor of me, my strong propensity for strolling. I seldom enjoy hours as I do these. I remember them in winter. I expect them in spring.
- Crossing a bare common in snow puddles, at twilight under a clouded sky without having in my thoughts any occurrence of special good fortune, I have enjoyed a perfect exhilaration. I am glad to the brink of fear.
- The sky is the daily bread of the eyes.
- I have heard a clergyman of Maine say that in his parish are the Penobscot Indians and that when anyone of them in summer has been absent for some weeks hunting he comes back among them a different person and altogether unlike the rest with an eagle's eye, a wild look and a commanding carriage and gesture. But after a few weeks off he is again into the indolent apathy which all exhibit.
- First be a good animal.
- Let him be not too eager to grasp some badge or reward and omit the work to be done. True success is in the doing.
- Fitness is so inseparable an accompaniment of beauty, it has been taken for it.
- We must be at the top of our condition to understand anything rightly.

● Do your thing: That which each can do best none but the Maker can teach him.

● All life is an experiment.

● Be no man's disciple. No one's satellite.

● On Waschutt I sprained my ankle. It was slow to heal and I went to the doctors. Dr. Henry Bigelow said, "Splint and absolute rest." Dr. Russell said, "Rest, yes. But splint, no." Dr. Bartlett said, "Neither splint nor rest, but go for a walk." Dr. Russell said, "Pour water on the foot but it must be warm." Dr. Jackson said, "Stand in a trout brook all day."

What I like best about Emerson is his ambivalence. He writes decisively about a subject, and then shifts ground and takes exactly the opposite position. A critic described this inconsistency well: "He asserts the absolute claims of self. Yet turn another page, pick up another essay and the disdainful Olympian turns into an egalitarian democrat, the scholar-hermit disdains books as crutches, the radical individualist demands that attention be paid to the claims of the world."

"Damn consistency," wrote Emerson, "it is the hobgoblin of small minds." So he spoke in words that were like cannon shot, and, while their sound was still in the air, he defended the opposite opinion.

Readers who are looking for a well-ordered world are likely to be unhorsed by this attitude. Having found certainty in one essay, they are unprepared for the rebuttal that takes place in the next. Lulled by an easy canter through some prescription for behavior, they are dumped on their behinds when Emerson then strongly recommends that it not be followed.

People have equally opposite reasons for not reading Emerson. Radicals find him too conservative; conservatives find him too radical. In a time when we are prone to give people labels, he is likely to turn up with any number of them. He seems to be many persons, but no precise and definite *one.* People do not like that. It makes them uncomfortable.

Emerson faced the same criticism himself. He never permitted it to bother him. More to the point, he refused to answer those who attacked him.

"There is no scholar," he wrote, "less willing or less able to be a polemic. I could not give an account of myself if challenged."

He acknowledged his lack of debating skill and the apparent weakness of his positions quite openly. "I delight in telling what I think but if you ask me why it is so, I am the most helpless of mortal men."

How does one deal with such a man? Just as he dealt with those with whom he differed. To one critic he wrote, "I shall read what you and other good men write, glad when you speak my thoughts and skipping the page that has nothing for me."

I do not skip pages in Emerson, although there are many there that have nothing for me. That lack is not due to what Emerson has written. It is due to my lack of the wisdom to understand it. I accept that.

"Ultimately, nobody can get more out of things, including books," wrote Nietzsche, "than he already knows."

What I seek in Emerson is the best statement of what I know to be true. And because he is so right in most matters, I suspect that there is truth also in those I do not yet comprehend: His changes in direction will surely be matched by mine. The fact is that the diversity of Emerson's moods is certainly just as much a feature of my own life, and if this kind of consciousness is his answer to the human condition, well, it is likely to turn out to be mine as well.

I can live with my own ambivalence because he lived with an even deeper one he could not express. "In silence, we must wrap most of our life," he wrote, "because it is too fine for speech, because also we cannot explain it to others, and because we cannot yet understand."

What Emerson was able to say and explain and understand is a sometimes difficult and frustrating path to follow. But no matter how it doubles back and around and back again, it is a journey worth the taking.

OUT OF TIME WITH THOREAU

"Thoreau lived," wrote Emerson, "*ex tempore*—from hour to hour, like the birds and angels; the only man of leisure in his town; and his independence made all others look like slaves."

Most of his leisure was spent in walking. Walking was his path to enlightenment. It was where he did his best thinking, his best writing. The length of my walk, he said, is the length of my writing. What he had to say about himself, his thinking, and his walking seems to have some relevance to many who have taken up another form of movement and meditation—running. Here are some thoughts from Thoreau that runners may recognize as true to their experience.

● An early morning walk is a blessing for the whole day.

● For many years I was a self-appointed inspector of snowstorms and rainstorms, and did my duty faithfully, though I never received payment for it.

● When you think your walk profitless and a failure and you can hardly persuade yourself not to return, it is at the point of success. For then you are in the subdued knocking mood to which nature never fails to open.

● I feel a little alarmed when it happens that I have walked a mile into the woods bodily without getting there in spirit.

● Now I yearn for one of those old, meandering, dry, uninhabited roads, which lead away from towns; where your head is more in heaven than your feet are on earth; where you can pace when your breast is full and cherish your moodiness; where you are not in false relations with men, and not dining or conversing with them; by which you can go to the uttermost parts of the earth; then my life will come to me, methinks; like a hunter I walk in wait for it. That's a road I can travel, six miles an hour or two, as you please. There I can walk and recover the lost child that I am without ringing any bell.

● A thinker's weight is in his thought, not in his tread. When he thinks freely his body weighs nothing.

● I do not know but I feel less vigor at night; my legs will not carry me so far; as if the night were less favorable to muscular exertion—weakens us somewhat as darkness turns plants pale.

● I do not know how to entertain those who can't take long walks. If they can't walk, why don't they take an honest nap and let me go in the afternoon? But come two o'clock, in the midst of a most glorious Indian summer afternoon, they sit, breaking their chairs and wearing out the house.

● I must be out-of-doors enough to get the experience of wholesome reality, as a ballast to thought and sentiment. I keep out-of-doors for the sake of the mineral, vegetable, and animal in me. Health requires this relaxation, this aimless life.

● I must let my sense wander as my thoughts, let my eyes see without looking. The more you look the less you will observe. . . . Be not preoccupied with looking. Go not to the object; let it come to you. What I need is not to look at all but a true sauntering of the eyes.

● I inhabited my body with inexpressible satisfaction: both its weariness and its refreshment were sweet to me.

● If a man does not keep pace with his companions perhaps it is because he hears a different drummer. Let him step to the music which he hears, however measured or far away.

● We should go forth on the shortest walk, perchance in the spirit of undying adventure never to return, prepared to send back our embalmed hearts only as relics of our desolated kingdoms. If you are ready to leave father and mother, and brother and sister, and wife and child and friend, and never see them again—if you have paid your debts and made your will, and settled your affairs, and are a free man—then you are ready for a walk.

A STROLL WITH WILLIAM JAMES

When I discovered the philosopher William James some years back, I began to note ideas and concepts in daily use that James had originated. People, it seemed to me, were forever taking paragraphs out of James and converting them into best-selling books. And he was special not only as a thinker but as a person—an authentic and seamless whole, as witty and spontaneous and concerned every minute of the waking day as he was in his books.

At the time, I was 45 years of age and smack in the middle of a personal life-meaning crisis. The best way to handle such questioning of the self is to find someone who is saying what you would say if you could. When I read James, I found for the first time the thoughts that make me different from anyone else—including him. Others helped, of course. Emerson and Thoreau, to name just two, and a few contemporaries, like sociologist Ernest Becker and Greek writer Nikos Kazantzakis. But it was James, himself an Emersonian, who set me free.

It was a freedom that demanded more of me than the authority that previously ruled my life, and in this James echoed our joint mentor Emerson, who wrote: "The natural situation for man may well be war. I do not mean that man is to man a wolf, but that man must be to man a hero."

I am not deterred in my reading of William James by the fact that most of what he writes is incomprehensible. I just do not have the mental capacity to understand much of what he is saying. The reason I go back again and again to his books are the parts that I *do* understand— those casual essays and lectures directed to ordinary citizens, the words he has for each individual. There, he is a delight to read, a joy to visit with. His sketches go right to my gut like passages in Beethoven. He knows me better, it seems, than I know myself.

American educator Jacques Barzun wrote a book, *A Stroll with William James*, expressing the same admiration. Barzun, however, had a mind capable of comprehending what James is saying. This book did much to reveal James's ideas in simpler words. One reviewer of the book said of its contents, "The seminal quality of James's mind opens avenues in nearly all directions, while the anecdotes of his wit and penetration seem inexhaustible."

I find James's work either too difficult or too inadequate. I long for more of his advice to students, or addresses to the Harvard YMCA, or the Boston School of Gymnastics. I wish that he had become an essayist in the Hazlitt and Stevenson tradition. He may well be America's greatest philosopher, but that is an arcane science to me. What I want from him is the art that he revealed in his letters and other lighter efforts.

James, who was unrelenting in his demand upon himself, expressed his need to strive in the most incisive words. He asked us to acknowledge that "the strenuous life tastes better." He wanted us to agree that "life is made in doing and suffering and creating." Aging he would have us admit that "most of us lead lives inferior to ourselves."

So when my spirits flag and my resolve begins to die, when I fail to see the humor in life and complain only of its difficulties, I go to James and am once again reborn. I reenter the fray, made for the moment—a seamless whole like that great man himself.

WORDS WITH A SAMURAI

After I became interested in Yukio Mishima's *Sun and Steel,* a friend questioned me about it. "I don't know how you can read Mishima," she said. "He was obsessed with death."

She was absolutely right. Mishima, a member of Japan's samurai class, was preoccupied with death. His life, in fact, has been described as a rehearsal for his death—a first principle of the samurai. *Sun and Steel* makes that evident. In a real sense, this book is a suicide note. In November of 1970, the year it was published, Mishima committed hara-kiri and was beheaded by four companions.

So death is a continuing presence in *Sun and Steel.* It is mentioned on almost every page. Death, the perfect death, is the motivation behind everything that occurs.

Yet when I read the book, I can look past this final fatal act, past all the thoughts on death woven into the text. What I see is that Mishima's preoccupation with death led to a preoccupation with life, and that preoccupation I can share.

Mishima saw that the perfect death required his perfection as an individual. "I cherished a romantic impulse toward death," he wrote, "yet at the same time I required a strictly classical body as its vehicle. The simple fact was that I lacked the necessary characteristics. Any confrontation between weak flabby flesh and death seemed absurdly inappropriate."

He therefore turned his life around. He began an all-consuming program of physical activity, a crash project toward physical development. If death was to be the ultimate peak experience, he must be the best body he could be.

I can see myself joining Mishima in this project. Am I not in the same position, not with death perhaps, but with life? If life is the ultimate peak experience, if it is to surprise me with joy, must I not be all the body I can be? Is not any confrontation between weak flabby flesh and life absurdly inappropriate? As I read the book, I see that I want no less than Mishima.

As Mishima prepared himself for the perfect death, I can prepare myself for the perfect life. The good life and the good death coincide. If I am to live beautifully and die beautifully, I can take Mishima's path for my own. If it is a disgrace to go to one's ceremonial death with less than a classical body, it is an equal disgrace to rise in the morning and face life the same way.

Thinking on death helps this rush toward perfection. Death creates urgency. Death makes every day count, makes every hour important, makes every second an opportunity. Because of death, we know that we do not have enough time. We cannot sit around and wait.

Mishima most definitely did not sit around and wait. He lived every day to the hilt, making each one a masterpiece.

Emerson, in his journal, speaks of this attitude. "Don't tell me to get ready to die," he wrote, "I know not when that shall be. The only preparation I can make is to fulfill my present duties. This is the everlasting life."

Mishima was one of those people we regard with amazement. They do not have views, they *are* their views. They do not have opinions, they *live* them. They do not write about theories, they make *realities*. They are heroes.

Mishima was a hero. This does not mean that he was right or rational, or to be commended for what he did. It does mean that he lived what he believed. In the course of that life, he did things that were childish and foolish and from our point of view incomprehensible. All his decisions and judgments came from inside himself. He was interested in nothing but the ideal life he had set in front of him.

Like most heroes, Mishima imposed his will on reality. And further, he saw his will as the will of the universe. He became body-mind-soul the creature he believed his Creator had in mind the day he was born.

He expressed this union of mind and spirit as few have done before him. One reason for this is that he saw the body with the unique perspective of another culture. He saw its perfection in much the same way a man blind from birth suddenly sees the world. *Sun and Steel* is no ordinary book on the role of the body in this life, not just another volume about the effect of sport and play on man. It is a testimony by the most ardent of lovers, the truest of believers, the convert who came late to the faith.

I have come to accept Mishima's truth. His "steel" is my running. His discovery of the body parallels my own. But where he translated his intensely individual interest into a philosophy of death, I have been able to translate mine into a philosophy of *life*.

CHAPTER

31

IMPORTANT PEOPLE

S*he came there once a week and made us feel clean, made us feel worthwhile — made us feel holy.*

DR. WILLIAM DOCK

"Once you visit Paris," a friend told me, "you will never be the same." He saw no need to explain why this should be. Perhaps he knew the futility of such explanations. I would have to *experience* Paris before I could understand how it would change my life — and when I did, I found that he was right.

Living in Paris even for as short a time as a week makes you deeply aware of something most Americans ignore — the past. Wherever I looked in this elegant city, I saw the past. History, tradition, culture are present in ways that no city in America can hope to equal.

Neither my friend nor I knew of another treasure I would meet in Paris — my former teacher and professor at Long Island College of Medicine, William Dock. Like the city, the experience of Dr. Dock changes a person's life. A Dock-taught student was never the same docile, authority-accepting schoolboy that first entered the great man's presence.

At the time I first met him, he was thin, wiry, and ageless, with the sharp, fine-boned face and questioning mind of a Yankee storekeeper. That questioning mind had been honed through the scientific rigors of appointments at Peter Bent Brigham Hospital, and subsequent years as professor of pathology at Stanford University and Cornell Medical College. In a profession where today's dogma quickly becomes tomorrow's heresy, Dr. Dock was like a lighthouse in a stormy sea—showing us where the safe and acknowledged truth was, and shedding light on the turbulent sea of speculation in the monthly medical journals.

Dr. Dock changed my life then. He made me take a larger view, concede the truth contained in history and tradition, and question the dogma proclaimed from the highest chairs in academia. My apprenticeship made me willing to say "I don't know," and impelled me to dispel that ignorance by going back to the basics.

In 1977, Dr. Dock, then 79 years of age, left his practice at Lutheran Hospital in Brooklyn and retired to Paris with his wife. I had not heard anything about him since. But when I was settled in my hotel room, I picked up the telephone book and there was his name. A phone call later, I was having lunch with this now 85-year-old master of storage, retrieval, and analysis.

Paris made me take a long look at the world. Dr. Dock made me take a long look at myself. Paris made me justify my view of history and culture and society. Dr. Dock made me justify my opinions on health and wholeness and purpose. An 85-year-old widower alone in what should be a foreign city, he is steadfastly pursuing his education. He is still thinking and growing, still focusing with unerring accuracy on the essential causes of illness and disease.

It was just as my friend had said. I had visited Paris and would never be the same.

DR. TIMOTHY NOAKES

One useful classification of our personality divides us into four categories: analytical, expressive, driven, amiable. Most of us have one primary characteristic. Many have two. A few have three. Dr. Timothy Noakes is one of the few people I have met who posesses all four in almost equal degrees.

He is completely disarming in debate because he is so amiable. He is rarely without a smile on his face. He is a driven man who pushes himself to the limit, both at work and in sports. He is a scientist devoted to exact proofs, an investigator who never allows emotion to get in the way of his judgment. At the same time, he is an expressive person who sees beyond all this logic and achievement to the nonrational areas of life. He allows himself to express the deepest and most fundamental human emotions. He is a rare combination, indeed, and that makes his book *The Lore of Running* an absolutely superb book.

Dr. Noakes has a training, an intelligence, a sensitivity, and an experience few writers on the athletic life can equal. On every page we can see the work of the scientist. He has studied the physiology and pathology of athletic training in depth. No problem in running, whether it be an intractable orthopedic injury or sudden death on the road, is foreign to him. He is not merely familiar with the medical literature—in many instances he *is* the medical literature. His published material covers running in virtually every aspect. And he has explored as well the areas of living beyond the physical: He has integrated the science and the art of living.

In Dr. Noakes's book we learn once again that the proper study of man is man. Each of us in some way follows that rule. Whatever we do for a living, we must know something about the human animal. Whether our art is selling or parenting, nursing or teaching, we are students of human nature and how it operates.

For the most part this specialization leads us to see only bits of man. Not, as English author D. H. Lawrence said, "the whole hog." We know man only in the scope of our own profession. The solution is to study ourselves. We must look inside and see all men. We must stretch our bodies and minds and spirits and thereby find our own limits.

Rarely do we do that. We may push ourselves to the limits of what we consider our roles in life, but, nevertheless, we remain specialists. The possibility of personal renaissance does not occur to us.

The Lore of Running should change that. The subject of this book is man fully functioning—and, at the same time, man cognizant of the problems to be encountered in the pursuit of excellence.

Timothy Noakes is a physician, intimate with the pathology of life. He has observed, diagnosed, and treated the diseases that visit the best of us. He understands that disease is not always inevitable. There are ways to prevent unnecessary morbidity and mortality. But should disease come, especially those that plague the athlete, there are rational and effective ways to deal with it.

Dr. Noakes is also a physiologist and an expert in human performance. He tells us how to become and remain athletes. His book instructs us on developing and maintaining our now-buried capabilities for athletic endeavors. It teaches us how the body can be trained to function at its best.

Dr. Noakes is a runner who has gone through the varied experiences of running: the contemplation, the conversation, the competition. He is familiar with both the joy and the boredom of running—its peaks and valleys, its elations and depression. If we are to study man, we must study man in all aspects. Body, mind, and spirit.

The result is a book that appears deceptively simple. Readers who have had the athletic experience may well say to themselves, I could have written this book had I had the time. This is the mark of writing that seriously influences us: It puts into words our own thoughts and leads us to insights not yet discovered. We all have within us the drive toward excellence. Timothy Noakes wrote of how he sought this excellence—and in so doing blazed a path for us all.

NOEL CARROLL

"I used to be an eccentric; now I'm an expert," wrote Noel Carroll in the opening chapter of *The Runner's Book*. "I was once tolerated; now I'm consulted. The oddity I practiced was running. The only wisdom I can now claim is that I continued to run."

Carroll is an expert. He is truly a wonderful runner, perhaps the best of his age in the world. For him, running always has been an absolute necessity. He has never stopped running since he was a schoolboy. And in the intervening years, he starred as a runner at Villanova and later as an Irish Olympian. When he retired from world-class competition, he continued with his daily sessions on the track and his weekend runs in the Wicklow Hills.

And Carroll is a fine coach. He knows firsthand all of the problems runners face. In this manual, he discusses what happens, from beginning running, on through the injuries and the ambitions and running's impact on family and social life. And all of this is done in a wise and witty way.

I would expect just this from Noel Carroll. When I was in Ireland, I spent time with him and found him full of humor, with an easy mastery of himself and every situation. His position as director of public relations for the city of Dublin requires those qualities. One has to be quick and agile with words to handle the Irish citizenry. The Irish use words the way the best painters use brushes. Carroll seemed never at a loss for one of those happy/sad, comic/tragic, utterly revealing responses that mark the Irish. And in his book, he has a way with a phrase that puts me in mind of what we American Irish must have been like before we were *assimilated.*

Runners, fortunately, are not yet assimilated, and Carroll knows it.

"Runners," he stated, "are an introverted lot. Their behavior is, at best, antisocial. At worst, it is utterly selfish. Runners feel comfortable only when talking to themselves or their kind. The true runner does not consider his obligations to the rest of humanity. He has to be badgered and bullied into everything from cutting the grass to putting out the [trash] bin."

To counterbalance this dreary picture of his fellow runners, Carroll pointed out: "Running is the classical road to . . . self-awareness and self-reliance. Independence is the outstanding characteristic of the runner. He learns that personal commitment, sacrifice, and determination are the only means to self-betterment. Runners only get promoted through self-conquest."

Nowadays, this self-conquest seems inevitably to include the marathon. Jogging for health, said Carroll, has a limited appeal. Eventually the masses look elsewhere for satisfaction, and along comes the marathon, "a challenge with charisma." The magnetism of the marathon, he claimed, is in this: "A heroic effort is needed, enough to excite the human spirit—a ready-made road to immortality."

As Carroll sees it, there is a specific way to prepare for a marathon. Three months to get fit. Three months to train. A schedule is based on time, not distance. Long days, in hours, alternate with short days, in minutes. When the six months are up, the runner is putting in eight hours a week on the roads. "The marathon," he wrote, "is a test of time, not speed. People who train themselves to run long enough in terms of time will run a marathon." Practically all runners who fail to finish fail, according to Carroll, because they run too fast early on, not because the distance is too far.

But there is more to the book than an expert telling us the secrets of the marathon. Carroll has some equally wise comments on other subjects of importance to runners.

In the chapter on style, for instance, he said, "Style is often an unnecessary preoccupation of the inexperienced runner. The seeking of this elusive 'style' often causes a runner to adopt a gait totally out of character with his physical makeup." And in a section on breathing: "Breathing is another function that commands a runner's attention to an unnecessary extent."

Carroll suggested that beginning runners take at least two days' rest per week. "All training is done while we rest. If the rest periods are not long enough the law of diminishing returns sets in. In other words increased effort produces decreased results."

So, with a sentence here and a sentence there, he absolves us of guilt about our schedule and our form and our periods of indolence. He does the same with our eating habits. "The great luxury of running is that it disposes of all sorts of junk foods, foods that the body would otherwise deposit on conspicuous corners in the form of fat. No serious runner has to worry about weight."

Carroll closes with a serious discussion of a serious subject: the runner's relations with other people. This is a topic which, quite rightly, he claims other writers on running have ignored.

"The reality of the runner's life," he notes, "is that somebody else is always affected by his running. It may be a spouse or a girlfriend, or a boyfriend, or a mother and father, or the children. To ignore the fallout is to court disaster. It can create an atmosphere that does nobody any good and certainly not the runner."

The solution? Never complain about being tired. Get your running in before you get home. Do not let running dominate your conversation. And do not insist on an early night Friday or Saturday night because of the next day's race or training. It is best to appear to comply with the rituals of socializing.

"The runner who clashes head-on with social convention is not doing himself a favor," said Carroll. "It is far more intelligent to yield to certain requirements than to insist on total rejection of conventions that no longer suit you."

Runners who read this book will find valuable information on every page and in the reading will come upon some genuinely priceless information—how they look to other people, and what to do about it.

BILL LOEB

Almost ten years ago, I received a letter from William Loeb, the publisher of the Manchester, New Hampshire, *Union Leader.* Loeb had read an article about me in a medical journal and liked it. Characteristically, he dictated a letter commenting on it. A short time later, I received another letter suggesting I allow the *Leader* to use my weekly column. I agreed, and have appeared weekly in that paper ever since.

I did not realize then that Loeb was a very controversial figure. I soon learned that he was disliked by people who read the *New York Times* and despised by those who read the *Village Voice*. When my friends learned I was writing for his paper, their reaction was usually one of disbelief. "How could you possibly write for that man?" they asked.

Well—I wrote for Loeb because I liked him. Or rather I liked his letters. I never met him in person.

His letters were bright and lively and filled with enthusiasm and exuberance. I think his newspaper had much the same spirit. "Mr. Loeb," wrote the *New York Times* in his obituary, "operated a crusading newspaper that campaigned furiously against official waste and corruption and probably printed more letters from readers than any other newspaper in the country."

This all made for interesting, if sometimes exasperating, reading. American journalist Hodding Carter said in the *Wall Street Journal* that Loeb was intemperate, bigoted, and ideologically constipated, but he was also a newspaperman who believed his journal was supposed to do more than deliver advertising to the subscriber.

"He cared deeply about big issues," said Carter, "fought passionately for his favored causes, and didn't mind what others thought of his belief or methods."

Carter went on to deplore the rarity of such men as Loeb among American newspaper owners. "What we have," he wrote, "are bottom-line boys who look upon their enterprise in much the same way McDonald's looks at Big Macs." Carter thought they might learn something from William Loeb and others—men like Greeley, Pulitzer, and McCormick—who held in contempt their more timorous and cynically detached brethren.

Loeb was neither timorous nor cynical nor detached. He was brave and optimistic and totally involved. He was alive and thinking every minute. I find that shining out of every letter I received from him over the years. Most of his comments, because of my column and profession, had to do with his views on physical fitness and sports. He wrote of his continuing physical activity well into his seventies. He loved to hunt and ski, found running a great bore and swimming likewise. He delighted in keeping his body fit and able to pursue his goals.

Perhaps the most interesting letter I ever received from him was in response to an idea I had of buying a weekly newspaper. This letter, written in 1980, spelled out some of his philosophy as a publisher. The following paragraphs are an exerpt from that letter.

"The trouble with most American newspapers today, which in turn is a reflection on the whole country, is that they are run by people whose only interest is the bottom line. They almost grudgingly carry news and a few editorials because that is apparently what you are supposed to do with a newspaper.

"As a result, the papers have become duller and duller. Also as a result of this preoccupation with merely the dollar sign, the left-wing journalism students and others have discovered that they have a free hunting ground, and so they keep pouring out their left-wing poison with impunity and happily go on undermining the business and financial sector that has allowed these silly owners to prosper at the outset.

"It was not always thus. My wife's grandfather, E. W. Scripps, founder of the Scripps-Howard newspapers, United Press International, and so on, and his contemporaries, such as Hearst and Pulitzer, were interested in making money, of course, and they made a great deal of money, but they were also editors and interested in their paper, and consequently their papers were lively.

"The owners of so many of these properties today are so utterly dull, and thus the papers themselves are dull. There is no understanding on their part that they are in competition just on the matter of *time* nowadays, and of course, especially with TV. If they don't make their papers dynamic so that people are waiting breathlessly for the next issue to come out, they are not going to sell papers.

"So, you are starting the situation with the right approach. Incidentally, a weekly paper such as this, if it is really made vital, is a much sounder investment sometimes than a bigger paper because it becomes a necessity to the community. It is the only way many people can find out what is going on in their community. Well run, economically run, well printed, it can be a money-maker and give you a great deal of fun at the same time. I think you are off in the right direction."

Loeb, of course, never doubted he was off in the right direction. Even when he was all by himself.

My column in the *Union Leader* frequently drew letters from Loeb. I have one in my file that was a response to something I had written called "Running is the Best Type of Exercise."

"That may be," wrote Loeb, "but Godfrey, it's dull. Like many other people I have a great many problems during the day so when I exercise I want to have fun while I'm doing it, along with having it good for my body, and running is no fun. I like skiing, horseback riding, tennis, etc., where there's an element of pleasure along with the exercise. Right now I am in Nevada where we ski two hours each morning and work in the afternoon. I feel ten years younger already. We ski at 8,000 to 10,000 feet and you really have to suck air. In December I will be 70 but my doctor feels it is my love for strenuous exercise, which ordinarily people of my age are not interested in, that keeps me fit."

I wrote back, thanking him for the letter. "I appreciate hearing of your experience," I said. "These things never seem to get into books. The real way men live is lost in considering achievements that never really interested them. Only truly great men live in idiosyncratic fashion. What they did as a daily routine may well have made them great."

Over the years I received other notes on Loeb's daily routine and personal habits that confirm this theory. Loeb's interest in physical activity and the care of his body undoubtedly contributed to his overall performance as a dynamic and crusading publisher.

"Nothing new with me," he wrote in 1974. "I will be 69 this year and I still play tennis, ride horseback, ski, and fish—just a very rugged lad, that's all. I know one thing: Keeping active and keeping busy never can hurt one's health and may improve it."

And again at the age of 70: "Here I am back in the East, stuck behind a desk with no more than two hours of skiing each morning to stimulate my aging carcass. Everybody feels better with exercise but I have never seen such effect on anyone as I get. My system is the type that would be naturally sluggish without exercise."

He was also willing to try anything. "There was an account in the *Lancet* by a lady doctor in Canada who had come up with a cure for leg cramps in the form of magnets placed under the mattress. When I suffered from cramps, my wife remembered this article and went out and bought some magnets and put them in the bed. That was the end of the cramps. My secretary and a doctor friend had the same experience. It sounds crazy but it works."

And on the subject of naps: "Your nap suggestion is a good one. I think one of the problems is that many people have forgotten their instinctive response to various physical situations. In other words, the problem of sleeping when one is tired. I have been very lucky in this respect. I am absolutely willing to bow to the need to sleep. Last night I went to bed before eight o'clock and slept until seven this morning. I just felt tired, and I know there is no use working when I am tired."

Loeb continued, "The late Roger Babson, the great economist and millionaire, always took a nap after lunch. When Mrs. Loeb and I visited his house, I remember his getting up from the table and in his autocratic fashion saying, 'nap time,' and everybody went and had a nap whether they wanted it or not. Roger lived into his nineties, as I recall."

And Loeb commenting on doctors: "In many years of going to some of the finest doctors I have yet to hear anyone make any comment on posture, general muscular condition and what other items go to make a really fit individual. When I happen to mention I feel better and get more work done when I engage in strenuous exercise—such as skiing at 8,000 to 10,000 feet in the High Sierras, and I am not doing it to prove anything but because I enjoy it—you can see that sort of tolerant look cross their faces as they mentally make note that this is another one of those physical fitness nuts. Whereas you and I know that everyone feels better when he (or she) is in top athletic condition."

TISH

Tish is dead. The brain hemorrhage she suffered two weeks ago finally took her away. And because she is gone, life will be a little more difficult, a little less joyful than it was before. Tish was a person who could light up your day. She carried another and better world around with her; she believed and made others believe as well.

Tish was our cleaning lady. For as long as I can remember, she had come once a week to put our house and our family to right. She was, I suppose, the same age as my wife and me. Age, however, was something I never associated with her. Tish was a little over average height, carried no excess weight, and seemed tireless. She was a handsome woman who smiled frequently and always seemed happy. It was a delight to have her around.

She had the ability to make a house shine—and the people in it as well. She would come every Thursday and revive our flagging spirits, make us proud of ourselves and our home and our way of being together.

We needed that pride. When you have 14 people living in a house, order gradually becomes impossible. There are times when it looks as if this experiment must fail. Times when you believe with Spanish thinker José Ortega y Gasset that the proper term for a family is "strife." Families learn to live together, he wrote, by avoiding the word or action that would bring on conflict. They were held together, he said, only by avoiding those things that would tear them apart.

Now, there is a lot of truth in that. Particularly if you have the number and variety of temperaments and personalities that we do. On any given day there is someone who is at odds with the rest of us, someone who has broken the code in some way—someone of this large self-fulfilling group of individuals who has become just too self-fulfilling and individualistic.

Tish never saw it that way. Whoever fell out of favor she would defend. Every boy was a good boy, and an even better boy when we were upset with him. "John is a good boy," she would say. Or, "George is a good boy." Or, "Timmy is a good boy." And so on down the line. She would hear nothing bad about anyone. She was so good herself she saw nothing but good in everyone else.

She was that way with the girls, too. Whenever one of our five daughters became obnoxious, Tish would see it quite differently. "Ann is a good girl," she would say. Or, "Sarah is a good girl." Whatever happened between the seven brothers and the five sisters was passed over as a temporary aberration, something that had no bearing on the persons they actually were.

She had the same feeling about the heads of the household. Mary Jane and I could do no wrong. There were times when I was in my own private hell, knowing my own private disgrace—times when I knew I had not measured up and had failed for the most miserable of reasons. Then I would meet Tish in the kitchen, or pass her in the hallway, and she would let me know that there was at least *one* person in this whole world who saw me as good.

For my wife, she was even more of a help. "We have to do better than others," Mary Jane told me. We could not use the 12 children as an excuse, only as an aid and responsibility to do better. Nevertheless, when you have 12 children, things do tend to go wrong. Especially when the bulk of them are males. English writer G. K. Chesterton once wrote about monasteries: "If men are to live without women, they must live with rules."

But rules or no, when you have eight men in the family, any woman would find it impossible to cope. And when you have six women living together, the one in charge has days when it all seems impossible.

Tish came into this situation once a week. She entered this home of restless egos and ids, this arena of teenage revolts and youthful escapades, of insubordination and outright defiance, and she helped hold us together.

First, she converted this old rambling house into a place of spotless order. She would take rooms that would dismay a Bowery street cleaner and turn them into a photograph from *House and Garden*. Each week she went through that house and restored our pride in where we lived.

She was awfully good at what she did. Cleanliness, they say, is next to godliness. Tish was the cleanest person I ever met. Even my trash, which no one is allowed to touch, she could rearrange so that it was neat and tidy, yet leave it so I could still find whatever I wanted.

But mainly what she cleaned was us. She came there once a week and made us feel clean, made us feel worthwhile—made us feel *holy.* And we believed her because we knew she knew. She knew the sinners we actually were. Knew everything about us. And had forgiven that, and anything else we might do, until she came back again.

I don't think we were that special to Tish, although we would like to have been. I think she felt that way about everyone. I am sure there are many others who have been touched by her, have been lifted up in the same way we were. For them, what I write is simply a confirmation of what they also experienced.

Tish, it appears, led the life we all should lead. She made herself irreplaceable. When she died, she left a void. She had taken what she did and made it so important that we are going to have difficulty living without her. Even the few of us left in this large house need her presence. We need the strength and assurance she dealt out to everyone she knew.

We will fill up that house again this week. That doesn't happen too often anymore. Holidays, perhaps, and the big summer weekends, but this time everyone will be back to say good-bye to Tish. Clean beds and clean closets and clean rooms are the smallest of our remembrances. What we will remember her for most are the clean hearts and minds and spirits we found in her gentle approval.

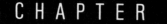

32

ME, MYSELF, AND I

Here were my sins and errors, my weaknesses and transgressions — there, the great gaping holes in my personality through which my life is leaking.

ME FOR THE MOMENT

Things that happen in my life are never due to well-laid plans. My days fall into place at the very last minute, and if I do undertake a long-range project, it rarely survives the first rush of enthusiasm. In short order, I return to my immediate tasks, perfectly willing to let tomorrow take care of itself.

And, usually, it does. This 24 hours just naturally leads to the next. A journal or a book or a lecture just gradually evolves. But there is never a blueprint. I seize the day, and when tomorrow dawns, it is today but better.

Paradoxically, by living without a future, I assure it. Not that this is appropriate for everyone: If making a living was my main purpose, I could be in big trouble. A business or professional career requires foresight. There are guidebooks and maps and well-charted highways that lead to success. Detours are taken at your own peril, and every move has import in the months and years ahead.

Not so when one follows the dictates of the present. The future requires no thought, there is no specific road to follow. I am without precedent, a unique individual whose future *has* to be different from everyone else who ever lived. I live in a labyrinth in which each detour is a learning experience. And though I live entirely in that present, every move *does* have import for the months and years ahead.

The reason is simple: My day is my life, and this present moment is forever. At this very moment, to make the point, I sit at my typewriter in the newsroom, oblivious to all other possibilities. The feeling: This is where I would be, this is what I would be doing. Writing this essay isn't competing with anything else for my attention. The newspaper's large working area filled with people gradually recedes from my consciousness, and I await the words and sentences that come through my fingers on the machine.

What comes, comes. At times there is nothing but silence. The probings of my mind bring no response. The self has nothing to say. But when you live without schedules or plans, it is of no matter. Whatever does come must always be followed by more.

I create my life the same way, just as I would a play or a novel or this book: I do today what can be done today. Each day I fill the allotted pages, and each day I use my entire being in this ongoing drama. I am always *in medias res*—completely engaged in the creative struggle of the moment. The future is hidden and must remain so: Looking ahead means less attention for the moment—for *now*.

So, you see, it is not my future that determines my present, it is my present that determines my future. What I do today and the way I do it assures me of the same quality of life down the road. When the future comes, no matter what it contains, I will be ready.

The question for me then is not whether to live in the present but *how*. Here the Stoic philosopher Epictetus had the best rule. "Let what appears best," he wrote, "be to you an inviolable law." In modern speak, that means trust your instincts.

THE MAN IN THE BROKEN MIRROR

Every week I go through the medical journals at the hospital library, reading case histories and looking for material for my column. And not long ago, I discovered a very interesting case history with some quite usable material in an article in the *American Journal of Psychiatry* entitled "Overview: Narcissistic Personality Disorder."

The interesting thing—the case was me, the material my life.

I had not seen myself described as accurately since reading William Sheldon's portrayal of the ectomorph in his *Constitutional Psychology*.

Drs. Salman Akhtar and J. Anderson Thomson had me right in their sights when they squeezed their scholarly triggers—they hit me simultaneously in the heart and the head and the gut.

They wrote as if firsthand about my failures in functioning. They understood my difficulties with self-image and interpersonal relationships. They were familiar with my troubles in social adaptation, and my deficiencies in ethics and ideals. They knew all about my inadequacy in love and sexuality, and were even cognizant of my problems in cognition—the inner tangles of my innermost thoughts.

Nothing that is wrong with me escaped them. Here were my sins and errors, my weaknesses and transgressions—there, the great gaping holes in my personality through which my life is leaking. Where most people saw only one or more of these deficits, these authorities had cataloged them *all*, lumping them under the single indictment, "a concentration of psychological interest upon the self."

I cannot deny any item in their litany. I might, it is true, admit to only minor tendencies in one area or another. But on the whole it is an all too accurate picture of the person I am—and God help me, will continue to be.

The narcissistic personality, the person in love with himself, is not a new psychiatric concept. It has been around as long as there were people. The Greeks discussed the condition millenia ago in the story of Narcissus. Later, Freud gave me official standing. The first detailed scientific description of my personality suggested three characteristics: condescending superiority, intense preoccupation with my self-respect, and a marked lack of empathy for others.

I am all of that and more. I admit to a self-knowledge brought on by the same qualities that are my undoing—thinking for thinking's sake and a preference for concepts over facts. I spend my time either thinking or writing about myself and my experiences. Eventually, the essential defects in my basic personality *had* to become evident. Blaming who I am and how I act on running and writing and my show-business life does not get to the heart or mind of the matter—a fundamental flaw in my personality structure.

Drs. Akhtar and Thomson nonetheless found some experts with a few good things to say about the narcissistic personality. Sigmund Freud wrote in 1931, "The subject's main interest is directed to self-preservation; he is independent and not open to intimidation. His ego has a large amount of aggressiveness at its disposal which also manifests itself in readiness for activity. In his erotic life, loving is preferred to being loved. People belonging to this type impress others as being 'personalities.' They are especially suited to act as support for others, to take on the role of leaders, and give fresh stimulus to cultural development, or to change the established state of affairs."

Mostly, however, the narcissistic personality has gotten a bad press, and rightfully so. What good can be said of an individual who can't love, lacks empathy, is chronically bored, and manipulates others?

Well, you might say, no one is perfect. But some people are closer to perfect than others. A Socialist author saw little good in the narcissistic personality and even less to hope for. The typical narcissistic, he wrote, "wants to be known as a winner, has little capacity for personal intimacy and social commitment, feels little loyalty and lacks conviction." And, he warned, "Once his youth and vigor, and even the thrill of winning are lost, he becomes goalless, and finds himself starkly alone."

Since the loss of youth, vigor, and the thrill of winning seems inevitable, those on the outside see no hope. Apparently, that is what one critic meant when he wrote of Emerson and "the impenetrable agonies of his loneliness." But nevertheless—as Emerson might have said—within the agonies and the loneliness are brief but splendid periods of joy. There are moments when even the narcissistic personality becomes fully functioning. At those times, I am filled with all those qualities I usually lack; and become for that instant a normal, healthy, loving, and playful human being.

And frankly, narcissism just isn't as bad as popular mythology would have it. "Narcissus is not a victim of vanity," wrote Dag Hammarskjöld, "but someone who responds to his unworthiness with defiance." Any thorough-going disciple of psychologist Alfred Adler would know that is true. A major inferiority complex is at the root of this preoccupation with the self.

Hammarskjöld put it all in perspective. Narcissists are simply responding to the human condition, he told us. We are born, he said, for success. But in life, the truth appears to be the opposite: We fail and meet failure upon failure along the way. And like it or not, we will go the way of the grasshopper. Given that, how can we feel anything but this fundamental unworthiness?

I see my preoccupation with myself as humility, not vanity. I do not deny my faults. I accept them.

And admitting that one has a narcissistic personality is not the end of the world. There are some very positive implications. I can see in myself all the negative qualities psychiatrists attribute to those with this disorder, but I see also that I'm not to blame: These faults come from low self-esteem.

How best is one to deal with this situation? I read conflicting advice, but most experts feel something must be done to reduce this overwhelming concern with self. But my medical experience tells me that this is going in *exactly* the wrong direction. The way to lessen the impact of a fault is to develop a strength. And, frankly, knowing who I am, with my own strengths and weaknesses, is the beginning of wisdom. My personal opinion: If I am fated to play life's game as a narcissist, I'd better be the best narcissist I can be.

The main thing is not to quit on myself. There are always critics — and none more insistent than the one inside. I know that full well. It is imperative to see the *good* me in the mirror, too. I must see *strengths*, not weaknesses.

What I *have* lost, or indeed never had, is an understanding of other people's feeling. The word is empathy. What I have in its place is endless self-doubt. If there are successes in my life, they are little more than temporary bivouacs. The fight against failure resumes again in the morning.

But meanwhile, wrapped up in my own concerns, I fail in my response to other people. I neither communicate nor receive communication. The world spins and I stand still, lost in thought. I take to the roads and become pure body. I sit at the typewriter and become pure mind. The day goes by and I discover I have not eaten. No wonder, then, this isolation that I feel: If one does not even break bread, what need is there for a companion? I am a rebel as solitary as Thoreau, a revolutionary whose cause is my own life.

Still, that may be the way to salvation — not the conformity sought by psychologists, but simply remaining original. What the narcissist needs is not less self-love but more: I have to reach the point of knowing that everything that lives is holy, including himself.

And only when I love myself can I love my neighbor.

33

MORE NOTES ON MYSELF

I *am no longer a knight on a white horse.*
I have become the ordinary, thoughtless,
absent-minded incompetent I am in real life.

THE ARM HANG MAKES EVERYONE EQUAL

We had just returned from an hour run through a park near the Houstonian hotel in Houston, Texas, when someone suggested we take the National Fitness Test. The Houstonian was sponsoring a fitness weekend and had set up a testing area in the gym.

I was reluctant. I knew in advance I would flunk it. I am an expert on fitness who cannot pass fitness tests. I have no strength, no flexibility, no coordination. But I see no *need* for them, really. I would like to be strong, to be more flexible, to have greater coordination, but I'm not willing to work at it. I settle for running and the endurance it gives me. Getting the most out of my 24-hour day depends on the *staying* power I have built into my body, not my musculature.

But my companion, much more athletic than I, was insistent: There is nothing that attracts true athletes more than tests that show

how good they are. So we trooped over and offered ourselves up as specimens.

There were, it turned out, five tests. The first one was the Harvard step test, which is based on the pulse response to steady quiet exercise. The subject steps up and down on a 12-inch bench in rhythm to a metronome for three minutes. The less your pulse goes up the more fit you are.

When I presented myself, my resting pulse was in the seventies despite the hour's run. "You don't need to take this test," said the physiologist. "We can give you a gold medal right now."

But that moment of glory was followed by several of ignominy. The next event was "the sit and reach." This is exactly what it sounds like. You sit and reach forward as far as you can. In demonstrating the test, the instructor reached 23 inches. My competitive friend got to 12 inches, and then was given two more tries to improve his score. And on the last attempt he pulled a muscle.

My turn came next. And since I have absolutely no pride—I know I can't stretch and accept it—I had *no* intention of straining my hamstrings to get another half-inch. I sat, reached forward, and heard the result: "Five and one-half inches." Definitely, rear of the pack.

I did only a little better on the sit-ups and, later on, the push-ups. I was clearly in need of remedial fitness if I were to conform to the standards of the National Fitness Foundation. I expected, therefore, only further proof of my inadequacy when I presented myself for the final test: the infamous arm hang.

The instructions for this test could not be simpler: "Hang from the bar as long as possible." The passing grade in my age group was 30 seconds. A gold medal went to those lasting 70 seconds or more.

I knew I was in for my fourth failure in a row, but there was no avoiding this final confrontation. I got up on the stool and grabbed the bar with both hands, the stool was removed, and the stop watch started.

Seconds later, I felt the pain in my shoulder. The test had hardly begun and I was already in trouble. There was no way I would last 30 seconds. But then I heard one of the physiologists whisper: "The key here is willpower. Eventually the grip weakens, but that comes later."

I found he was absolutely right. The arm hang is a measure of your ability to handle pain. Your score actually depends on determination, and has very little to do with strength. Hanging there, the pain increasing in my shoulders with each passing second, I began to think better of myself: Pain is something I know about.

Runners develop two basic qualities. One is endurance. The other is determination—dogged determination. So putting both to work, I hung there and contemplated the pain. I followed the old athlete's dictum, "Where it hurts, make it hurt more." I took all that pain now spreading through both shoulders and localized it in a small area at the tip of the right collar bone. I closed my eyes and felt my whole being mobilized, pushing the pain into that little corner. And then I hung there, just allowing the time to go by.

"Forty-five seconds," the examiner called out. A minute went by. My pain and I kept up the battle. No quarter given, no quarter asked. But now I could feel it in my hands. My grip was beginning to go. At 90 seconds, it *did* go: My hands gave way and I fell to the floor. But I never gave in to the pain.

My overall mark on the National Fitness Test was barely passing. I expected that. What I did not expect was that they could devise a test that would show that the weak, inflexible, uncoordinated runner is, nevertheless, an athlete to be reckoned with.

The arm hang makes everyone equal.

HOW THE MIGHTY ARE FALLEN

In certain circles, I have celebrity status. I am invited to speak to large gatherings of runners or health-care specialists. When I fly into a city, I am met at the airport. My whole visit is *arranged:* Things happen like clockwork. I am chauffeured around, housed and fed, catered to. Then, after a day or two of verbal fitness advocacy, I am taken back to the airport and shipped home.

That's when the trouble begins. I am no longer the conquering hero, but an also-ran. The all-star expert becomes the all-star dummy. From being someone who can do no wrong, I move to being someone who can do no right. I preach taking charge of your life, but when *I* do, the result is disaster.

Moments after my new friends drop me at the gate, I begin my search for the tickets. I go through the briefcase I call my office, the one that gapes open with books and papers and requires two hands to lift. Before I find the tickets, I have to empty out all the notebooks, five or six paperback books, a volume of Emerson, some half-finished columns, assorted reprints from medical journals, and the airline magazines I accumulated during my incoming flight.

The tickets, once found, are not found permanently. Periodically I look for them again, just to be sure they are still in my possession. And each time, I have to repeat the original procedure: books, papers, magazines, and columns strewn elsewhere. I'm in the 60-and-over category but still haven't learned: There is a place for everything, and everything in its place.

Sometimes, I *don't* find them. In Kalamazoo, they had spilled out of the bag along with my car keys in the trunk of my friend's Renault. They were not found until the next day: I had to buy new tickets and have someone meet me at Newark with an extra set of car keys.

While waiting for a flight, I also have to be careful not to daydream or become engrossed in a book: If I lose track of time, I can miss the plane. I've often looked up to find the plane gone and everyone else in the lounge with it.

After I reach Newark, I am still not home free. First, there is the anxious search for the car keys. I pat each pocket, go through the jacket, and then the last resort—the two zippered compartments of the briefcase. But both are *unzippered,* so the keys could have slipped out, anyway—they have in the past.

I put my hand in one pocket: no keys. The whole ball game now rests on the next move. If the keys aren't there, I'm not sure there is another set in existence. This is the last try. It is the bottom of the ninth, two out, bases loaded, and a full count. But amazing grace—the keys are there.

But finding the keys is not enough, I still have to find the car. Often, it's been a week since I put it in the long-term lot and I have only a hazy idea of where it is. I sort of remember that the car is in a line that ends in zero: 20, maybe 80, just across the street, but possibly a quarter-mile away.

Sometimes I remember exactly where I parked it, only to go there and find it gone. My first reaction is that it's been stolen. But then I realize that this spot is where I had put my car on *last* week's trip. More often than not, I spend a quarter of an hour searching through rows of parked cars looking for my little Honda, all the while promising myself that next time I will write down the car's exact location when I park it.

Eventually—disheveled, exhausted, and my life completely out of control—I find the car. The question now is, Did I really want to? The car is just as I left it—patiently waiting to be cleaned. It is filled with empty Coke cans, coffee cups, old newspapers, and running gear. Later, I say to myself, and wait nervously for the engine to turn over. Once, I left the lights on and returned two days later to be greeted with a dead battery.

Finally, after anxious moments searching for enough money to pay the parking fee, I am on my way home. I am no longer a knight on a white horse. I have become the ordinary, thoughtless, absent-minded incompetent I am in real life. And all I have to prove the trip ever happened is a check from my sponsor.

That check, as you already suspect, is never seen again. I have to call the next day to have them stop payment and issue another one.

THE GREAT MAN STUMBLES—AGAIN

It is 7:15 A.M. I stop by Dunkin' Donuts for my second cup of coffee. There is a long line of people waiting for service. The woman at the front is selecting a dozen doughnuts, one by one. Just behind her is another woman holding a coupon from the paper: It allows her a dozen doughnuts at a special price. And despite a truly *passionate* desire for a second cup of coffee, I turn around and walk out.

Strange behavior? True, given that I literally live from one cup of coffee to the next. But *nothing* is worth standing in a line.

I am at my worst standing in a line. The old Adam comes out, the bad me emerges from the subconscious. As I shift from one foot to the other, I become more and more aware of my impatience and hostility, my inner tensions, and my increasingly ill humor.

This is a side of me few people see. Usually, I keep this person concealed. I pass as a simple workaholic instead of the Type-A personality I really am. I have acquaintances who have never seen me ruffled, colleagues who do not believe I have a temper. A woman who spent years at the desk next to me at the local newspaper said she had never known me to get upset. But all these people who have marveled at my equanimity have *never* seen me waiting in line.

Experts on the science of *queuing*—the mathematics and probabilities of waiting in line—describe two specific negative responses to the situation. One is balking, which is what I did at Dunkin' Donuts. Balking usually occurs when the length of the line or the established waiting time discourages a person from even trying to wait.

I balk easily. Even a short line with a short waiting time discourages me. Time in line is time that's just plain *wasted*. "Take my money," said Thoreau, "but not my afternoons." I feel the same. Time is my most precious possession, and I do not use it fruitfully while waiting in line.

So I've become very *good* at balking. Thoreau said a man's riches are based on what he can do without. Mine are based on lines I refuse to join, which is pretty much the same thing: Here, I'm a *very* wealthy person.

That philosophy has also made me a veteran of the second negative maneuver—reneging. This is simply leaving a line after joining it. I rarely see other people renege, but I do it regularly. People in line for five minutes seem to think that they have invested too much time to leave. To me, however, waiting longer is like spending good money after bad. I simply reevaluate my needs, eliminate from the list whatever I am waiting for, and walk away a free man.

In so doing, I avoid the confrontation with the old Adam, the person in line who is the real me—a spoiled brat. I want what I want and I want it immediately. In my sixties now, I am still immature, a Type-A personality with "hurry sickness": I regard everyone else in that line as the enemy.

Every line, then, is an invitation for me to grow up. The list of things I *could* do in line is a long one: I could pursue mentally anything I might think of in more favorable surroundings. I could read or converse. I might observe my fellowman, or slip into a reverie, or plan the future. I may be in line, but I am not in chains: Lines require my body, but my mind can be anywhere in this world or the next.

If I am to grow up, I must *join* lines, not avoid them. Self-control is not achieved by avoiding the sources of anger and irritation, it is gained by exposing myself to the irritant and refusing to be upset.

"It is difficulties that show what men are," wrote Stoic philosopher Epictetus. "Therefore when a difficulty falls upon you, remember that God, like a trainer of wrestlers, has matched you against a rough opponent. For what purpose? you may say. Why, that you may become an Olympic conqueror. But it is not accomplished without sweat."

Tomorrow morning, I am going to get in that line at Dunkin' Donuts and *sweat it out*.

COFFEE CAPERS

When I conduct a clinic for runners, I am frequently asked about the value of drinking coffee before the race. My answer is short and simple.

"It gets me to the line."

Race or not, coffee gets me going. I cannot start my day without it. Should I somehow forget to have that first cup of coffee, within an hour I am becalmed—engulfed in apathy, going nowhere, and not even caring.

Coffee is my universal starter. I have to put it in my tank or the engine just won't kick over. Ideas refuse to flow, no plans are made. But with coffee comes thought and the ambition to act on it.

I am addicted to coffee. Or, perhaps better put, I am addicted to the caffeine in the coffee. I'll take caffeine any way I can get it, in coffee, tea, cola, or chocolate. But I *prefer* coffee, and especially in the morning. I am now of an age when my body wakes up before I do, and when I awake, I like it to be to the sound of coffee perking and to the aroma of coffee being made.

Which, of course, leads us to the next question: Can something so good be bad? The answer, basically, is *no*. Decades of research have failed to produce conclusive evidence of any long-term repercussions from coffee drinking.

But it is essential here to distinguish between coffee and caffeine. In almost every instance where an individual has a problem, it is the *coffee*, not the caffeine, that causes it: Should the person shift to decaffeinated coffee, the symptoms will persist. So it is the coffee that should be eliminated, not the caffeine.

This intolerance to the caffeine in coffee can cause difficulties ranging from palpitation to diarrhea to hyperacidity. If you are sensitive to coffee, you could suffer from any of a variety of disorders. Nevertheless, coffee and the caffeine it contains are harmless to the general population.

The likelihood, in fact, is that caffeine is actually *good* for you. An internationally known physiologist once studied nine competitive cyclists and found that caffeine increased their time to exhaustion by nearly 20 percent. The mechanism for this appears to be better use of fat and consequent conservation of sugar supplies in the body.

So coffee probably makes me more efficient physically. But it definitely makes me more efficient mentally. After I have my coffee, I feel like the mathematician who described himself this way: "A mathematician is a machine for converting coffee into theorems." That is surely where the real source of addiction to coffee lies—in just living more effectively. I convert my morning coffee into the obligations and duties of day-to-day life.

To be fair, I should put in a word here for tea, too. When I was in Dublin, Ireland, years ago, I became a tea drinker. There, tea was served in an enormous pot with an accessory pot of hot water on the side. Once served, you were set for an hour of uninterrupted conversation. And one of the best things about tea is that it is never bad.

Tea, in fact, is almost uniformly *good*. At the worst, a cup of tea may be mediocre, but it is never *bad*. The same cannot be said for coffee. Coffee ranges from superb to absolute dregs. I have had coffee that I was certain would eat a hole in my stomach. Only the fact that my gastrointestinal system is living tissue that repairs itself allowed me to survive.

But finally, one major advantage that coffee has over tea: aroma.

And not only when it is perking. I remember as a youngster going to Bohack's or the A&P and smelling the coffee being freshly ground. That aroma is pure assurance that a good cup of coffee is in the offing. Freshly ground coffee is almost always of superior quality. An addict will, to be sure, be satisfied with anything. We cannot all be like Juan Valdez. But there is no better way to start the day than with the best cup of coffee money can buy.

PERSONAL BESTS

There are two generally recognized truths about records: (1) They are made to be broken, and (2) when they are, it is not by much. When we set goals for ourselves, the likelihood is that we will not exceed those goals to any great degree. The strength and determination mustered to achieve success dissipates once success is achieved.

Message: Winning a race means you beat someone else. It doesn't mean that you did your best.

I went through this very experience recently in Dallas. The day before a speaking engagement, I visited Kenneth Cooper at his clinic in Texas. Dr. Cooper, who was the first to turn the country toward aerobic exercise, has people come from all over the world for fitness testing.

This particular week he had a very fit and very distinguished visitor—John Kelly, the 76-year-old wonder from Cape Cod, who has run the last 52 Boston Marathons. He was undergoing a series of tests that would culminate in a try for the Cooper clinic treadmill record for 70-and-overs.

That word *record* set my juices flowing. I had just turned 65 and was ready to do battle in that age category. "Would it be possible for me to try for the 65-and-over record?" I asked. Cooper immediately set an appointment for seven the next morning. The mark I had to shoot at, he told me, was 28:15—a time I associate with a race a little short of 5 miles.

Promptly at seven I went into action. I felt insecure at first because I was not allowed my prerace coffee. I felt an additional insecurity as the grade on the treadmill increased steadily, 1 percent a minute. This was to be a hill test and I am never at home on hills. During a race I invariably lose ground on hills. So I instantly felt at a disadvantage against the other runners who had taken the test.

Dr. Cooper was very helpful: "Walk as long as possible, it's more economical." It was true. I could walk at the 3.3-mile pace. I did not need to jog. If I did I found that I paid for it with a quickening of my pulse. Walking was the best way to handle the grade. It was just the way an old-timer told me years ago: "Walk the hills. You won't lose that much time."

By now, I was in the 17th minute and feeling the rising tide of lactic acid in my legs—a burning sensation. My breathing was also getting faster. If it were a race, I would have about a mile and a half to go. And in a race, I could console myself with the thought that I would never feel worse than I did now. But with this ever more demanding treadmill, I knew it was only going to get worse and worse.

At 22 minutes, Dr. Cooper informed me I had just passed the elite in the 50-and-over group. I gave a wave of my hand. "So long, guys," I said. A minute or so later, I left the elite 40-year-olds in my wake. Then, at 25 minutes, I forged ahead of the elite 30-and-over cohort. I was now up with the best, regardless of age.

But the end was approaching. It had become a matter of *when* I would crack, not *if* I would. I was on a course to utter exhaustion, to a state where I could not take one step more. The machine never loses.

It did not lose this time, either. My pulse was now beyond the predicted maximum. Every alarm system in my body was sounding. At 27 minutes, I could no longer maintain my speed by walking. I was forced to run. This was the beginning of the end.

I was using the kick I have at the end of races. It can be astonishingly swift but it is also very short in duration. For 30 seconds or so I can sprint as if the race had just begun, but that is it—collapse is seconds away.

Fifteen seconds away from the record, everything began to tighten up—my neck and chest, my arms and legs. But I knew nothing could stop me now. I had become pure willpower. My protesting body would just have to do it. Then I heard Cooper say, "Twenty-eight minutes 16 seconds, a new record."

Suddenly, I had nothing left. Whatever had propelled me that last minute was gone. I no longer felt that desperate need to go on. When Cooper asked me whether I could make it to 28:30, I nodded yes, but didn't do it. That was it, and I wrapped it up for the day.

Later, when I was told the 50-and-over record was 31:24, I wondered why I had been so foolish as to stop. With the passing of the pain and fatigue, it seemed it would have been easy to go another three minutes. But the truth is that I did what I came to do, and only that. I also know that someone—and it could well be me—will do better in the near future.

But not by much.

34

AGING, PART ONE

In a world without mirrors or the reflection from others' eyes, would I be old?

THE ME I ALWAYS WAS

"There are no specific sensations of old age," wrote E. M. Glasser, a retired physiologist, in the *British Medical Journal. "If you are well, you are just yourself, as you always have been."*

This thought came to him in a month during which he climbed to the top of Ben Nevis, Britain's highest mountain, hiked some of Scotland's most remote glens, spent hours in the saddle, and reached his 71st birthday.

A few years his junior, I have come to the same conclusion. One ages and is unaware of it. Changes in your appearance go unnoticed. I am, as far as I can tell, the same me I have always been. The body I take into the shower feels the same as it did a decade back. When I run or race, I am repeating experiences I had last year and the years before. I am as young as ever I was.

Only when I look in the mirror to shave am I aware of any change. What change I see then seems as much for the better as for the worse. This morning glimpse of me as others see me is quite soon forgotten. The ensuing hours are lived by a body I cannot distinguish from the one that years back took me to school, and later, on rounds at the hospital. Now it takes me with the same stride and energy to the newspaper office and the lecture hall.

I am in my body as it was and will be, yesterday and today and forever. I arise with a body that does my bidding. The hours pass as they always have. Tasks contemplated, tasks accomplished. Is age then only in the eye of the beholder? In a world without mirrors or the reflection from others' eyes, would I be old?

"I don't feel like an old man," some elder said. "I feel like a young man with something the matter with him." Not so with me: I feel like a healthy young man or, even better, an *ageless* man. My health and well-being and competency are never altered permanently or inevitably. They are within my control. I can allow myself to age, if that is the word, at any age. I can also become younger whenever I determine to do so.

Even when this aging or return to youth occurs, I remain in the same ageless state. What actually occurs is a change in energy. What is potential in me becomes actual. Regardless of chronology, this flux back and forth exists.

My autobiography, the book of life I am writing, is a record of the evolution of my inner and outer lives. Everything I now am has always been resident in me. Psychoanalyst Erik Erikson's eight stages of man are present at every stage, every virtue operating but one dominant. Every stage is simply the self with a slightly different focus.

This ageless me is no delusion. I am capable of feats of endurance I never accomplished in my early years. I could still develop my strength to a level it has never reached. I have resources in my body I have never used.

And now, in my sixties, I am *aware* of the unused capabilities resident in my body. I know full well that I have yet to reach my peak. I operate at a physical level others might consider extraordinary — but I don't. Dr. Glasser's life makes the point. He had been completely sedentary until his retirement eight years ago. His only exercise was little more than an occasional walk of one-half to two miles. Contrast this to his present activity — climbing mountains, hiking for miles. He is still, in his seventies discovering what his body can do.

Too often we see our bodies as beyond our control, obeying inexorable laws of decay. In one respect this is true: The body follows inexorable laws—*but not necessarily of decay.* There are also laws of growth and function, and they actually put *us* in control.

Aging may be inevitable, but if a person trains properly, the body is not even aware of this process. When a person follows the laws of the body, aging occurs so slowly that one must take quite precise measurements to demonstrate that changes have taken place.

Dr. Karl Spangler, for example, is an 82-year-old competitive runner who started running at 57. He wrote, "My life is so changed [by running] that I am miserable if I am not able to get my 5 to 10 miles in every day. My health has never been better. I have a new zest for living."

The word *health* comes from the same root as whole and healed. The body healthy is the body whole, the body healed. All these concepts apply to us regardless of age. The body I have, whatever length of time it has spent on earth, can still become healed and whole and healthy.

My best advice on this is to *listen* to your body. The body is its own best guide in training. It will tell you how much and how fast and how often. It will decide on smoking and diet, on alcohol and stress management. It will tell you when to push and when to coast, when to reach for a peak and when to survive in peace and quiet.

The body has a mind of its own. Mine is telling me (and Dr. Glasser's is telling him) that I am no particular age. I am an athlete capable of infinitely more activity than I ever suspected. The differences between the body I had in my thirties and forties and fifties and the one I have now may be detected through the use of sophisticated physiological tests. But it is *not* apparent to me in operation.

A great man in his seventies once said, "On any particular day I am as good as ever." He could still reach his peak, just not as often. I have had the same experience. I am the me I always was and perhaps better. I know I could rewrite my own athletic record book if I would only set to work. In that respect, I am truly the me I always have been—lazy and undisciplined. I need a marine drill instructor to make me get the most out of the marvelous body entrusted to my care.

AGE AND OUR ENVIRONMENT

I have been reading psychologist B. F. Skinner's strategies for managing old age. Dr. Skinner's previous concerns had been with the manipulation of human beings. His books had been on conditioning people in much the same way as laboratory animals are conditioned. Behavior, in his judgment, is controlled not by free will, but by positive and negative reinforcements of the environment and our culture.

Now, he was attempting to assert his own autonomy. By his own free will, he is trying to push back the "decay and rot" of old age. He still wants to think big thoughts and express them well.

"It is characteristic of old people," said Dr. Skinner, "not to think clearly, coherently, logically, or creatively." Even when he did, he reported, he was distressed to find that he was making the same point he had made in something published a long time ago.

One response to this difficulty is to dwell in the past. This is nonproductive and self-defeating. Ernest Hemingway put it succinctly: "Chasing yesterday is a bum show."

Dr. Skinner said the same. "I have been wallowing in reminiscences lately in my biography," he admitted. "The trouble is that it takes you backward. You begin to live your life in the wrong direction."

Another practice that will take us in the wrong direction is to seek out people and audiences that will flatter us. "If you are very successful," Dr. Skinner stated, "the most sententious stupidities will be received as pearls of wisdom and your standards will instantly fall."

Dr. Skinner's tactics for handling his own failing memory and intellectual powers were quite simple. Success, he said, lies in creating a stimulating environment and giving the brain plenty of rest between serious intellectual exertion. He works fewer hours and thus adjusts his mental efforts. He makes the necessary concessions to the tricks of his memory by jotting down thoughts as soon as they come to him.

To rest his brain further, he tried to use leisure time in a "relaxing" way. Many people, he noted, maintain their self-image by doing intellectually demanding tasks during their free time. Dr. Skinner suggested an alternative—that we try reading detective stories and watching sitcoms on TV.

Dr. Skinner believed that much of the depression and boredom of old age is due to the reduction in our five senses. I find this arguable. Nerve conduction is the last of the body's capabilities to diminish. Nevertheless, Dr. Skinner listed ways in which we can heighten these contacts with the world around us. He suggested that by increasing the stimulus, our senses will respond as they always have. Presumably, if we turn up the music, brighten the lights, spice up the food and so forth, our senses will respond.

These were the words of a sly old fox who has learned to live in a new part of the country. Dr. Skinner had used his enormous problem-solving powers to set up positive and negative reinforcements of his own behavior. He was the director of this project and its sole subject. He was, as all of us are, an experiment of one.

One need not be as old to be aware of the astuteness of Dr. Skinner's observations on himself. He was reporting on research we all must do, whatever our age. He was telling us that "a day in the life" is little different whatever your age. Whether age 28 or 48 or 78, Dr. Skinner's experience is also yours. Are you thinking clearly and coherently and creatively? Is that thought you just expressed something you said even better some months back? Is yesterday the topic of your conversation? Trivia the meat of your discourse? Nostalgia your game? Are you living your life backward?

Dr. Skinner, in condemning himself, was unrelenting on the rest of us, regardless of age. We seek audiences who agree with us. We surround ourselves with people who say "Yes, yes." We do not admit that we like common things. We may listen to obscure Italian composers, we may claim to adore opera and understand ballet. But we are reluctant to reveal our interest and delight in what is *popular.*

You do not need to be old to be bored and depressed. We do horrible things to our minds. And frankly, it is not age but the *self* that causes mental decay and rot. We live in ignorance of our energies and how to use them. If we are to outwit old age, we must learn to outwit youth and middle age as well. When you read this sly old fox, you will learn at least one thing. The hunter's horn sounds for *all* of us.

MENTAL MUSCLES

When British philosopher Bertrand Russell was in his eighties, he wrote the essay, "How To Grow Old." He began by denying the title. "This article will really be on how *not* to grow old," he wrote.

The proper recipe for remaining young, Russell thought, was to be so busy you never have time to notice that you are growing old.

A National Public Radio show, "I Can't Talk to You Now, I'm Too Busy," was a series of conversations with artists in a variety of fields who are over 70 years old.

The talks are marked by the intense absorption of these individuals in whatever their forms of expression. They have apparently avoided what Russell calls the two psychological dangers of growing old: First, undue absorption with the past, and second, clinging to young people in hopes of sucking vigor from their vitality.

"It does not do," wrote Russell, "to live in memories, in regrets for the good old days, or in sadness about friends who are dead."

The busy people are the young-old who direct their thoughts to the future, toward something to be done. Their message: We must always, young or old, be in pursuit of the grail. Life is the quest.

And in age as in youth, you must be ready to do it on your own. In age, there is the temptation to live in your children and grandchildren.

And it is true that for some, life would be empty without these concerns. Nevertheless, age is a time of achievement. A time to utilize the gifts of experience.

In age, you have the accumulated gifts of every other stage in life. You no longer have to go through the pain and effort of gaining them. Only on looking back does one realize how painful these acquisitions were. Knowing that pain, few people want to be younger than they are.

A Boston University psychologist discovered this in her life-span classes. Her students interviewed thousands of people and asked them what age they considered the prime of their lives. Not one person they talked to wanted to be a teenager. Only a few wanted to be in their twenties. Psychologists tell us the thirties and forties are the ages of greatest stress for breadwinners and homemakers. People, it seems, are into their sixties before they begin to live creative lives of their own making. Prior to that, they are generally employed at what is obligatory. Now they are free, free to do something with the person they have made.

I recall a story of when Supreme Court Justice Oliver Wendell Holmes, then in his nineties, was out walking with a friend and passed an attractive woman. Holmes turned to his friend and said, "Oh, to be 80 again." I think that being ten years younger is the maximum anyone would want. The thought of repeating more of that daily travail of trial and error is just too much.

Age in many ways is a reward for the ceaseless exploration that preceded it. Few of us are inclined to give up the possession of the completed person that results. Better to look ahead than repeat the errors of the past, to have to relive all that anxiety and guilt. Spanish thinker José Ortega y Gasset is said to have gone through life saying, "This is not it, this is not it." For such a person, today is the only chance to get it right.

How best not to grow old? Do something with the person the past decades have molded. There are cycles of creativity. Studies of 70 thinkers have identified at least two cycles, the first occurring at 38 years, the second in the early sixties. A later resurgence is also evident. Examples are evident all around. Extraordinary old people abound: Picasso, Chagall, Buckminster Fuller, Grandma Moses, perhaps one's own grandparents. There is always an elderly family member or neighbor whose physical or mental or social performance puts you to shame.

Not that age is all positive. Poet Archibald MacLeish, who found the sixties a marvelous experience and expected no less from his seventies, had his negative thoughts. The elderly may be in the prime of life in experience and judgment, but the poets still make hymns to youth. And there's some truth to their elegy-making. I may know more about life and with a depth no younger person can know, but I have lost forever some of the experiences that gave me that knowledge.

Ralph Waldo Emerson had a suggestion for those depressed by the apparent loss of the joys of youth. "A walk is one of the secrets for dodging old age," he wrote. "I recommend it to people who are growing old against their will. The forest awakes the same feeling it did when I was a boy. *It is the old trees who have all the beauty and grandeur.*"

BRAIN SWEAT

When Eric Hoffer was 70, he began a journal. Hoffer was alarmed by what he perceived as loss in his mental functions. So he decided to make a daily entry of his thoughts on the human situation.

Six months later, he decided his fears about his ability to reason and to remember were unfounded. His recorded observations were up to the standards he had always set for himself. Age had not diminished his powers of observation or his ability to express the conclusions he drew from them.

I suspect one significant reason for his maintainance of the usual Hoffer performance was the exercise the journal provided. The mind is not different from the body. It requires daily training. Only through regular use will it continue to function well. Just as the body maintains its power and endurance and agility through regular exercise, so does the mind.

Mental fitness, like physical fitness, encompasses diverse capabilities of the mind: memory, creativity, reasoning, observation. Studies suggest that losses vary in individuals. Men may have more problems with vocabulary, women with problem solving. But all of us can fight back, if we plan our days so that our minds are put through their paces the same way we train our bodies.

We are told of any number of old people who produced works of genius at an advanced age. On inspection, they prove to be people who attended to the care and feeding of their minds. They developed the muscles of their brains.

"As long ago as 1911," wrote a psychologist in the *New York Times,* "Santiago Ramón y Cajal, a pioneering neurobiologist, proposed that cerebral exercise could benefit the brain." The psychologist was discussing a recent report that the development and the growth of the brain go on into old age. Experiments on elderly rats put in an enriched environment showed that their brain cells increased in size and activity.

What Cajal proposed was, of course, not new. Read Cicero or Seneca on old age and you will see that. The Greeks held to the holistic concept of the body/mind machine. Each must be trained, each requires exercise. Age is held at bay, and even conquered, by remaining active. What it requires is maintenance—the daily renewal of our powers, the regular use of our mental faculties.

We need a gymnasium for our *minds* as well as our bodies. Our first duty, as Thoreau has said, is to make to ourselves perfect bodies. But our second is to make fit minds.

The untrained brain might be said to be tireless. And in one sense, the body is, too. Both can operate in the low (untrained) gear indefinitely. But the sedentary body is limited. It lacks strength and stamina and speed. And so it is with the mind. Tireless it may be, but productive it's not. Unexercised, creativity ebbs away. And the less time we spend in our mental gymnasiums, the more we lose in mental function.

Unquestionably there is a loss in brain function with age. I don't have the rapid recall I had when I was younger. But I am not running races at the same speed either. Still, the word finally comes, and the race does come to an end. Except for speed, the quality of my thinking and the quality of my running remain the same. I share with the runners up front an experience that has no qualitative difference. So, too, with thinking, remembering, imagining. What I do, however longer it takes, is a match for what others do.

And for much the same reason, I remain competitive in running because I train my body as I always have trained it. By doing so, I have slowed the toll taken by time. I train my mind in the same way. Daily I demand performance. My brain is not a passive instrument any more than my body. My brain must wrestle and run, must climb and strain, must stretch and dance.

"The legs go first," the old baseball players used to say. The reasons the legs went was that those old-style athletes let them go. Now there are 70-year-old marathon runners whose legs will get them to the finish line faster than runners 40 years younger. "Use it or lose it" applies to everyone's bodies whatever the age, and the brain follows exactly the same rules. "The memory goes first," say our children. But it need not. "I never knew an old man," wrote Cicero, "who forgot where he hid his money."

The body's most important quality is endurance, but the brain's is attention. Hoffer's concern was just that awareness. Some loss of attention is natural. Things don't seem as important as when we are young.

Why bother noticing them? For just that reason: Realizing their unimportance makes us aware of just how funny life is. From the vantage of age, one can observe all the high comedy going on around us. "Life is so funny now," said an aged colleague of mine, "that I rarely stop laughing at what's going on."

Attention can also bring us moments of joy when we suddenly see meaning and happiness in what we are and do in life. But attention comes only to those who work at it, those who daily practice their skills, keep in touch with themselves and their functions. Chance, they say, favors the prepared mind. It also favors the trained mind. Whatever your age, when your brain is in trim, you are prepared for a great thought or a moment of illumination that can make your day and— when it becomes a regular experience—can make your life.

THE FINAL BATTLE

"I can't remember names," said psychologist Rollo May, "I can't run as fast, and my joints are stiffer. But I can call up my experiences, and I have the wisdom that leaves the details out and goes right to the point."

May's answer to those who view aging in a bad light is to be creative. "Think new thoughts," he advised.

Remaining fresh, continuing to be creative—these options are always available to us whatever our age. We can have a rebirth, a resurrection, no matter how old we are in years. We must, however, accept responsibility for our lives, for our health. We must realize that living is an art, and life is an achievement. It is *not* a gift or a possession, it is our final battle.

How can one think then that aging is a period to retire from life? It is quite the reverse. When all else are saying, "You have earned this rest," we are filled with divine discontent. We have earned our spurs, we are warriors to reckon with. Yet friends and family would have us seek rest and recreation. They would muster us out of the ranks of the militants and cause us to become *spectators*.

There is a case for being relieved of the daily combat of making a living, but not from the daily combat of making a self. The war outside may be ended, but the war inside will never be. This is a battle to the death, and for all we know, beyond as well. The major campaigns in our lives are not over. In all probability we have yet to face them. What has gone before now provides the experience, the insight, the creativity, the endurance—and the courage—to fight this final duel with death.

At the age of 60, British author John Powys wrote in his autobiography, "My life's about to begin." He had the superior education of the upper-class Englishman. He could write at length on society, in all its aspects, social, political and literary. But at the age of 60, the object of his life became a search for personal meaning.

Sculptor Eric Gill in his autobiography spoke on the same subject. Of his book he said, "It's more concerned with meaning than events." And ultimately, that is what we want to know about other people's lives. Not the facts, not what he or she accomplished, but what they *learned* about life—the hard-bought kernels of truth that come with the passage of years.

I believe with seventeenth century English poet John Dryden that "none would live past years again." But not for his reasons—that life is a cheat that promised us joys and pleasures that never came. For me the past was pleasant and at times joyful. But today and tomorrow hold the opportunity to be better and become more. I would not relive the past because it was simply the beginning of the process—still ongoing—of molding and making a self.

I am no different from Rollo May. I can't remember names. I can't run as fast. My joints are stiffer. But if I cannot stay young, I can stay fresh. If I cannot get younger, I can get better. Age brings problems; it also brings solutions. For every disadvantage there is an advantage. For every measurable loss there is an immeasurable gain.

And that is *my* new thought for this new day.

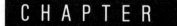

CHAPTER

35

AGING, PART TWO: MEDICINE AND MEDITATIONS

W*e should not accept the generosity of medical advisors who allow us to weigh more and have a higher cholesterol because we are too old for it to matter. It* always *matters.*

THE MEDICAL MENACE

The elderly Polish woman lying in her hospital bed was telling me her story. The broken hip had become the least of her problems. If they would only let her go home with a walker she could handle that. She could get active again. But now, except for a brief trip to therapy each day, she was confined to bed.

She could feel her energy ebbing away. She was on seven different types of pills. Her appetite was gone. She was no longer in control of her activities, her day, or her life. Her only salvation would be escape from the health-care system designed to save her.

Fortunately, a broken hip does not require a lengthy stay in the hospital. Most patients do escape. Then, back at home, they can return to an independent and *healthy* existence. Other patients who end up in hospitals and nursing homes are not always as fortunate: The care of the elderly is not something every doctor does well.

The difficulty begins right at the beginning of their careers as medical students and then later, as interns. The budding physician knows that old patients are the worst. Treating the chronically sick elderly patient is a no-win undertaking. "They think of them," says one doctor trained in the care of the elderly, "as hypochondriacal, foolish, demented, incontinent, unreasonable, pains in the neck."

If they are *not* all of these, the treatment given the elderly frequently will bring about such conditions. Medications can easily cause psychological changes in older people. They can also result in the spectrum of side effects listed after almost every drug in the pharmacopoeia — side effects the average doctor responds to by ordering up additional drugs, which cause additional side effects. The patient becomes agitated, is put in restraint, and, finally, diagnosed as a victim of senile dementia.

The alternative to this tragic sequence is rehabilitation. The elderly must be approached with a positive attitude. Everyone should be assumed to be capable of independent living. "In geriatrics," said the director of the Jewish Institute of Geriatric Care in Long Island, "the general rule is that improvement in function is everything."

We live to the extent that we function. The woman with the broken hip knew that, even if her doctors seemed unaware of it. Perhaps they assumed that such function would follow automatically after the hip pinning and the appropriate drugs for her medical condition. It never does. Function comes from movement, and it follows training. It is the result of a lifestyle that includes daily exercise, a diet the body responds to, and *avoidance* of as many drugs as possible.

This should be the rule for everyone, regardless of age. This simple nonpharmacological therapy should be the first resort. Nothing good is going to happen to a patient in bed. People know that. My barber, who had a hernia repaired, told me of his own efforts to get moving. The nurses kept ordering him back to bed. But on the fifth day, he'd had enough. He asked his doctor for a release so that he could go home and get well.

USE IT OR LOSE IT

How old I look is important to me. Physicians, however, are primarily concerned with my biological age. How old are my arteries? What is the age of my kidneys? Is my heart becoming senile? Those are questions that run through a doctor's mind when faced with a patient who looks older than would be expected. In my practice, I saw numbers of people who had lifestyles that accelerated their biological aging. Our probable optimal life span is a little over 100 years—some say 120. But we begin quite early in life to diminish our longevity and ultimately settle for much less.

Part of this loss is due to our gene pool. Some people come from short-lived stock susceptible to the major killers: heart disease, diabetes, and cancer. Some have body types that are vulnerable to diseases of the arteries and high blood pressure. These people have to be *very* diligent if they are to maintain their normal biological age.

But we also have a physiological age, an age that is measured by our physical fitness, and on this scale the average American is *30 years older functionally* than he or she is in actual years. The sedentary 30-year-old, in other words, is actually *60* years old in endurance and stamina. A trained 60-year-old and an inactive 30-year-old will have equal physical work capacity.

At one time physiologists thought people aged functionally from 10 to 15 percent a decade. The new reality: This is *far* from the truth. Fit individuals show about 5 percent loss in endurance per decade. The world's record at the age of 40 in distance races is within 5 percent of the actual world's record. At 50 it is within 10 percent. At 60 is it close to 15 percent—clear evidence that apparent aging is due more to inactivity than loss of work capacity.

How old would you be if you didn't know how old you are? The unfortunate truth is that the average American would be much older than he or she actually is. It's accepted as normal to look, perform, and have the arteries of a person 20 to 30 years older. A truly normal individual seems younger than she or he is.

Yet, we are all capable of staying young—we can all hold the aging process at bay. We have 85-year-old ballerinas who *prove* we can remain lithe and supple.

We should not accept the generosity of medical advisors who allow us to weigh more and have a higher cholesterol because we are too old for it to matter. It *always* matters. The noted physician Paul Dudley White said we should not gain a pound after 25. And, I would add, we shouldn't gain a milligram of blood cholesterol, either.

The way to do it? Start *doing*. Forget whatever ravages age has done to your body and simply put it into action. In use, the body grows young. And over time we can regain the physiological losses we have incurred by sitting around on our duffs. "Life is motion," said Aristotle. To restore life to your life, to defeat aging, to regain the youth you still possess, you must get your body in motion.

There you have it. A prescription to make your chronological and biological and physiological ages coincide. But one note of caution: When that occurs you may find other people your age now view you as an oddity.

"Why don't you act your age?" they will ask. And you can reply, "I am."

THE AGING GAME

To play the aging game well, there are certain imperatives. Fitness is one of them. Consider the alternative. The unfit youth or young adult or even middle-aged person can still be independent and enjoy life. The aging cannot. The normal loss of physical powers that occurs with inactivity makes fitness a *necessity.*

A study published in the *New England Journal of Medicine* makes just *how* necessary crystal-clear. This report on "active life expectancies" forecasts how many years individuals 65 years of age and over will remain functional. Function was defined as the ability to handle the activities of daily life.

When I was 65, my average life expectancy was 13.4 years, but the average *active* life expectancy was only 9.3 years. Translation: If my life took the average course for a man my age, I could expect to spend almost 40 percent of my remaining years in a dependency state. I will need someone to take care of me. A woman my age has a longer life expectancy, it's true—17.5 years—but her active life expectancy is only a little lengthier than mine—10.6 years. Almost 50 percent of the rest of her life will require the services of other people.

I find these figures personally alarming and generally appalling. Clearly what is needed is a concerted program of exercise and activity for the aging and aged. We need to be prodded and pushed and forced into movement. People are killing us with kindness when they allow us to take it easy and not do for ourselves.

We are being groomed for a prolonged senescence. Great efforts are being made to keep us alive—but little or none to encourage us to *live.* Fitness is a human right. No one should be deprived of it.

The best way to play the aging game is to concede nothing. Never make it easy for yourself. Should your body suggest it is too old for this effort, say "Nonsense!" Should your mind decide it is too late to learn new tricks, say "Balderdash!" Should your soul say it needs a respite from duty and obligation, say "Rubbish!"

In time, regardless of how we play, we will all depart. What we must avoid is to have our actual leaving precede that departure—to die in *effect* before we die in truth, to live out our years in joyless, dependent existence, our body and mind and soul already waiting for us on the other side of the divide.

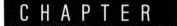

AGING, PART THREE: A MASTER'S TALE

M*ourn with me for my lost youth. . . . Help me bury the runner I once was, and then we can talk about what the future holds.*

SEPTEMBER SOLILOQUY

The baseball season is a series of individual baseball games, one just as important as the other. A loss in April shows up in the standings the same as a loss in September. The statistics make no distinction between a win in May or one in the final weeks of the season. A base hit is a base hit, a double play is a double play, a shutout is a shutout, no matter when they happen. When you look at the record all you will see are the cold facts. Winning the pennant, playing in a World Series, getting out of the cellar, whatever the outcome, depends on a final reckoning that includes everything from the time some public figure throws out the first ball.

That is logic. But it is *not* baseball. Baseball, maybe, is a spring game. It is surely a summer game. But mostly, it is a September game: It's *when* you play that counts.

An error in the newborn season is quickly forgotten, but one in the last weeks is remembered for a player's career. A timely base hit, a marvelous catch, a shutout, all take their significance from the months in which they occur. The September game demands the very best. It allows for no excuse, it provides no opportunity for redemption.

The September game is no game for rookies. The spring is for the young, but when the shadows lengthen and the leaves change and everywhere there are hints that time is running out, when the import of everything that is done is raised to epic proportions—it is time for the veterans, the older men in the league, tempered by time and season after season.

And as it is with baseball, so it is with life. The best of baseball is played in September, the best of life comes in life's September. And no more than baseball is *life* a game for rookies. Life is played best by a veteran, understood best by the master. Life is the supreme aging game.

Some may not agree with this analogy. They have difficulty seeing the 50- and 60- and 70-year-olds around them as being in the equivalent of a pennant race, or playing for great stakes. They agree that life gets more and more challenging, but *not* into those advanced years. Life is over at the ages they view as *elderly.*

I'm here to report from the land of the 60-year-olds: The World Series and the Super Bowl and Masters still exist. The seventh game and the two-minute warning and the seventy-second hole have their counterparts in every waking day. The excitement and tension and rewards of life are raised to the nth degree, the player and the game finally and forever engaged.

In September, the baseball player has become what May and June and July taught him to be. He knows things that were a mystery when the season began. He has developed a concentration that was absent earlier in the season, and he no longer has time for nonessentials. The game has become all.

Life is no different. In the September of my life I am all that the past has taught me. I know things that were a mystery before. Every year has become an asset, every experience a treasure. I am no longer a rookie, no longer a neophyte. And I no longer look to veterans for guidance—I *am* a veteran, a master at my own game.

LESSONS OF THE LONG MILE

I first came upon age in the race.

I felt no sense of advancing years in my day-to-day activity. My work week was unchanged: I wrote, I traveled, I lectured. Some people marveled at my energy and endurance. It was my weekend race that finally told me I was no longer young.

The changes that come with age are subtle—but not to a runner. My 10-kilometer time measures me quite accurately. Any change in performance dictated by age is precisely recorded in minutes or seconds on the digital clock at the finish line.

"Crumbling's not an instant act," wrote poet Emily Dickinson. And the physician in me knows that almost 90 percent of my liver has to be damaged before its impairment is apparent. The body has enormous reserves to call upon. But in the race, I call on *all* my reserves. I am operating at full throttle. The least diminution in function becomes evident.

The race, therefore, is the litmus test for aging. Long before anything else goes, race times signal the approach of the last stage of life. Any look at my weekly race results will tell you bluntly that I am no longer middle-aged. I am now a full-blown citizen of the country of the aged.

Some three years ago when this happened, I refused to believe it. Running had been my fountain of youth. For years I thought it was inexhaustible, like the never-empty cup of coffee some restaurants offer. After I began running in my forties, I quickly became 32 years old and stayed that way. Decades came and went and I was still in my prime.

When my 10-kilometer times slowed down and I began to run personal worsts instead of personal bests, I took stock. It was not age, I told myself. I had been 32 years of age for the previous 20 years and did not intend to get older. All I needed was more training, some hills and speed work, and I would be back to my best.

I took up arms against age. I increased my training and within a single Thanksgiving holiday ran four races. Each race I ran a little faster than the previous one but never near the times I had registered just a year before. And I was no longer in the top third of the field— now, I was well back in the last half of the pack.

How did I feel about all this? Terrible. And don't remind me that most people my age have run up the white flag. Do not tell me I can still outrun the average person 20 years younger than me. Do not point out that age has compensations that will more than pay for the lost few minutes in the race. I am rebuilding my life on those thoughts. But first, mourn with me for my lost youth. Attend the wake for the death of the abilities I once had and will never have again. Help me bury the runner I once was, and then we can talk about what the future holds.

Apparently, it still holds plenty. My initial depression has receded.

I realize now there are more things at stake then setting a personal best in a road race. I can even answer truthfully (and this is the most difficult part) when someone asks me, "What time did you do, Doc?"

My times continue to get slower and slower. And, therefore, the "me" that I am is different. But the me that I am has developed insights and wisdom I did not have before. What I have lost I can afford to lose. What I have gained is something I cannot do without.

The race, however slow my times, remains an everchanging learning experience. Whenever I race I learn something new about myself and those who race with me. I will never be 32 years old again, but it no longer matters because I've learned that winning doesn't matter, it's *running* that counts. And when I push to the limit, I am a boy again—an untried youth listening to the wisdom of my body.

WE'RE ALL EQUAL HERE

Age has caught up with me. Time's winged chariot is leaving me in its wake. When I race these days, I am not a patch on what I was a few short years ago.

This past summer I ran in the Asbury Park Classic, a 10-kilometer event. I came to the halfway mark in just under 25 minutes, almost a minute a mile slower than last year's time. In fact, I was running at last year's training pace.

I was asked about this in a runner's clinic. "How does it feel to be setting personal worsts every time you run?" My answer then was "Embarrassing." It also can be annoying when people in the trailing edge of a race pack ask me, "What are you doing back here, Doc?" My first impulse is to say something about what can a runner on drugs for cancer expect.

The truth is, I expect a great deal more. But as we all know, there are no bad experiences. Running back in the pack at Asbury Park was enlightening and inspiring. I had always *written* as a representative of the also-rans but, in truth, I was always an elite runner—one of the winners. I rarely came home from a race without a trophy and more often than not was a winner in my age group.

When I ran in my prime, everyone around me was at flank speed. Everyone had the throttle down as far as they could handle. If I beat anyone, it was because they had nothing left. What I discovered at Asbury Park was that this is *universal* in a race: From leader to last man, the runners are running at the fastest pace they can.

The eight-minute milers, for example, were taking no prisoners.

They were not—as I once suspected—lollygagging along, engaged in conversation about last night's pasta party. They may not have the maximum oxygen capacity of those averaging two and even three minutes a mile faster, but it was costing them the same effort. They were paying with an equal amount of pain. And for me, gaining in this flow was just as difficult as it had been a year or so back at a much faster pace.

Running back of the pack was an experience that affirmed that all runners are indeed equal—only their times are different. Talent may separate us in a race, but I like to remind myself and my running friends once more of what William James said: "Effort is the measure of a man." The eight-minute-mile club passes that test. And so will the ten-minute-mile club when I join it.

THE RACE

No matter how old I get, the race remains one of life's most rewarding experiences. In a race, age changes only place and time. I see my placings get higher and higher, my times become slower and slower. But the experience of the race is unchanged: Each race a drama, each race a challenge, each race stretching me in one way or another. And each race telling me more about myself and others.

In yesterday's race, it was a matter of fine-tuning my form, getting the most of what I had. I kept at the edge of what was possible, always trying to go with anyone who passed me—and always keying on an older runner some 25 yards ahead whom I knew to be in my age group. I suspected he was the leader in our bunch but I couldn't be sure.

It didn't matter. If there was someone to beat up ahead I would have to catch him first anyway, and as mile after mile went by, I couldn't do it. Occasionally he would put on a spurt and get even farther ahead. Then on the hills I would reel him back in. So it went. Sometimes he was 100 yards ahead, but never less than 30—until we went into the last mile.

When he made the turn into the loop for the final mile, I began counting. I reached the turn 15 seconds later. A lot to make up in a mile. And for half of that distance, there was no change. I had to make a move and I did. I picked up the pace and began closing on him. It was too fast to hold for any length of time, but I had to get close before the last 100 yards of the race if I were to have *any* chance at all.

But as I pushed to catch him, I had this wish that I wouldn't. I was hurting that bad, I could not *imagine* how bad it would be if I drew even with him. Then it would be a battle to the death. Nevertheless, want to or not, I gained on him until I was on his shoulder.

There was still a quarter-mile to go, much too far for a move, but I had to find out. I inched past him. It turned out to be a bad move. He put on a spurt that sent him 15 yards in front. The race was apparently in his hands. But I hung on, and again got back to him. This time I waited until I could see the last turn, and a hundred yards beyond that, the finish line.

This time I didn't inch past, I pulled the trigger. I was running better and faster than I had the entire race. I blew past him and he had no response. I rounded the turn and saw the crowd ahead. Now I was paying for the effort. My chest was burning, my legs were getting heavy, I couldn't get enough air, I was losing my form. I took a look over my left shoulder. He was a good 15 yards back, but I was slowing perceptibly. It was all I could do to get to the finish line. I had absolutely nothing left—but I got there first.

At the end of the chute I turned and shook his hand. "Great race," I said. "Good job," he said in reply. It was a meeting that happened to any number of runners that day in that race. It mattered little that we were 83d and 84th. Whether you finish in the top ten or the middle or bring up the rear, whether you are 20 or 40 or 60, whether you are male or female, a race is a race is a race. Time and place are incidental.

DEATH AND DYING: THE FINAL COMBAT

Death *makes the everyday magical, the ordinary unique, and the commonplace one-of-a-kind.*

A DEADLY DRAMA

In one hour I will know whether the nodule in my prostate is benign or malignant. In another 60 minutes, the urologist who did the biopsy will be calling on the phone with the result. In a very brief time my future will be decided.

This drama began only a week ago. I was in Dallas to give a talk at a fitness festival. The day before, I went over to challenge Dr. Ken Cooper's treadmill at the Cooper Institute for Aerobic Research. I had set a record for my age group the year before and someone had come along and broken it. I was of a mind to get it back. I did, and by a large margin. Afterward, as I lay on the table recovering, I felt as if I were joining the immortals: Despite my age, I had performed in the 99th percentile of the 70,000 treadmill tests done at Cooper Institute for Aerobic Research.

But then Dr. Cooper told me he was going to do a physical examination of me. Before I could protest, I was stripped down in his examining room and subjected to everything ordinary people go through when they go to a doctor. And that was when he discovered the suspicious area in my prostate. The news was paralyzing: I had just joined the immortals when suddenly I was made aware of my mortality.

It hardly seemed possible that only a week ago I had been fretting and worrying about the normal vicissitudes of life. My running, for one: My times had deteriorated over the past year. I was running a minute slower than usual in 5-mile races—running 6:20 miles instead of 6:10s. I had rarely thought of my aging before, but now I was becoming preoccupied with it. I had finally reached a point where no amount of training made me improve.

The worst part was that aging as a runner meant aging as a person. I live in social circles that are one and two generations younger than I am. I had never felt that difference to any great extent, and neither had they. But lately, I'd become resigned to being no longer a contemporary in body or even in mind. I had become a bore, and I'd found that I was even boring myself.

My writing was proof. Many times before, I had thought that I was written out. This time it was really true. When I took on a new subject I almost uniformly found that I had done it *before*, and better. I started writing years ago with the pledge—for years, easily kept—never to repeat myself. The phrases would leap onto the typewritten page. Now, none appeared that did not land with a thud and then lie there lifeless. I could no longer come up with a sentence that made me laugh or cry.

But all these defeats I had also known in the past. One loses loves at 50. One ages at 55. One has writer's block at 60. The cycles come and go. One finds another love. One recaptures one's youth. One writes an absolute best-seller as age continues.

I know all this and fret still. I look for causes of rhythms that are as natural and fundamental as the seasons—and just as unchangeable. I should make up my mind not to complain about those rhythms but to enjoy them. The best of all know the worst of times—and then use those experiences when the bright, beautiful, and productive days return.

The big question: How should one live one's life? Basque philosopher Miguel de Unamuno y Jugo had this answer: "Our greatest endeavor must be to make ourselves irreplaceable—to make the fact that each one of us is unique and irreplaceable, that no one can fill the gap when we die—a practical truth."

In the past week, I learned that I have done that. If not always as well as I could, I still have made that fact a practical truth—I will be irreplaceable, I will leave a gap. Each day, family and friends have affirmed my importance to them.

But I also learned the corollary of that truth. There are people in my life who are irreplaceable. No one can fill the gap when they are gone. And I know now who they are. When you are between the sword and the stone, you know whom you want standing beside you. When time becomes short, those who are essential to your life become obvious.

That is what I will take away from this experience, even before I hear the result of the biopsy. My future has been decided: Whether this nodule turns out to be benign or malignant, my life has been unalterably changed. The lesson: I've made every day count. But what I have *not* done is make every person count.

HIDDEN BLESSINGS

In many ways, cancer is a blessing. You see life as a gift, and every day becomes precious—and that's a lesson you never forget.

Paul Tsongas, for example, quit the U.S. Senate when he found he had cancer. He has now apparently been cured of it. But Tsongas said he prefers not to think of being cured.

"The problem with the notion of cure is that I don't want to go back to the assumption of immortality," he said. "I think I am better served by being aware of life's fragility than going back to the assumption that we are all going to live forever."

Most of us do assume exactly that, however—that we're going to live forever. I know I did. Like writer William Saroyan, I knew that everyone must die but an exception would be be made in my case. Death may have been a fact of life, but not in my life. It simply did not concern me.

Except on Ash Wednesday, and while attending funerals, I have never thought much on death. Now, however, every day is Ash Wednesday. I am constantly reminded that I am dust and unto dust I will inevitably return.

Death will not take me unawares. I expect now to be cut down in my prime, doing well at what I do best. Cancer has put urgency into my life. I, still unworthy, am about to return to my Creator. And I am learning something critically important about the human condition: No one, no matter their age, should *ever* retire from life.

We must be forever *enlarging* our lives, not diminishing them. "Sin is closing the circle," wrote a contemporary theologian. Once we exclude anything or anybody we cease to grow. We join forces with sin and age and death.

Emerson made this the theme of one of his greatest essays, "Circles." He invited us to see that only by ever enlarging our circles of life and endeavor do we progress toward the perfection that always seems beyond our reach.

When we cease to do that, we age—and we age irrespective of our years. Conversely, we grow younger as we aspire to be more and more.

All around him, Emerson saw forms of old age—rest, conservatism, inertia. "We grizzle every day and I see no need of it." He urged us to live as when we were filled with zeal, fired with enthusiasm, always going beyond what we have already thought or done.

Now that death has entered the picture, I am no longer in danger of grizzling. Death makes the everyday magical, the ordinary unique, and the commonplace one-of-a-kind. And all this is done without introducing anxiety. Once I accept death, I center on the present. I concentrate on this new day, this—in Emerson's words—"everlasting miracle" I am presented with each dawn.

Living has now become a matter of life and death. The imperative? Meaning. To have a death worth dying, you must have a life worth living. And that can only be done by giving meaning to our lives.

According to another thinker, the real cause of our anxieties and depression, our inability to be happy and feel joy, is a life that lacks meaning.

Each day for me is now a separate life. I arise, take my morning swim, and prepare for battle. The cancer is always at the gates. "I feel like Israel," said Tsongas. "I *have* to win every war."

There is no sense now in faking anything. When I was in the Navy I did that. I always carried papers so it would appear that I was working on something. Now I truly am, and that something is me. Because I now have cancer and can see death plain, I have begun to live. And when the big sleep comes, I'll sleep—but not a minute before.

TO STRIVE AND NOT TO YIELD

When I learned I had inoperable cancer of the prostate—inoperable because it had spread to the bones—I went through a familiar sequence: Panic, then denial, and finally depression. I lay awake nights thinking of this alien eating up my body. I stopped scheduling talks. I began to live with death.

But in time I realized that this was not the end. If one is lucky—and I was lucky—prostatic cancer is testosterone-dependent. Remove this male hormone from the body and the tumor stops growing—even regresses. In time, cancer cells that do not need the hormone for growth will take over. But that can be far down the road—several years, perhaps, or maybe even a decade.

I was one of the lucky ones. Offered the choice of castration, female hormones, or a daily injection of hypothalamic hormone GhRH, I chose the last—and it worked. In fact, it was almost miraculous. The pain disappeared, the bone scan improved, and serial tests for prostatic specific antigen—proteins the body manufactures in response to prostate cancer—showed only a negligible amount of cancer tissue in my body. Still I remain apprehensive. If there is one guarantee on any form of castration, it is that the cancer will eventually break through. The enemy within will win the war.

I also had to worry about the other life-limiting conditions that come with my age. Some, perhaps with more immediate consequences. "People with prostate cancer," said my son, the endocrinologist, "usually die of something else."

There is good reason for people with prostatic cancer to die of another disease. Their average age is 67 years old. And the average 67-year-old is unfit, and carrying around all sorts of other risk factors for heart disease and stroke—cigarettes, for example, or too much weight. Many have already incurred life-threatening disease. So considerable numbers succumb to heart attacks, strokes, and pulmonary diseases.

But I remembered something basketball player-turned-politician Bill Bradley said about his attitude when training for basketball: "I might lose because I wasn't tall enough, I might lose because I wasn't fast enough. But I wasn't going to lose because I wasn't ready." I decided then and there: I might die of prostate cancer but I was certainly not going to die of anything else.

I chose the Bradley approach: Become an athlete, develop all the functions my body possesses, and let the cancer look for help elsewhere. So I went about the business of making myself the best body possible. I wasn't going to die because I wasn't ready, and what I could control, I would control.

I also chose to ignore most of the modern medical community—those doctors who allow elders like myself to have higher cholesterols, more body fat, and high blood pressure.

At what they consider my advanced age, health-care professionals ease up on restrictions—especially for cancer patients. They justify it on a lost-cause basis; why worry when the patient's going to die anyway? Enjoy what's left of life is the attitude.

"I prepare my patients for death," one oncologist told me. As if I would enjoy it more and be better prepared if I suddenly discarded my athletic life—stopped running, gained 15 pounds, drank myself into oblivion every night, and took up smoking cigarettes. Is that the way my life should end?

I admit, there is some temptation toward complete self-indulgence. But true self-indulgence is the reverse. The athletic life is the good life. Becoming the best you can be makes you feel the best you can feel. And from that renewed body comes a renewed attitude that would satisfy the most ardent proponent of mind over matter—important when you're battling an opponent like cancer.

My daily injections have not given me a reprieve: My cancer has not been cured. In other cases, radiation or surgery or chemotherapy may eradicate the tumor, in which case the person is returned to the land of the living. But I am still under sentence. I have been given a stay of execution. Time to set things right—I was about to say, get things right, which is part of it, too—and achieve what I was sent here to do.

FINAL PAGES

Last week the *British Medical Journal* ran a short notice urging their readers to submit self-written obituaries. Please include, the *Journal* suggested, accomplishments that might otherwise go unnoticed. The editors were dissatisfied with the literary and personal level of the current crop of death notices. They were incomplete, quickly thrown together, and frequently missed the import of the deceased's life.

This is a capital idea. The obituaries will undoubtedly improve, but more than that, so will the lives of those who wrote them. Such an obituary would be autobiographical—and, done with zest and candor, autobiography is the best form of writing.

Obituaries can take various forms. Montaigne's essays, Thoreau's journals, Pascal's *Pensées*—all are obituaries. They are an individual's attempt to present his thoughts, words, and deeds in some coherent form. The best model of all might be Greek writer Nikos Kazantzakis's *Report to Greco*, written when the author's death was quite clearly on the horizon.

What might begin as a few paragraphs for the *British Medical Journal* could become the bright book of our lives, an ongoing record of our search for meaning—a mixture of the quite ordinary events of our days with those quite extraordinary occurrences that illuminate our inner landscapes like a lightning bolt.

And writing one's obituary will inevitably lead to a more lengthy exploration of one's reason for being. Journals will be started, diaries begun. Daily examinations of the self will lead to essays and novels and collections of aphorisms.

But most of all, tackling our own obituary will teach a person that he can *write*. The self-written obituary allows us to write about what is the most interesting thing in our lives—us. And through it, we can tell how we became the artists and heroes and saints that we are. And if we're not, it will alert us while there's still time to get our act together for the triumphant finale.

The auto-obituary is a ready remedy for the unexamined life. Writing one's death notice could lead to some very profitable soul searching. This seal of the life finished could become a chance to start life anew: I am here for a purpose. Have I fulfilled it? I was to deliver a message. Have I delivered it? I was to bear a particular fruit. Has that harvest occurred?

Each day is a separate life, said one of the great Stoics. And each evening a time to review it, said the great Greek philosopher and mathematician Pythagoras. There is the stuff of obituary—the events of daily life that, written down in a journal, describe the evolution of you. And always, emphasizing not *what* was done but *why*.

The usual obituary does quite the opposite. It tells us *what* a person did, not why. But the good obituary is short on deeds and long on motivation. The object is to learn from the deceased, not to praise them.

More than anything else, authoring my own obit gives me a chance to follow the philosopher Søren Kierkegaard's advice to be objective about yourself and *subjective* with others. What was the worst mistake I made? My greatest achievement? Was I a success or failure? Really—who could answer these questions but me and my Creator? And in my own obit, I'm finally free from the necessity of apologizing for myself. Let someone else do it if they feel the need. My only concern is a fair presentation of the facts of my life.

But I hope the *British Medical Journal* will have no immediate use for it.

NOT JUST THE FACTS

Almost simultaneously with the *British Medical Journal*'s request for self-written obituaries, the *Journal of the American Medical Association* (JAMA) announced a change in its obituary column. Unlike the *British Medical Journal*'s present essays, which at least mention the deceased's family life and hobbies, the JAMA has traditionally offered little more than death notices. A list of names with age, medical school, and cause of death.

These Boot Hill epitaphs are to be replaced with reports the JAMA regards as more seemly. Physicians will now be memorialized with a recital of their awards and achievements. The future JAMA obituary intends to be a realistic portrayal of the late doctor's impact on the profession.

The *Journal* points out that much of the great American and English literature was written to memorialize the dead. Its readers, however, should not look for a present-day equivalent of Milton's "Lycidas" or Tennyson's "In Memoriam." The JAMA takes a different attitude: "Today, writing that praises the dead is much less sentimental and more to the point. Contemporary readers are interested in facts: when and where did the person die and what did he or she accomplish in life."

I guess I'm just not one of those contemporary readers. I am much more interested in what a person learned about living, how an individual pursued happiness, and what gave meaning to that particular life, than I am in reading about honors and awards, or when and where the death occurred.

My own self-written obituary is not concerned with what I did but why I did it — not the surface of my life, but the inner reality; not the public figure, but the private personality. Life is the greatest of all games. And as in every game, it is not the statistics that are important. It's how we play that really counts.

Some time back, a friend introduced me to an audience with a string of superlatives citing my books and lectures and races. When I began my talk, I told the audience I felt like Indian Joe listening to my own eulogy.

And it may in fact have been my eulogy, but it was not *me*. All those accomplishments were past and unimportant. Having goals is necessary. They lend urgency to living. They demand a productive lifestyle. But having goals is much more important than attaining them. They teach us the frequently repeated truth that the journey is more rewarding than the arrival.

I've learned a great deal about living from reading other men's last words. One such was Sir William Osler, the Canadian physician who revolutionized American medicine.

At his farewell dinner at Johns Hopkins University in Baltimore, Osler gave a talk that was, in effect, his last testament. He spoke of his two ambitions — to become a good clinical physician and build a great clinic. These are the twin drives we see in most successful lives — to do one's best and to help others in the process.

When Osler died, his obituaries emphasized the results of the first ambition — his drive to do his best — spelling out his many accomplishments in detail. But his talk in Baltimore had contained much more, of much greater importance. It revealed what the routine death notices failed to disclose—the man himself.

"I have three personal ideals," he stated. One, do a day's work well and don't bother about tomorrow. Two, act the Golden Rule. And finally, cultivate equanimity (one of his personal ideals) so as to bear success with humility, enjoy the affection of friends without pride, and meet sorrow and grief with courage.

Nothing new, you might say. Merely reinforcement of what we have been told for centuries. But we can never be reminded too often of what's really important. "The wise of all ages," wrote philosopher Arthur Schopenhauer in his *The Wisdom of Life*, "have always said the same thing and fools have done just the opposite."

The importance of today rings through all of Emerson. In "Immortality," he wrote of one famous man who caused to be written on his tombstone, "Think life." That is a message that straightens one up. And indeed, it recalls Thoreau's remark when asked on his death-bed how it looked on the other shore. He replied, "One world at a time."

Thinkers over the ages have left us the same message. The future either in this life or the afterlife should not be our major concern. Do your best and what happens will be for the best.

"If I work to the best of my ability until my death," wrote the German thinker and poet Johann Wolfgang von Goethe, "Nature is bound to give me another form of existence when the present can no longer contain my spirit."

The Irish poet William Butler Yeats, who fought age and dying down to his final breath, also thought there must be a provision in the afterlife for his unfinished work: "I feel sure we take up our half-done labors in other lives and carry them to conclusion."

The message of all these men? It is not achievement but the unremitting *effort* to achieve that marks the successful life. The pursuit of happiness *never* ends.

"It is not death I'm afraid of," wrote the French essayist Montaigne, "it's dying."

DEATH—THE MIDDLE WAY

Is it the act we fear, or the hereafter? People differ. If you have trouble handling pain but love solitude, you are probably one with Montaigne. If pain means little to you and you love to be with people, it would not be the dying that brings dread but death itself.

Yet when death actually comes, fear isn't evident. I have seen death come many times in my role as a physician. Rarely does fear accompany it. People fight the *thought* of death, but when it actually comes it is no longer the enemy.

When the great Roman orator Cicero grew old, he said he had had enough of living. "My soul seemed to understand that its true life would only begin after my death." And if some god granted him the powers to cancel his advanced years and return to boyhood, Cicero said he would firmly refuse. "Now that my race is run, I have no desire to be called back from the finish to the starting point."

If life is the big race, then each race is a separate life. Yesterday, for instance, I went through the continual and at times excruciating torment of racing 10 kilometers in Central Park. Every hill brought with it a little death, but then on the downhill came the rebirth—the breath coming back, the pain receding, and the consciousness, which had been reduced to the length of a stride, now expanding to take in my fellow runners and this miracle of grass and trees in the middle of a city.

All this was prelude to the last two hills. By the time I crested the first, I was *in extremis.* "There comes a time," said Cicero, "when one has had enough." I had reached that point, but life and the race continue their demands. So I went up that final hill and tried to sprint those last 200 yards. Ahead, just past the digital clock, were peace and warmth and friends—the runner's Eden. I entered it with my last breath.

A race or any other athletic experience puts life and death in perspective. Some people make too much of living, others make too much of dying. Some see life as all-important and trivialize death. Others see life only as a preparation for death and therefore trivialize life. Properly, we should steer the middle course.

EPILOGUE

It is Saturday morning, and a little to the north of us at Lake Takanassee they are having a 5-mile race. Ordinarily nothing short of an injury would have kept me from being there. But I'm on my way south toward Spring Lake to join a group that meets for a leisurely run on the boardwalk every Saturday morning at eight o'clock. I have added another dimension to my running life. I have become a social runner.

I still compete, of course, and on a regular basis—but the social self is growing. There was a time I rarely ran with anyone else. I wanted to be alone with my thoughts when I was out on the road. Without a companion who might interrupt my stream of consciousness, I could follow any idea at any pace.

In my middle years running was an escape from people. And in that solitude, my writing was born. But where there were once too many people in my life, now there are too few. There was a time when I would have told anyone who asked to run with me that I had already run, when that was not true. Now I look forward to running with people. I need people to talk to. I need people to listen to. I need people to be with.

I went through a transition period when the person who ran with me was little more than an audience. After one run a friend told me, "That was a great conversation you had." He had let me pour out my ideas without interruption during our hour on the road.

Now I have real conversations. I have revived what had become a dying art in my life. I actually listen to what people have to say instead of simply waiting until they stop so I can talk.

On the pleasant Saturday runs, there are no monologues. The ideas bounce from person to person. Topics surface and are gone. Paces vary. Places change. I run next to someone for a while, and then someone else takes his place.

A prayer we say at the beginning of our run makes us instant kin. We join hands in a little ceremony that had its origin years back when this coming together first started. Then we jog off, sharing feelings and thoughts, successes and failures, our joys and our woes. And at a deeper level we share the competent rhythms of our bodies. This innermost nonverbal communication makes everything else we share possible. Our efforts bind us together.

Later, most of us go to a pancake restaurant that is a mile or so back from the ocean and share again in food and laughter. This is what the Dairy Queen was to my Little League sons, the part we will remember best when we get older: who was there and what they said and what we ate. This is the time for guilt-free pancakes and waffles with all the toppings. We have paid for this enjoyment with our sweaty hour on the boards.

In the past I defined myself as a runner and did not realize what that fully meant. I was the runner deep in thought on the ocean road. I was suffering in the race. Now I am the runner sharing my life with other runners. I have come full circle. I have become, in the words of Blake describing age, "a child grown wise."

If not grown wise, I have at least come to understand how important friends are. I knew that well when I was a child. Social animals, children rarely do things alone. They find their friends are at the hub of a frictionless existence. That may be idealizing the childhood experience, but it comes close to what happened as I entered the final stage of my life. People have again become important.

For years I looked at this Saturday gathering with wonder. Why would anyone waste time on a leisurely jog on the boardwalk when there were races available? Why would anyone subject himself to an hour of banter when there were great ideas to be discovered alone?

Now I know that while competition and solitude are both sources of happiness, there is yet another source of happiness to be found in running—a return to the companionship of youth and childhood. I now have comrades. I am a member of a gang.

What has happened to me proves the truth of English writer Hilaire Belloc's words:

*From first beginnings
out to undiscovered ends,
nothing's worth the winning,
save laughter and the love of friends.*